D1526703

Aboriginal Consultation,
Environmental Assessment,
and Regulatory Review
in Canada

Aboriginal Consultation, Environmental Assessment, and Regulatory Review in Canada

KIRK N. LAMBRECHT Q.C.

U OF R PRESS

Printed and bound in Canada at Friesens.
The text of this book is printed on 100% post-consumer recycled paper with earth-friendly vegetable-based inks.

Cover and text design: Duncan Campbell, University of Regina Press.
Editor for the Press: Donna Grant, University of Regina Press.
Copy editor: Dallas Harrison.
Index by Patricia Furdek.
Cover photo: *Smoke 4* by Brian Lary.

Library and Archives Canada Cataloguing in Publication

Lambrecht, Kirk N., 1955—
    Aboriginal consultation, environmental assessment, and regulatory review in Canada / Kirk Norman Lambrecht.

(Canadian plains studies, ISSN 0317-6290 ; 66)
Includes bibliographical references and index.
ISBN 978-0-88977-298-4 (pbk.)

1. Environmental impact analysis—Law and legislation—
Canada. 2. Native peoples—Canada—Government relations.
3. Native peoples—Legal status, laws, etc.—Canada.
4. Environmental law—Canada. 5. Economic development—
Government policy—Canada. I. Title. II. Series: Canadian plains studies ; 66

KE7709.L34 2013   342.7108'72   C2013-901806-9
KF8210.E78L34 2013

10 9 8 7 6 5 4 3 2 1

University of Regina Press, University of Regina
Regina, Saskatchewan, Canada, S4S 0A2
TEL: (306) 585-4758 FAX: (306) 585-4699
WEB: www.uofrpress.ca

We acknowledge the financial support of the Government of Canada through the Canada Book Fund for our publishing activities, and the Creative Industry Growth and Sustainability program which is made possible through funding provided to the Saskatchewan Arts Board by the Government of Saskatchewan through the Ministry of Parks, Culture and Sport.

*This work is dedicated to
my children, Shannon and Michael,
and my grandson, Viggo.*

SUMMARY TABLE OF CONTENTS

CASES

STATUTES

Acknowledgements

I wish to acknowledge the privilege afforded to members of the Law Society of Alberta for experiences and a vantage point unique to barristers. I had the opportunity over many years to engage on the issues discussed in this book with Indian and Métis persons, regulators, judges, experts, environmental assessment and regulatory review practitioners, scientists, policy makers, academics and ordinary citizens. All shared valuable perspectives.

The University of Regina Press—formerly the Canadian Plains Research Center (CPRC) at the University of Regina—requires special acknowledgement. This book is the direct result of the interest of publications manager Brian Mlazgar, now retired. The Center provided funding that allowed the assistance of Jonathan Clark and Tracie Scott during early development of the manuscript and also submitted the manuscript to the Canadian Federation for the Humanities and Social Sciences. Comments of readers engaged by the Federation were instrumental in shaping the final form of the work.

Bruce Walsh, director of the University of Regina Press, supported the work enthusiastically upon taking up his position, with the result that the book will be amongst the first to be published by the Press. Designer Duncan Campbell formatted the charts from my sketches. Senior Editor Donna Grant was instrumental, and unfailingly helpful, in guiding the manuscript through the final stages of production. Diane

Perrick of the Press adapted the maps of the historical and modern treaties. I hope that the book advances the mandate of the Press in giving voice to Aboriginal issues.

Barristers James Kindrake and Ellie (Elle) Venhola took time from their personal lives to read a mature draft of the manuscript and offer helpful views on its style.

On a personal level, I wish to especially recognize the support and encouragement of my family and friends, especially Yves and Lynn Lagimoniere. Thank you for the space and time needed to write and revise this work.

The manuscript was prepared in accordance with the Code of Conduct of the Law Society of Alberta, which encourages lawyers to contribute to professional publications and education. The views expressed here, and any errors of fact, law or interpretation, are mine alone in a personal capacity.

Although the manuscript was written when I was with the professional staff of the Justice Department of Canada, it was written entirely during personal time in accordance with the policies of the Department as they were at the time. All sources cited are in the public domain, and many are made available through the Internet. Hyperlinks are used to facilitate access to these Internet sources in the public domain. No use has been made of information sheltered by solicitor-client or other privilege. Nothing here is intended to convey, directly or indirectly, the views of the Justice Department of Canada or the Government of Canada.

I joined the law firm of Shores Jardine LLP upon retiring from public service after 30 years of continuous service. The partners and associates of Shores Jardine LLP all contribute actively to professional publications and education. Their support for this book, and the labour it has involved, is appreciated.

Prologue

T his book describes, through functional and contextual analysis, how Aboriginal consultation can be *practically* integrated with environmental assessment and regulatory review processes of tribunals in Canada to foster relationships among Aboriginal peoples, project developers, tribunals, the Crown and the courts. Such a multi-faceted relationship-building dynamic can advance reconciliation with Canada's Aboriginal peoples. It should, at a minimum, ensure that project planning, approval, and regulatory oversight take meaningful account of Aboriginal concerns.

The Supreme Court of Canada recognizes the law of Aboriginal consultation in its 2004 decision in *Haida Nation v. British Columbia (Minister of Forests),* but the Court defines only a general framework of broad principle, leaving development of details by the courts to the future:

> This case is the first of its kind to reach this Court. Our task is the modest one of establishing a general framework for the duty to consult and accommodate, where indicated, before Aboriginal title or rights claims have been decided. As this framework is applied, courts, in the age-old tradition of the common law, will be called on to fill in the details of the duty to consult and accommodate.[1]

As of the date of publication of this book, five judgments of the Supreme Court of Canada define the national framework for the duty to consult and accommodate. *Haida Nation,* and its contemporaneous companion judgment *Taku River Tlingit First Nation v. British Columbia (Project Assessment Director),*[2] originate in the distinctive legal regime of unextinguished Aboriginal rights in British Columbia. The Court extended the framework to the regime of Treaty rights under the historical numbered treaties through its decision in *Mikisew Cree First Nation v. Canada (Minister of Canadian Heritage.*[3] Then, in *David Beckman, in His Capacity as Director, Agriculture Branch, Department of Energy, Mines and Resources, et al. v. Little Salmon/Carmacks First Nation, et al.,*[4] the Court further considered the framework in the context of a modern treaty regime. Finally, in *Rio Tinto Alcan Inc., et al. v. Carrier Sekani Tribal Council,*[5] the Court considered the role of tribunals in the general framework. Taken together, these five cases complete the general framework. They do not fill in the details of the duty to consult and accommodate as it may apply to environmental assessment and regulatory review associated with project development.

There is, as yet, no consensus or doctrine for how the duty to consult may be applied in project development. Instead, in keeping with the common law, adversarial perspectives are taken. The "age-old tradition of the common law" results in conflicting points of view, promoted by an adversarial system embedded in Western traditions. This seems to be anticipated in the Court's acknowledgment that "hard bargaining" is not offensive to the right to be consulted.[6] As a result there has been an explosion of courses, conferences, publications, workshops, and symposiums addressing Aboriginal consultation in the context of project development. Indeed, an Aboriginal consultation industry has been created in the first decade of the twenty-first century, just as an environmental assessment industry was created from the environmental initiatives of earlier decades.

Aboriginal consultation, environmental assessment, and regulatory review intersect in respect of project development. This book recognizes the positive potential arising from that confluence. It points to the potential for contribution to reconciliation by an integrated process. The focus here is on how relationships can be practically built as projects proceed through the development process of planning, approval, and control— despite discordant adversarial dialogue, and while the common law develops. By analogy, and adapting language used by the Supreme Court, this book offers a practical signpost on the long path to reconciliation.

This book will interest anyone generally concerned about sustainable development, environmental protection, and reconciliation with

Aboriginal peoples. Since the subject matter is rooted in legal processes, those particularly interested will include Aboriginal persons, businesses engaged in project development, regulators, staff of regulatory agencies, barristers and solicitors, legislators, policy-makers, scholars, and students. The book might also be of value to the thousands of people from all walks of life who today, and in the future, will engage in Aboriginal consultation during the course of project development in Canada. Their work advances reconciliation.

A GUIDE TO THE DIGITAL LINKS USED WITH THIS BOOK

In traditional legal publishing, source materials are made available to the reader by reproducing them in the body of the book and then adding commentary of the author or editor. The tradition of making source materials available to readers is followed here, but in a new way. The book itself is commentary based upon sources placed in the public domain by others and accessible through hyperlinks. In this way case law, constitutional documents, statutes, and secondary sources are all made available to the reader, an accomplishment that could not be economically done in the traditional method of publishing.

To maximize the value of this book to those who may use it, the University of Regina Press has facilitated reference to source materials via the Internet. Through this action the Press allows every reader to conveniently locate and view the references cited in this book from any Internet connection at any location in the world, no matter how remote. Internet technology makes information sources available to readers in a more immediate way than ever before in history.

The Press maintains the Endnotes, and the hyperlinks there, on its website. Those who have a hard copy of the book, and who have access to the Internet from any point in the world, can go to the website of the University of Regina Press at http://www.uofrpress.ca/lambrecht and access source materials through the hyperlinks there. Readers who are using the hyperlinks will find that "clicking through" will successfully open most of the source documents; however, the links to pdf files will open more easily if the web address is copied and pasted into the browser, rather than attempting to click through.

The book will also be available in digital format. The hyperlinks in the endnotes will be live for those who use the digital version of the book.

In the future, as links given here become outdated, the Internet archives at http://www.archive.org/ may allow continuing reference capacity.

CHAPTER ONE

Relationships in the Project Development Process

Good measure for all.

—after Arthur J. Ray and Donald B. Freeman, *'Give Us Good Measure': An Economic Analysis of Relations between the Indians and the Hudson's Bay Company before 1763* (Toronto: University of Toronto Press, 1978).

THE PROPOSITION AND THE METHODOLOGY OF PROOF

The fundamental proposition here is that Aboriginal consultation and environmental assessment/regulatory review of projects by tribunals can be integrated so as to operate effectively and serve the goal of reconciliation. To borrow a phrase from Abella J., writing the judgment of the Supreme Court of Canada in *R. v. Conway*, "...it is time to consider whether these universes can appropriately be merged."[1] I propose that they can be integrated because each is a *process* that informs decision making. I offer proof through a survey, or observation, of the constitutional law of Aboriginal and Treaty rights in Canada, the law of Aboriginal consultation, and the function of tribunals in environmental assessment and regulatory review. I then explore integration via case studies involving the National Energy

Board of Canada. In the conclusion, I discuss observations of general application and some outstanding questions.

Aboriginal law, environmental assessment and regulatory review law, and the law of Aboriginal consultation, are specialized subjects. Of course, Canada is too large a country, and the applicable legal regimes too contextual, for an encyclopedic analysis of all asserted Aboriginal rights in Canada, all historical and modern Indian treaties in Canada, or all environmental assessment and regulatory regimes in Canada. Some focus is required for the analysis in this book, and this is achieved through (1) reliance on Supreme Court of Canada jurisprudence, (2) use of the numbered treaties,[2] with particular reference to the Prairie provinces, as an illustration of rights under historical treaties, and (3) reliance on case studies to illustrate the detailed mechanics of integrating Aboriginal consultation into the environmental assessment and regulatory process of tribunals for asserted Aboriginal rights and rights under historical and modern treaties.

I rely on Supreme Court of Canada jurisprudence because this Court is responsible for setting national direction and policy in the law through the doctrine of *stare decisis*. Judgments of the Court are applicable in all jurisdictions in Canada. As the Court itself states in *Wolf v. The Queen*:

> A provincial appellate court is not obliged, as a matter either of law or of practice, to follow a decision of the appellate court of another province unless it is persuaded that it should do so on its merits or for other independent reasons. ... The only required uniformity among provincial appellate courts is that which is the result of the decisions of this Court.[3]

Reference to the historical numbered treaties, with particular reference to the Prairie provinces, is simply a convenient way of focusing the scope of the work on a geographical area where the interaction of the laws of Aboriginal consultation, environmental assessment, and regulatory review is engaged. It also allows for consideration of the constitutional protections conferred by the *Natural Resource Transfer Agreements*.

Métis also have a heritage in the Prairie provinces, tracing back to pre-Confederation and the economic industry of the fur trade. Use of the Prairie provinces therefore also facilitates inclusion of both Indian and Métis Aboriginal peoples in the analysis.

I present the National Energy Board (NEB) in the case studies of Chapter 5 for several reasons. First, the NEB is centrally engaged in significant project development across Canada.[4] Second, protection of the environment and contribution to sustainable development through robust environmental assessment/regulatory review and oversight are central to its function. Third, its transparency affords ease of reference to its role and function in Aboriginal consultation and, where necessary, accommodation. And fourth, its role and function have been the subject of judicial consideration. It is a mature tribunal that well illustrates the subject matter discussed in this book.

From the Court's decisions I derive the proposition, central to this book, that Aboriginal consultation, environmental assessment and regulatory review are processes. Process has sufficient elasticity to accommodate the merger discussed by the Court in *R. v. Conway* and illustrated in the case studies. In its 2010 judgment in *Rio Tinto Alcan Inc. v. Carrier Sekani Tribal Council*, the Court describes Aboriginal consultation as a *process*—of "a 'generative' constitutional order" [5]—corollary to Crown decision making with a dynamic function intended to reconcile prior Aboriginal occupation of the land with the reality of Crown sovereignty.[6] In its 1991 decision in *Friends of the Oldman River Society v. Canada (Minister of Transport)*, the Court describes environmental assessment as a *process* of decision making that reconciles development desires with environmental protection and preservation.[7] In its 1994 judgment in *Quebec (Attorney General) v. Canada (National Energy Board)*, the Court recognizes that regulatory review and oversight comprise a *process* of control spanning the life cycle of a project.[8]

Integration of these processes allows for more fully informed decision making, which I propose is both effective and efficient. The ultimate goals of environmental assessment (sustainable development and protection of the environment[9]) and Aboriginal consultation (reconciliation[10]) are different. Environmental assessment and regulatory review cannot achieve reconciliation of all matters with all Aboriginal peoples. But, at minimum, protecting the environment from project effects can protect Aboriginal practices in that environment. Finally, if the objectives of the laws of environmental assessment/regulatory review and Aboriginal consultation in relation to project development are to be met without unnecessary and expensive duplication of effort by Aboriginal peoples, courts, and governments, then environmental assessment/regulatory review by tribunals and Aboriginal consultation should be integrated with one another rather than isolated from one another. There is one sovereignty in this approach, not multiple solitudes.

FUNCTIONS OF GOVERNANCE: PLANNING, APPROVAL, AND CONTROL

I propose that the project development process in Canada inherently involves three essential functions: planning, approval, and control, in that sequence. I also propose that there are three basic Crown or government functions that correspond to that sequence in the project development process: environmental assessment/regulatory review, project approval, and regulatory oversight. Rather than review the details of these functions as they may exist in any given legislative regime, this book uses contextual analysis to emphasize function (rather than form) in the project development process.

Characterization of environmental assessment as a planning mechanism is articulated on the United Nations University's Wiki page.[11] Environmental assessment can be seen as an aspect of the "increased environmental awareness that swept the globe in the late 1960s."[12] In the United States, the *National Environmental Policy Act (NEPA)* was signed into law on January 1, 1970.[13] In Europe, *Council Directive 85/337/EEC* was issued on June 27, 1985.[14] In Canada, the Governor in Council adopted the *Environmental Assessment and Review Process Guidelines Order* in 1984.[15] This Order was superseded in 1995 when the *Canadian Environmental Assessment Act* came into force.[16] Today environmental assessment legislation and policy exist at all federal and provincial levels, and modern treaties define tribunals with environmental assessment responsibilities.[17]

Regulatory review and regulatory oversight predate the 1970s. Prior to that time, governments had created tribunals, and conferred on such tribunals the obligation to undertake planning and control functions in regard to project development. The National Energy Board of Canada is an example at the federal level.[18] The Energy Resources Conservation Board of Alberta (Alberta Energy Regulator) is an example at the provincial level.[19]

In *Friends of the Oldman River Society v. Canada (Minister of Transport)*,[20] the Supreme Court of Canada judicially considered the fundamental principles of Canada's environmental assessment regime. Writing for the Court, La Forest J. opened the judgment with a statement that captured the contemporary reality: "[t]he protection of the environment has become one of the major challenges of our time." The Court describes the fundamental relationship between environmental assessment and environmental protection by referring to the former as a planning tool. The Court reaffirms this passage in *MiningWatch Canada v. Canada (Fisheries and Oceans)*, stating that environmental assessment legislation "provides a process for integrating environmental considerations into planning and decision making."[21]

In much the same way as *Charter* protections associated with freedom of expression protect the right to a general process of collective bargaining, but do not provide a particular model of labour relations or a specific bargaining method,[22] the division of governance processes into planning, approval, and control *functions* defines stages of project decision making without guaranteeing either a specific process or a particular decision. Application of these principles in domestic law results in legislation that varies in detail with regard to circumstances specific to legislative initiatives as introduced and amended over time. The objective, protection of the environment by use of environmental assessment or regulatory review as a planning tool used in aid of sustainable development, remains the same, but the way in which it is to be achieved has evolved and will continue to evolve.

Seen through this functional lens, there is a *planning process* (described here as environmental assessment or regulatory review) that informs *control process(es)* (described here as project approval decision making, and subsequent regulatory oversight decisions during project construction, operation, and decommissioning). There can be significant overlap between the planning and the control processes, since environmental appreciation does not necessarily terminate with project approval. Rather, some form of environmental assessment of major projects will certainly be undertaken after project approval, during the life cycle of the project, to monitor impacts and inform adaptive management.

THE PROJECT DEVELOPMENT PROCESS IN CANADA
An Emphasis on Function Rather Than Form

The doctrine of integration proposed in this book rests upon the premise that the development process for major projects, whether undertaken by corporate business or by government, relies upon this sequence of *functions*: planning, approval, and control. I propose that this sequence remains standard, even though the details at each stage may and will vary significantly. I further propose that placing an emphasis on *function* in the project development process, rather than *form*, allows for appreciation of the potential for common purpose with Aboriginal consultation. To clarify the functional stages of project development discussed in this book, Figure 1 illustrates how the governance functions of *planning, approval,* and *control* (Figure 1a) correspond both to the corporate business model (Figure 1b) and to the government regulatory model (Figure 1c).

Figure 1a. General governance functions for major projects.

Figure 1b. Corporate business model for project development.

Figure 1c. Government regulatory model for project development.

At a basic corporate level of decision making, described here as a corporate business model (Figure 1b), a project proponent first plans for a project at a conceptual level. Based on the planning, and on whatever other criteria may to it seem appropriate, the corporate board then makes a decision whether to approve the project. If approved, the project may then be developed.

The corporate exercise of planning for a major project may take several years and involve hundreds of millions of dollars. The development cycle of a project that proceeds may take decades and involve millions or billions of dollars. Hundreds or thousands of persons may be directly and indirectly employed. Economic benefits can amount to millions or billions of dollars over time.

If corporations always acted independently to plan, approve, and control projects, then there would be no Crown decisions capable of attracting the duty to consult. However, project development in Canada will normally require some form of government, or Crown, responsibility in the project development process. The law of Aboriginal consultation can introduce a constitutional imperative into this process. Where Crown decisions in the project development cycle have the potential to adversely impact Aboriginal rights or interests, Aboriginal consultation will be required and accommodation may be required. The scope and nature of Aboriginal consultation and, where necessary, accommodation, will vary with the context of each case.

Integrating the Corporate Business Model and Government
Regulatory Model for Project Development

Legislation usually requires that environmental assessment or regulatory review precede and inform project approval decisions. The two may overlap in whole or in part. Environmental assessment and regulatory review have common purpose, and are used as interchangeable terms here, insofar as they are seen as processes that perform a planning function intended to inform decision making. The actual degree of their interchangeability will depend upon the particular wording of the legislation which governs each.

Environmental assessment and regulatory review are mandated in legislation of many jurisdictions as a precondition to project approval. Responsible project proponents welcome robust and efficient environmental assessment and regulatory review during the planning stage of major projects. This evidences the corporate contribution to the purposes of sustainable development, generally.

In a government regulatory model (Figure 1c), the function of environmental assessment/regulatory review is to inform a government decision whether to "approve" the project, and to identify appropriate conditions of approval, if any. Project approval refers to the decision to allow a project to proceed. This approval is normally subject to conditions, and may be time limited. Project approval, therefore, does not confer an absolute right to develop, but a licence to develop that is subject to conditions. Failure to comply with the conditions of project approval may give rise to administrative sanction, prosecution or, indeed, to revocation of the approval.

After obtaining government project approval, project proponents will normally then make a final decision on whether or not to proceed with the project, having regard to market conditions, cost, and other considerations as they may then exist. Financing is obtained for projects that do proceed, enabling contracts to be finalized and labour and equipment to be mobilized. With these resources in place the project then advances in stages from concept to detailed engineering and construction plans, to construction, operation, decommissioning, and reclamation.

If the project is approved both by the Crown and by the corporate proponent and is actually developed, government entities will typically exercise regulatory oversight during construction and operation. The phrase "regulatory oversight" refers to government permitting and licencing activities, including enforcement, taken after project approval. Government licences or permits of various kinds will usually be required after project approval and during project development. The decision whether to issue such licences is not predetermined by a prior decision to approve the project at a conceptual level. Rather, specific permit and licencing decisions are taken with respect to criteria outlined in enabling legislation. Criteria for issuing a permit or licence may be further refined by policies of different kinds.

Conditions of project approval, and the conditions of permits or licences issued during project development, are primary mechanisms by which government exercises a degree of control over development in order to achieve public purposes embodied in legislation. The essential function of regulatory oversight is to ensure compliance with the conditions of approval and to enable adaptive management should the development result in effects that vary from those predicted during project planning.

Figure 2 illustrates how the planning, approval, and control functions of both the corporate business model and the government regulatory model are integrated.

Legislatures or Parliament may delegate some or all of the responsibilities for environmental assessment, project approval, and regulatory oversight to specialized tribunals. This is depicted visually in Figure 3. The case studies described in this book focus on instances in which environmental assessment and regulatory review were conducted by a quasi-judicial tribunal created by the legislative branch of government.

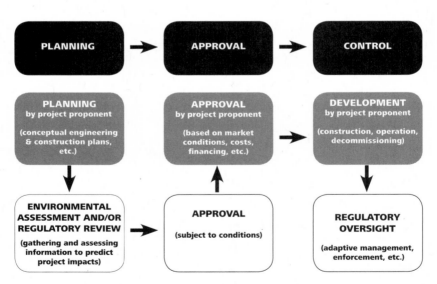

Figure 2. Integration of the planning, approval, and control functions of the corporate business model and the government regulatory model for project development.

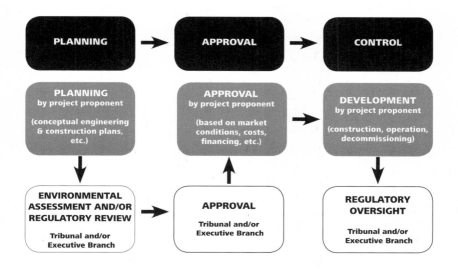

Figure 3. Functions that a Tribunal may perform in project development.

Both environmental assessment and regulatory review perform a planning function. That is, the purpose of both environmental assessment and regulatory review is *to inform* subsequent decisions in the project development process. This planning exercise is conducted early in the project development cycle, recognizing that the project at that time is at a conceptual level and that funding is not always sufficient, or will not have been yet marshaled, so as to allow for detailed "as built" engineering plans and specifications to be developed. Extensive modeling, therefore, may be relied upon in this predictive exercise. The process of gathering and assessing information on proposed projects informs Crown decision making on whether to approve the project, and how best to regulate the project through conditions of project approval and subsequent licencing or permitting.

The government regulatory model can, of course, take many forms. Legislation can confer responsibility for project planning on a tribunal, on other government entities more closely related to the executive branch of government, or on both. A project approval decision can be delegated to the tribunal, to the executive branch of government, or both.

What I propose in this book is that relationships with Aboriginal peoples can be positively developed throughout the development process for projects. Integration of Aboriginal consultation into project planning, approval, and control is therefore not a one-time activity, but a distributed and ongoing dynamic. Corporations, tribunals, the Crown, and the courts will all contribute, with the nature and extent of that contribution varying according to the context in which it occurs in the stages of project development.

INTEGRATING ABORIGINAL CONSULTATION INTO THE PLANNING PROCESSES OF PROJECT DEVELOPMENT

The law mandates integration of Aboriginal concerns into Crown decision making as a constitutional imperative, but it is also practical. As the Supreme Court states in *Canada (Attorney General) v. TeleZone Inc.*, "People who claim to be injured by government action should have whatever redress the legal system permits through procedures that minimize unnecessary cost and complexity. The Court's approach should be practical and pragmatic with that objective in mind."[23] Today, then, legislative branches of governments have created environmental assessment/regulatory review processes that are often implemented by tribunals. Where these are mandated to consider the potential impacts of projects on Aboriginal peoples, it seems consistent with the honour of the Crown to rely on such regimes to fulfill this statutory mandate. Aboriginal peoples who assert harms from project development may engage in the process to express those concerns prior to project approval and have them heard in a meaningful way by proponents, tribunals and by the Crown.

Tribunals are moving in this direction. Where a project might adversely affect Aboriginal peoples, tribunals such as the National Energy Board or the Energy Resources Conservation Board require evidence of Aboriginal consultation by a proponent as a precondition of making a regulatory application.[24] The Ontario Energy Board, drawing from the NEB experience, has adopted a similar practice.[25] To the same effect is Ontario's *Draft Aboriginal Consultation Guide for Preparing a Renewable Energy Approval (REA) Application*[26] supported by *Ontario Regulation 359/09.*[27]

Governments are also moving in this direction in formal policies. Ontario, for example, encourages Aboriginal consultation by mineral project proponents.[28] Canada's most recent policy on Aboriginal consultation also promotes harmonization of Crown Aboriginal consultation with existing regulatory processes.[29]

Aboriginal peoples do not necessarily agree with or accept this approach. Aboriginal groups often assert the *right* to be consulted by the Crown in a process separate from Aboriginal consultation by a proponent and preceding environmental assessment or regulatory review process.[30] Some commentators suggest that it is still appropriate for Aboriginal consultation procedures to be worked out on a case-by-case basis for each project or each Aboriginal group potentially affected by a project.[31] This reflects fundamental disagreement over how to correctly apply the broad statements of policy underlying the law of Aboriginal consultation.

The paradigm discussed in this book—that is, reliance on an integrated process during project planning—practically means that project proponents, tribunals created to discharge environmental assessment and regulatory review functions, the Crown, and the courts all have a role to play in reconciliation with Aboriginal peoples. Many hands therefore serve the purposes of reconciliation.

Project Proponents

Reconciliation with Aboriginal peoples can be advanced by project proponents themselves in the environmental assessment and regulatory review process, just as proponents themselves can reconcile environmental protection with project development in these processes. Industry can liaise with Aboriginal peoples well in advance, often years in advance, of making a regulatory application. As noted, such engagement of this kind is mandated by tribunals such as the National Energy Board. These require evidence of Aboriginal consultation by the proponent as a precondition of making a regulatory application. This approach is well supported by international organizations.

Industry is far advanced in its development of, and support for, Aboriginal engagements on many fronts.[32] The project in its early design phase may be cost effectively altered by the proponent in response to Aboriginal concerns about potential negative impacts, or the economic aspects of the project may be positively structured by the proponent to meet Aboriginal concerns. Case studies demonstrate that this certainly has the capacity to reconcile at least some Aboriginal interests with the project.

Environmental Assessment/Regulatory Review Processes of Tribunals

During project planning, tribunals assess project impacts on Aboriginal peoples. Where Aboriginal peoples are not satisfied with proponent responses to their concerns, they can seek redress from the tribunal by asking it to impose conditions of regulatory approval or even to deny approval. Case studies demonstrate that tribunals do not necessarily favour project approval.[33] These case studies also illustrate that tribunals themselves, by adopting and imposing conditions of regulatory approval or subsequent regulatory oversight, are capable of accommodating Aboriginal concerns. The National Energy Board's Reasons for Decision in the Southern Lights Pipeline Project explain how the Board's environmental assessment functions were integrated into its regulatory oversight functions and were responsive to potential project impacts on Aboriginal interests.[34]

In regard to relationships, tribunals that engage in continuous process improvement will be capable of modifying process sensitivity to Aboriginal peoples as necessary. Foreseeable accommodations include provision of translation services, location of public hearings with regard to accessibility for Aboriginal witnesses, and creation of information initiatives by the tribunal itself and directed specifically to Aboriginal peoples to ensure that they are informed of tribunal process.[35]

The Crown

The Crown is responsible for the duty to consult but is not the ultimate source of all information and responsibility regarding projects and project development. Proponents have the best information on the project and the capacity to develop and implement project accommodations for Aboriginal peoples. Tribunals have specialized planning and control knowledge and capacity, defined in their enabling legislation. Integration of Aboriginal consultation into corporate and tribunal planning, approval, and control processes will engage these entities directly with Aboriginal peoples and allow these entities to apply their specialized and specific knowledge and capacity to the cause of reconciliation, at an early stage of project development—during project planning. Integration, then, fosters multilateral dialogue.

If the proponent and the tribunal have not effected reconciliation themselves either prior to or through the tribunal processes, it may then fall to the Crown itself to do so prior to project approval decision making. Of all the entities of the executive branch of government with project approval decision making responsibilities, Cabinet, or ministers assisted by Cabinet, most clearly represent the Crown as a whole and have both (1) the obligation to balance Aboriginal concerns with broader societal requirements and (2) the capacity to direct resources as required in regard to accommodations for Aboriginal peoples, or avenues of consultation outside the tribunal process.

It may be anticipated that Aboriginal peoples will look to the Crown for accommodations where adverse effects of a project on Aboriginal practices are likely significant despite the implementation of mitigation measures, such that the capacity of a proponent or the statutory jurisdiction of a tribunal to meet Aboriginal concerns by implementation of mitigations or other measures is exhausted. In cases where a government cabinet or minister makes a project approval decision after receipt of a report from the tribunal, there might be a temporal separation between the gathering and assessing of information about a project by the tribunal and potential consultation or accommodation by the Crown of outstanding Aboriginal concerns, if any, as illuminated by the tribunal report. Such a temporal separation might be criticized by Aboriginal peoples for lack of Crown responsiveness—effectively, lack of Crown accommodation—during the preceding tribunal process. But Crown responsiveness may be most effective in terms of accommodation once information on project impacts on Aboriginal or treaty rights has been gathered, assessed, and presented by a tribunal.

In regard to relationships, Crown entities that have project approval authority flowing from a statute will also have the responsibility to be satisfied that Crown consultation has been adequate before that authority is exercised. These entities may develop reasons. These reasons may articulate the rationale of the Crown entities regarding whether constitutional consultation obligations have been satisfied before the statutory decision is taken. This is in keeping with the generative nature of the law of Aboriginal consultation.

Project-specific consultation by a project proponent, and by the Crown, will also arise after project approval, through regulatory oversight during the life cycle of the project, from construction through operation and decommissioning approval.

Project-specific consultation should not be seen in isolation from other initiatives by the Crown before and after a project is reviewed or approved (assuming that it is) by a tribunal. Complementary initiatives before, after, or in parallel with tribunal work can include political negotiation, delivery of economic development and social programs directed to Aboriginal peoples, land use planning or zoning exercises, and direction of Aboriginal concerns broader than project-specific concerns into other specialized processes such as treaty negotiations or comprehensive or specific claims. All can serve to advance the interests of reconciliation and be complementary to, but not duplicative of, integration of Aboriginal consultation into a tribunal's project planning process.

Aboriginal Peoples

Aboriginal engagement in environmental assessment or regulatory review is not a certainty. If Aboriginal peoples do not engage in the tribunal process to express their outstanding concerns about a project, then who will communicate to the tribunal such concerns? Clearly, it is best that Aboriginal communities affected by a proposed project express their concerns directly. I therefore suggest, with the greatest of respect, that Aboriginal persons engage in tribunal planning processes where these are intended to gather and assess project impacts on Aboriginal rights or Treaty rights.

Tribunal proceedings are often described as adversarial and therefore unacceptable by some Aboriginal groups. However, the law provides that administrative law principles are material to the duty to consult. Tribunal process may confer extensive procedural fairness and natural justice rights on Aboriginal parties to a tribunal proceeding, including the right to obtain information from the proponent, present witnesses, make motions, cross-examine other witnesses, present arguments, receive reasons for a decision, and appeal any ultimate determination. These are powerful tools. All are evident in the case studies.

Finally, as is evident in the tribunal registries cited in the case studies, the tribunal process is well designed to develop a public record. Should Aboriginal peoples believe that the tribunal process was not meaningful, the record will be helpful to a court in subsequent judicial oversight.

The Courts

The Supreme Court confirms that "it is open to governments to set up regulatory schemes to address the procedural requirements of consultation at different stages of the decisionmaking process" with regard to a resource project.[36] Courts may supervise planning and decision making for adherence to procedural fairness, natural justice, and constitutional law, but will respect the authority of tribunals and the executive branch of government to make decisions consistent with Canadian constitutional law and within the ambit of their authorities. Questions about project impacts on Aboriginal peoples are likely mixed questions of fact and law, well within the mandates of high-level tribunals to determine through environmental assessment/regulatory review. The case studies show that tribunals are capable of gathering information on and making decisions about project impacts on the actual or asserted rights of Aboriginal persons. Judicial oversight of such decisions will be probing and reasoned. Courts, then, ensure that planning and approval functions in any given context operate according to law and reasonably in the circumstances. The common law develops in this time-honoured way.

Defining Aboriginal Rights and Treaty Rights

There is no doubt that aboriginal and treaty rights differ in both origin and structure.

—*R. v. Badger*, [1996] 1 S.C.R. 771 at para. 76.

METHODOLOGY

Aboriginal and Treaty rights can vary dramatically across the vast expanse of Canada. The first step in the relationship-building exercise associated with project development is to locate the project geographically and then consider whether it is to be located in an area of Canada where a treaty has been concluded. Understanding the basic distinction between Aboriginal rights and Treaty rights in Canada is the first step in understanding how project development can affect such rights and therefore the first step in building relationships with Aboriginal peoples whose rights are integral to their identities.

Figure 4 shows where historical treaties have been concluded, while Figure 5 shows where modern treaties have been concluded.[1] Modern and historical treaties can overlap in their spatial dimension because the negotiation of modern treaties is undertaken on a policy basis with those who assert comprehensive land claims.

Figure 4. Map of Historical Indian Treaties in Canada.

Adapted from the historical Indian treaties map available on the website of Aboriginal Affairs and Northern Development Canada at http://www.aadnc-aandc.gc.ca/. Used with permission of the Minister of Public Works and Government Services Canada, 2012.

If a project is being undertaken in an area of Canada where the provisions of a treaty apply, then the treaty itself will likely define the nature of the constitutionally protected rights and title that may be enjoyed by Aboriginal peoples. This can include ownership of land, referred to here by the term "title." The term "Treaty rights" is therefore used here to refer specifically to rights and title recognized in an historical or modern treaty. This assumes that, for most of Canada, the conclusion of an historical or modern treaty means that any Aboriginal rights and title that preceded the treaty have been extinguished and replaced with rights or title founded in the treaty instrument itself.

If the project is being undertaken in an area of Canada where there are no applicable treaties, and this is the case today for most of British Columbia, then the definition of the rights that are claimed by Aboriginal peoples will fall into one of two categories. The phrase "asserted Aboriginal rights" (or "title") is used here to refer to rights (or title) that are claimed by Aboriginal peoples but that have not yet

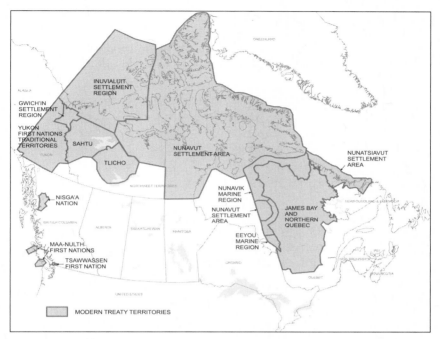

Figure 5. Map of Modern Treaties in Canada.

Adapted from the modern treaties map available on the website of the Land Claims Agreement Coalition at http://www.landclaimscoalition.ca/. Used with permission.

been recognized by a court in Canada with jurisdiction to do so. The phrase "actual Aboriginal rights" (or "title") is used here to refer to Aboriginal rights that have been recognized by such a court.

There are differing perspectives on this approach. Aboriginal peoples who assert Aboriginal rights and titles do so on the basis that they are actual rights and titles. Aboriginal peoples who enjoy Treaty rights may also assert unextinguished Aboriginal rights and title, as if the treaty were merely declaratory of a subset of the underlying and still unextinguished Aboriginal rights and titles. Many commentators use the term "Aboriginal rights" to refer indistinguishably to all rights of Aboriginal persons in Canada, whether or not defined in a treaty.

For clarity, then, the distinctions presented in this chapter are taken from jurisprudence of the Supreme Court of Canada. In 1987, Brian Slattery published an article comparing the subject of Aboriginal rights to a poorly explored archaeological site:

The subject of aboriginal rights is like an overgrown and poorly excavated archeological site. Most visitors are content to wander around the ruins, climb to the top of the highest mound, or poke about in the dust for souvenirs. Others, prompted by curiosity or official duty, select a likely spot and sink a trench through the layers of historical deposits, uncovering, perhaps, the severed foot of a colossal statue, or a worn inscription. But the meaning of these objects is unclear. Even when they can be identified and dated, their larger import escapes us.[2]

In 2000, Slattery observed that

Little-known areas have been brought to light and apocryphal seas dispelled. We now know broadly what is terra firma and what is not, and the monsters have been largely tamed or banished to the decorative margins. Nevertheless, the first fruits of the Court's labours amount to a series of explorer's charts, enlightening so far as they go, but covering different areas, drawn in varying projections, and sometimes bearing an uncertain relation to one another. We lack a reliable mappamundi.[3]

Since that time, there have been further judgments from the Supreme Court dealing with Aboriginal and Treaty rights, and the Court has also recognized the law of Aboriginal consultation. Peter Hogg concludes "that no area of law has been so transformed in such a short period of time as the law of Aboriginal rights."[4] And this evolution continues. Most recently the Court applied the concept of the Honour of the Crown to Métis in *Manitoba Metis Federation Inc. v. Canada (Attorney General)*.[5]

In 1990, the Supreme Court describes its occasion in *R. v. Sparrow* "to explore for the first time the scope of s. 35(1) of the *Constitution Act, 1982*, and to indicate its strength as a promise to the aboriginal peoples of Canada."[6] The Court extends this consideration in *R. v. Van der Peet* where it describes the issue before it:

This appeal, along with the companion appeals in *R. v. N.T.C. Smokehouse Ltd.*, [1996] 2 S.C.R. 672, and *R. v. Gladstone*, [1996] 2 S.C.R. 723, raises the issue left unresolved by this Court in its judgment in *R. v. Sparrow*, [1990] 1 S.C.R. 1075: How are the aboriginal rights recognized and affirmed by s. 35(1) of the *Constitution Act, 1982* to be defined?[7]

Aboriginal law was further developed by the Court in *R. v. Nikal*,[8] *R. v. Gladstone*,[9] *R. v. Côté*,[10] *R. v. Adams*,[11] *Delgamuukw v. British Columbia*,[12] *R. v. Marshall*,[13] *R. v. Sioui*,[14] *Mitchell v. M.N.R.*,[15] *Kitkatla Band v. British Columbia (Minister of Small Business, Tourism and Culture)*,[16] *R. v. Powley*,[17] *R. v. Marshall*; *R. v. Bernard*,[18] *R. v. Sappier*; *R. v. Gray*,[19] *R. v. Morris*,[20] and *R. v. Kapp*.[21]

From this list, *Sparrow, Van der Peet, N.T.C. Smokehouse Ltd., Nikal, Gladstone, Delgamuukw, Kitkatla Band,* and *Kapp* all arise from the unique British Columbia context, which has significantly influenced the development of the Court's consideration of the protections of constitutional law conferred by section 35 of the *Constitution Act, 1982.* But most of Canada is covered by treaties, whether historical or modern. Although the Court's consideration of the nature of the constitutional protections of section 35 has national application, the actual Aboriginal rights (or claims to title) considered in these BC cases do not have national application and are applicable only to the BC Aboriginal peoples who assert the rights and title.

Cases reaching the Supreme Court from the Prairie provinces—*R. v. Horse*,[22] *R. v. Horseman*,[23] *R. v. Badger*,[24] *R. v. Sundown*,[25] and *R. v. Blais*[26]—define Treaty rights in the historical numbered treaties and discuss a second source of constitutional protection for these Treaty rights: the *Natural Resource Transfer Agreements,* which are schedules to the *Constitution Act, 1930.*

The analytical model that I adopt here therefore attempts to identify the broad *terra firma* spoken of by Slattery: the basic definitions of Aboriginal and Treaty rights. The discussion is intended to identify first principles without exhaustively narrating the law. I recognize that the information in this chapter is limited, but I present it nevertheless because of its fundamental significance to the subject matter of the book. The duty to consult arises in respect of Crown conduct that has the potential to adversely affect Aboriginal and Treaty rights.

The cases cited in this chapter do not include the Supreme Court cases recognizing and developing the contours of the law of Aboriginal consultation, because these are specifically discussed in Chapter 4. Nor does this survey extend to all cases touching Aboriginal peoples. Excluded from this discussion are cases that consider the impact of the section 15 equality provisions on Aboriginal people,[27] those that consider the tax liability of Aboriginal people,[28] the boundaries of reserves,[29] or the duties of the Crown in regard to Indian reserve land.[30] Even this list of exceptions is not exhaustive, omitting applications for leave to appeal that were dismissed, or appeals that became moot,[31] most pre-

1982 cases,[32] and cases from the Privy Council era (ending in 1949), which introduced truly difficult terms such as "usufructuary rights."[33]

I begin the analysis with a discussion of the constitutional law principles applicable to both Aboriginal and Treaty rights. I then discuss the creation of modern treaties through land claim processes, the contemporary regime of claims to unextinguished Aboriginal rights in British Columbia, Métis rights, and finally the historical numbered treaties.

I use the historical treaty regime under the numbered treaties in the Prairie provinces as a primary comparator for the regime of unextinguished Aboriginal rights in British Columbia or modern treaties across Canada. I therefore explain historical treaty rights primarily, though of course not exclusively, with reference to the numbered treaties and the significant body of Supreme Court jurisprudence arising from them. I also refer to modern treaties where the Supreme Court jurisprudence considers modern treaties from Quebec and the Yukon in the context of environmental assessment and regulatory review,[34] and via a case study of a natural resource development in the Northwest Territories.

BASIC PRINCIPLES APPLICABLE TO BOTH ABORIGINAL AND TREATY RIGHTS

Constitutional Status Conferred by Section 35 of the Constitution Act, 1982

Aboriginal and Treaty rights of the Aboriginal peoples of Canada are recognized and affirmed in section 35 of Part II of the *Constitution Act, 1982*.[35] The phrase "Aboriginal peoples" includes Indians, Inuit, and Métis. In *R. v. Adams*, the Supreme Court of Canada describes the purpose of section 35 as being "to extend constitutional protection to the practices, customs, and traditions central to the distinctive culture of aboriginal societies prior to contact with Europeans."[36] Constitutional status limits the ability of the legislative branch to infringe section 35 rights. It also informs the reciprocal obligations inherent in the law of Aboriginal consultation.

The *Constitution Act, 1982* also created the *Canadian Charter of Rights and Freedoms*. Since section 35 is not within that part of the *Constitution Act* creating the *Charter*, Aboriginal and Treaty rights are not "*Charter* rights." The Aboriginal and Treaty rights recognized and affirmed under section 35 are referred to as "section 35" rights.

Section 35 Rights Vary in Nature and Scope

Section 35 rights vary because the practices, customs, and traditions central to the distinctive cultures of Aboriginal societies prior to contact with Europeans, or to the identity and practices of Métis thereafter, were not and are not the same across the vastness of Canada.[37] This variance has important implications for the contextual analysis associated with the duty to consult. The ambit of these rights is ultimately defined by the judicial branch of government as a result of litigation, or by treaties negotiated between the Crown and Aboriginal peoples, or both.

Aboriginal Rights and Treaty Rights Are Not Absolute

Section 52 of the *Constitution Act, 1982* operates in regard to section 35 rights and, on its face, section 52 makes section 35 rights paramount over conflicting law. However, in *R. v. Sparrow*[38] the Supreme Court of Canada rejected an argument that Aboriginal rights and Treaty rights were therefore "more securely protected than the rights guaranteed by the *Charter*."[39] As a result, infringement of Aboriginal and Treaty rights can be subject to a justification test that allows legislation or government action to prevail over these rights where that is justifiable. The Court recognizes that, in Canada, no rights are absolute. When dealing with section 35 rights, some balancing with other societal interests is required. This reality was described by the Supreme Court in *R. v. Badger*, where the Court cites with approval the Ontario Court of Appeal in *R. v. Agawa* in which Blair J.A. states that "... Indian treaty rights are like all other rights recognized by our legal system. The exercise of rights by an individual or group is limited by the rights of others. Rights do not exist in a vacuum and the exercise of any right involves a balancing with the interests and values involved in the rights of others."[40]

Prior to 1982, Aboriginal rights or Treaty rights could be adversely affected by ordinary legislation. After 1982, something more was required given the constitutional protection afforded to these rights by section 35. The Court in *Sparrow* ultimately cited Slattery in regard to the need for a justificatory scheme, which it then introduced.[41] In *Mikisew*, the Court confirms the impact of its decision in *Sparrow*: "*Sparrow* holds not only that rights protected by s. 35 of the *Constitution Act, 1982* are not absolute, but also that their breach may be justified by the Crown in certain defined circumstances."[42]

Infringement of Section 35 Rights May Be Justified

Where Aboriginal rights or Treaty rights are said to be breached, and this is most often the case with legislation, Aboriginal peoples can challenge the validity, applicability, or operability of the legislation. In *Sparrow*, the Court addresses the burdens of proof and criteria to be considered in regard to challenges to the constitutional validity of the infringing legislation. There are two stages: first, proof of infringement, the onus for which rests on the Aboriginal person(s) asserting the right or practice; second, justification of infringement, the onus for which rests on the Crown.

The Court places the onus of proving a *prima facie* infringement on the individual or group challenging the legislation. There are three criteria to be considered in relation to the question of whether an asserted right has been interfered with such as to constitute a *prima facie* infringement of section 35(1): "First, is the limitation unreasonable? Second, does the regulation impose undue hardship? Third, does the regulation deny to the holders of the right their preferred means of exercising that right?"[43]

At the second or justification stage, the Court places an onus of proof on the Crown to justify the infringement. There are two primary stages to the process of justification, but the list of criteria to be considered is open. The Crown must show, first, a valid legislative objective and, second, that the infringement is consistent with the honour of the Crown. Criteria material to the second stage of Crown justification include whether "there has been as little infringement as possible in order to effect the desired result; whether, in a situation of expropriation, fair compensation is available; and, whether the aboriginal group in question has been consulted with respect to ... measures being implemented."

Although *Sparrow* was a case of unextinguished Aboriginal rights, the Supreme Court confirms in *R. v. Badger* that the same principles apply to Treaty rights under the numbered treaties.[44] The Court supports the obligation to justify *prima facie* infringements of Treaty rights with the observation that Aboriginal rights were extinguished at the time of treaty: "The rights granted to Indians by treaties usually form an integral part of the consideration for the surrender of their lands."[45]

CREATION OF MODERN TREATIES IN QUÉBEC, THE YUKON, THE NORTHWEST TERRITORIES, NUNAVUT, AND LABRADOR

The decision of the Supreme Court of Canada in *Calder v. The Queen*[46] left open the question of whether Aboriginal title in British Columbia was extinguished. Following the *Calder* decision, the federal government brought forth a formal policy to negotiate modern treaties with Aboriginal peoples across Canada. Canada maintains a website that describes its comprehensive land claim policies and the status of negotiations.[47]

These modern treaties are often referred to as land claim agreements because they were negotiated following the development of a comprehensive land claims policy by the Government of Canada. To come into force, a modern treaty must be negotiated. The final negotiated agreement must then be ratified by the membership of the Aboriginal signatories and then be given the force of law binding the Crown by legislation enacted by Parliament and the legislature with jurisdiction over the subject matter of the treaty. Regardless of nomenclature, modern treaties with Canada's Aboriginal peoples have constitutional status by virtue of section 35(3) of the *Constitution Act, 1982.*

Modern treaty making is intended to give "some precision around property and governance rights and obligations."[48] Modern treaties normally involve extinguishment of asserted Aboriginal rights and title in return for formal recognition of Treaty rights and title to land as defined in the treaty itself. Modern treaties also create tribunals through which Aboriginal signatories exercise governance of land and resources as defined in the treaty and the enabling legislation. These tribunals enable Aboriginal signatories to modern treaties to exercise governance responsibilities—planning, approval, and control functions. Consultation can certainly be addressed by these treaties, but an examination of their details is required to assess how consultation may be addressed in any given instance. The Supreme Court goes so far as to say, indeed, that "the parties themselves may decide therein to exclude consultation altogether in defined situations and the decision to do so would be upheld by the courts where this outcome would be consistent with the maintenance of the honour of the Crown."[49]

After the Supreme Court judgment in *Calder,* the first modern treaty concluded was the *James Bay and Northern Quebec Agreement,* which was concluded in 1975 and amended since. It was followed by the conclusion of modern treaties in the Northwest Territories, Yukon, Nunavut, and Labrador. The *James Bay and Northern Quebec Agreement,*[50] the various Yukon agreements, the *Inuvialuit Final Agreement,*[51] the *Gwich'in Comprehensive Land Claim Agreement,*[52] the *Nunavut Land Claims Agreement,*[53] the *Tlicho Land Claims and Self Government Agreement,*[54] the *Labrador Inuit Land Claims Agreement*[55] and the *Nunavik Inuit Land Claims Agreement*[56] together encompass a significant geographical area of Canada.

Project development in the regions covered by these treaties can be impacted, depending on their location, by the terms of the treaty. The precise nature of the impact has to be assessed with reference to the terms and provisions of the treaty itself. In *Beckman,* the Court observes that modern treaties are concluded by "adequately resourced and professionally represented parties" who "have sought to order their own affairs."[57] Rights defined in each modern treaty will therefore vary considerably, recognizing the complex and varying nature of the Aboriginal rights that gave rise to the claim, the nature of the give and take in the negotiations, the language in the final treaty itself, and the implementing legislation.

The provisions of the *James Bay and Northern Quebec Agreement*, and the project governance tribunals created by it, were first considered by the Supreme Court in *Quebec (Attorney General) v. Moses*.[58] The *Agreement* was given effect, federally, by the *James Bay and Northern Quebec Native Claims Settlement Act*.[59] It provided, *inter alia*, that "All native claims, rights, title and interests, whatever they may be, in and to the Territory, of all Indians and all Inuit, wherever they may be, are hereby extinguished. ..." The National Assembly of Québec also enacted enabling legislation, an *Act Approving the Agreement Concerning James Bay and Northern Quebec*.[60]

In the Yukon, an *Umbrella Final Agreement between the Government of Canada, the Council for Yukon Indians, and the Government of the Yukon* was concluded in 1993.[61] In 1994, Parliament enacted the *Yukon First Nations Self-Government Act* to bring self-government agreements into effect.[62] More specific and individual agreements have been concluded under the *Umbrella Agreement* with the Champagne and Aishihik First Nations (1995), the Teslin Tlingit Council (1995), the First Nation of Nacho Nyak Dun (1995), the Vuntut Gwitchin First Nation (1995), the Little Salmon/Carmacks First Nation (1997), the Selkirk First Nation (1997), the Tr'ondëk Hwëch'in (1998), the Ta'an Kwäch'än Council (2002), the Kluane First Nation (2004), the Kwanlin Dün First Nation (2005) and the Carcross/Tagish First Nation (2006).[63] Three other Aboriginal groups remain in negotiation. The Supreme Court judgment in *Beckman v. Little Salmon/Carmacks First Nation* involved judicial consideration of the *Little Salmon/Carmacks First Nation Final Agreement*.[64] The process of creating tribunals was still in progress when the litigation that ultimately reached the Court began, and had a material influence on the judgment of the Court.

In 1984, in the Northwest Territories, Canada and the Inuvialuit concluded the *Western Arctic Claim: The Inuvialuit Final Agreement*.[65] This was given effect by Parliament when it enacted the *Western Arctic (Inuvialuit) Claims Settlement Act*.[66] In 1992, Canada and the Gwich'in concluded the *Gwich'in Comprehensive Land Claim Settlement Agreement*,[67] given effect by the *Gwich'in Land Claim Settlement Act*.[68] In 1993, Canada and the Sahtu Dene and Métis signed a *Comprehensive Land Claim Agreement*,[69] given effect by the *Sahtu Dene and Métis Land Claim Settlement Act*.[70] The *Tlicho Land Claims and Self Government Agreement*[71] followed some years later, given effect by the *Tlicho Land Claims and Self-Government Act*.[72] The *Mackenzie Valley Resource Management Act*[73] was enacted by Parliament to structure the regulatory apparatus in the Northwest Territories accordingly. The case study of the Mackenzie Gas Project in Chapter 5 discusses a project-specific effort to harmonize the responsibilities of these tribunals. The tribunals with a public hearing process in regard to such a project are listed there.

The Northwest Territories was divided, and the territory known as Nunavut created, by the *Nunavut Land Claims Agreement Act*[74] and the *Nunavut Act*.[75] The *Nunavut Waters and Nunavut Surface Rights Tribunal Act*[76] created the Nunavut Water Board[77] and the Nunavut Surface Rights Tribunal. Other tribunals created in this initiative include the Nunavut Impact Review Board, the Nunavut Planning Commission, and the Nunavut Wildlife Management Board.[78]

The *Labrador Inuit Lands Claims Agreement*[79] was concluded with Canada, the Government of Newfoundland and Labrador, and the Nunatsiavut Government in 2005 and was given effect by the federal *Labrador Inuit Land Claims Agreement Act*[80] and the provincial *Labrador Inuit Land Claims Agreement Act*.[81] It was amended in 2010 to incorporate an *Overlap Agreement* reached in November 2005 between the Labrador Inuit and Nunavik (Quebec) Inuit.[82]

The Supreme Court has twice considered Aboriginal consultation in the context of modern treaties created by the negotiation of land claim agreements.[83] In both cases, the Court divided, with a majority judgment[84] and a dissenting minority judgment.[85] In both cases, the dissenting minority approached the modern treaty as more definitive regarding the rights of the parties than did the majority. Yet even the majority judgment in *Beckman* states that, "Where adequately resourced and professionally represented parties have sought to order their own affairs, and have given shape to the duty to consult by incorporating consultation procedures into a treaty, their efforts should be encouraged and, subject to such constitutional limitations as the honour of the Crown, the Court should strive to respect their handiwork: *Quebec (Attorney General) v. Moses*. ..."[86] This suggests that the contours of the duty to consult and, where necessary, accommodate will have definite limits where modern treaties define consultation obligations.

THE BRITISH COLUMBIA TREATY NEGOTIATION PROCESS

In British Columbia, modern treaty making has not enjoyed the success that it has in other provinces and territories of Canada. In a 2006 report, the Auditor General of British Columbia comments on the negative consequence of the *Calder* decision from an economic perspective in British Columbia: "It creates a state of uncertainty about land and resource management."[87]

Historical treaties are few in British Columbia. In *R. v. Morris,* the Supreme Court describes how "[b]etween 1850 and 1854, 14 treaties were concluded with bands living on Vancouver Island. These came to be known as the *Douglas Treaties,* named after James Douglas, Governor of the Colony of Vancouver Island at the time."[88] Treaty 8 extends into the northeastern corner of British Columbia. The first modern Treaty concluded in British Columbia is the *Nisga'a Final Agreement.*[89] This was brought into force by the *Nisga'a Final Agreement Act of Canada*[90] and by the *Nisga'a Final Agreement Act of British Columbia.*[91]

In 1992, the Governments of Canada and British Columbia "and the First Nations Summit, representing the First Nations involved in the process, created the BC Treaty Process."[92] The British Columbia Treaty Commission was created by legislation.[93] The Commission oversees the process and allocate funding from the federal and provincial governments to the First Nations involved in the negotiation process.[94] It publishes annual reports that document its activities.[95] The negotiation of modern treaties in British Columbia therefore occurs within a unique, six-stage process.[96] The first modern treaty negotiated under the British Columbia Treaty Process, with the Tsawwassen First Nation, came into effect on April 3, 2009.[97] A second, with the Maa-nulth First Nations of Vancouver Island, came into effect on Vancouver Island on April 1, 2011.[98]

The status quo regarding these negotiations under the BC Treaty Process was discussed in the *2006 November Report of the Auditor General of Canada.*[99] This audit was conducted in collaboration with an audit by the Auditor General of British Columbia, who also produced a report.[100] The Auditor General of Canada also describes the general lack of progress, as measured by the conclusion of treaties, in the negotiation process:

> Initially, the federal government expected that all claims in B.C. would be resolved by the year 2000. Today, about 40 percent of eligible B.C. First Nations, or *Indian Act* bands, representing about 30 percent of their population, do not participate in the process. ... [T]he process has not yet resulted in any treaties with First Nations. After spending hundreds of millions of dollars over more than 12 years of negotiations, the results achieved are well below the three parties' initial expectations.[101]

The causes of this lack of progress are many but include, in the views of both Auditors General, differing visions and perspectives:

Successful negotiations require that the participants share a common vision of their relationship and of the future. Our two audits found that the participants have differing views on the nature of the treaties being negotiated. For example, the two governments base their participation in the treaty process on their own policies, and do not recognize the Aboriginal rights and title claimed by the First Nations. Many First Nations base their participation in the process on the assertion that they have Aboriginal rights under Canada's Constitution and that these rights should be acknowledged before negotiations begin. Additionally, the governments see treaties as a full and final settlement of the Aboriginal rights and title claimed by First Nations, whereas First Nations see them as documents capable of evolving as the relationship between the parties develops.[102]

If a modern treaty is not negotiated in regard to asserted Aboriginal rights and title, then these rights and titles must be proven before a court.

PROOF OF ABORIGINAL RIGHTS

The Supreme Court describes how unextinguished Aboriginal rights and titles can be proven if negotiation fails and litigation is necessary. This jurisprudence applies to any context in which an Aboriginal person may be required to prove an asserted Aboriginal right or title.

Burden of Proof for Establishing Aboriginal Rights

Aboriginal rights and title are subject to necessity of proof. The burden of that proof was defined in *R. v. Van der Peet*.[103] The Court selected the time prior to contact with Europeans as the time for assessing Indian aboriginal practices that fall within the protections afforded to Aboriginal rights by section 35.[104] The Court made it clear that the alleged practice making up the right had to be rooted in the pre-contact period and must continue to the present day. In summary, the term "pre-contact" is specific to the "integral to a distinctive culture" criterion that the Court established as the essence of Aboriginal rights.

Burden of Proof for Aboriginal Title

The assertion of Aboriginal title is fundamental to Aboriginal claims to land in British Columbia and to the negotiation of land claim agreements resulting in modern treaties. The relationship between Aboriginal rights and Aboriginal title was discussed by the Supreme Court in the companion judgments of *R. v. Adams*[105] and *R. v. Côté*.[106]

Both cases originated in Quebec. The Court defined the issue before it as "whether aboriginal rights are necessarily based in aboriginal title to land, so that the fundamental claim that must be made in any aboriginal rights case is to aboriginal title, or whether aboriginal title is instead one subset of the larger category of aboriginal rights, so that fishing and other aboriginal rights can exist independently of a claim to aboriginal title."[107]

The Court held that Aboriginal rights (for example, fishing or hunting) could be proven to exist in circumstances where proof of Aboriginal title was not asserted or made out.[108] The Court added a proviso, noting at paragraph 30 that,

> [e]ven where an aboriginal right exists on a tract of land to which the aboriginal people in question do not have title, that right may well be site specific, with the result that it can be exercised only upon that specific tract of land. ... A site-specific hunting or fishing right does not, simply because it is independent of aboriginal title to the land on which it took place, become an abstract fishing or hunting right exercisable anywhere; it continues to be a right to hunt or fish *on the tract of land in question.*

Delgamuukw demonstrates some of the difficulties associated with litigated resolutions of claims to Aboriginal title. In this case, a claim of asserted Aboriginal title went to trial in British Columbia. The trial itself involved 318 days of testimony and a total of 374 days of evidence and argument combined. The trial judgment, in printed format,[109] was almost 400 pages long, with an additional 100 pages of schedules. In the result, the case reached the Supreme Court, which ordered a new trial.

The Court recognizes the possibility of, and limitations inherent in, Aboriginal title. The Court described the single issue before it as "the nature and scope of the constitutional protection afforded by s. 35(1) to common law aboriginal title."[110] In the course of reaching its decision, the Court offered an answer to the question "What is the content of aboriginal title, how is it protected by s. 35(1) of the Constitution Act, 1982, and what is required for its proof?"[111] The Court upheld the concept of Aboriginal title, summarizing at paragraph 124 that "the content of aboriginal title is not restricted to those uses which are elements of a practice, custom or tradition integral to the distinctive culture of the aboriginal group claiming the right. However, nor does aboriginal title amount to a form of inalienable fee simple."

The most direct approach to *Delgamuukw* is through subsequent decisions of the Court that articulate the *ratio decidendi* of the case. In

R. v. Marshall; R. v. Bernard,[112] the Court confirms that *Delgamuukw* "enunciated a test for aboriginal title based on exclusive occupation at the time of British sovereignty" but that "[m]any of the details of how this principle applies to particular circumstances remain to be fully developed." Regarding the specific requirements for title, the Court states in *R. v. Marshall; R. v. Bernard* that

55 This review of the general principles underlying the issue of aboriginal title to land brings us to the specific requirements for title set out in *Delgamuukw*. To establish title, claimants must prove "exclusive" pre-sovereignty "occupation" of the land by their forebears: *per* Lamer C.J., at para. 143.

56 "Occupation" means "physical occupation." This "may be established in a variety of ways, ranging from the construction of dwellings through cultivation and enclosure of fields to regular use of definite tracts of land for hunting, fishing or otherwise exploiting its resources": *Delgamuukw, per* Lamer C.J., at para. 149.

57 "Exclusive" occupation flows from the definition of aboriginal title as "the right to *exclusive* use and occupation of land": *Delgamuukw, per* Lamer C.J., at para. 155 (emphasis in original). It is consistent with the concept of title to land at common law. Exclusive occupation means "the intention and capacity to retain exclusive control," and is not negated by occasional acts of trespass or the presence of other aboriginal groups with consent (*Delgamuukw*, at para. 156, citing McNeil, at p. 204). Shared exclusivity may result in joint title (para. 158). Non-exclusive occupation may establish aboriginal rights "short of title" (para. 159).

58 It follows from the requirement of exclusive occupation that exploiting the land, rivers or seaside for hunting, fishing or other resources may translate into aboriginal title to the land if the activity was sufficiently regular and exclusive to comport with title at common law. However, more typically, seasonal hunting and fishing rights exercised in a particular area will translate to a hunting or fishing right.

Regarding what must be proven, the Court confirms that "[a]ll that is required is demonstration of effective control of the land by the group, from which a reasonable inference can be drawn that it could have excluded others had it chosen to do so."[113] Such evidence can be tendered by a nomadic or semi-nomadic people, but there must be continuity in that, "[t]o claim title, the group's connection with the land must be shown to have been 'of a central significance to their distinctive culture': *Adams*, at para. 26. If the group has 'maintained a substantial connection' with the land since sovereignty [and to the present day], this establishes the required 'central significance': *Delgamuukw, per* Lamer C.J., at paras. 150–51."[114] The Court concludes that, typically, "Aboriginal title is established by showing regular occupancy or use of definite tracts of land for hunting, fishing or exploiting resources: *Delgamuukw*, at para. 149. Less intensive uses may give rise to different rights."[115]

Delgamuukw establishes that, once proven, Aboriginal title has limiting qualities. Such land "cannot be put to such uses as may be irreconcilable with the nature of the occupation of that land and the relationship that the particular group has had with the land which together have given rise to aboriginal title in the first place."[116] The implications for project development on lands subject to Aboriginal title are significant. If such development is not consistent with the special bond held by the Aboriginal people in relation to that land, then it is prevented. The Court states at paragraph 131 of *Delgamuukw* that, "[i]f aboriginal peoples wish to use their lands in a way that aboriginal title does not permit, then they must surrender those lands and convert them into non-title lands to do so."

MÉTIS RIGHTS

Métis are Aboriginal people whose asserted Aboriginal rights to hunt were the subject of consideration by the Supreme Court in *R. v. Powley*[117] and *R. v. Blais*.[118] The result confirms that section 35 of the *Constitution Act, 1982* can afford constitutional protection to Métis hunting rights where such rights are proven and the claimants are properly identified as Métis. The Court modified the test for Aboriginal rights slightly to define how Métis rights could be asserted. The Court confirms that Métis rights, like Indian rights, are contextual and site specific. The Court applies the *Van der Peet* test for proof of Aboriginal rights to proof of Métis rights but modifies the pre-contact test "to reflect the distinctive history and post-contact ethnogenesis of the Métis, and the resulting differences between Indian claims and Métis claims."[119] It was necessary, of course, for the Court to modify the pre-contact time used as the basis for assessing claims to Indian Aboriginal rights because "[t]he unique status of the Métis as an Aboriginal people with post-contact origins requires an adaptation of the pre-contact approach to meet the distinctive historical circumstances surrounding the evolution of Métis communities."[120] The Court concludes that pre-control, rather than pre-contact, should be the relevant time period for defining the asserted right, reasoning that "[t]he focus should be on the period after a particular Métis community arose and before it came under the effective control of European laws and customs. This pre-control test enables us to identify those practices, customs and traditions that predate the imposition of European laws and customs on the Métis."[121]

A claimant to a Métis right also carries a burden of proof that he or she is Métis. Paragraph 10 of *Powley* defines the term "Métis" to refer "to distinctive peoples who, in addition to their mixed ancestry, developed their own customs, way of life, and recognizable group identity separate from their Indian or Inuit and European forebears." With regard to communality, the Court describes Métis rights as Aboriginal rights, that is, "communal rights" that "must be grounded in the existence of a historic and present community, and they may only be exercised by virtue of an individual's ancestrally based membership in the present community."[122] The Court states that "proof of shared customs, traditions, and a collective identity is required to demonstrate the existence of a Métis community that can support a claim to site-specific aboriginal rights."[123] As with Indians, there must be "some degree of continuity and stability in order to support a site-specific aboriginal rights claim."[124] Membership in the community, what the Court describes as Métis identity, must be proven "on a case-by-case basis" until such time as Métis communities "organize themselves more formally … such that membership requirements become more standardized."[125]

The Court does not therefore "set down a comprehensive definition of who is Métis for the purpose of asserting a claim under s. 35." Instead, it endorses guidelines to be applied by the lower courts on a case-by-case basis with particular reference to three factors: "self-identification, ancestral connection, and community acceptance."[126] The claimant must self-identify as a member of a Métis community, must present evidence of an ancestral connection to a historical Métis community, and must demonstrate that he or she is accepted by the modern community whose continuity with the historical community provides the legal foundation for the right being claimed.[127]

The potential for Métis claims to Aboriginal title remains unclear in Canadian law. Land grants or scrip issued for Métis, and said to be towards the extinguishment of the Indian title, were made pursuant to the *Manitoba Act, 1870* and the *Dominion Lands Act*.[128] In litigation cited as *Manitoba Metis Federation v. Canada (Attorney General)*, the Supreme Court of Canada ultimately issued a single declaration: "That the federal Crown failed to implement the land grant provisions of the Manitoba Act, 1870 in accordance with the Honour of the Crown." The Court noted that the Métis litigants "seek this declaratory relief in order to assist them in extra-judicial negotiations with the Crown in pursuit of the overarching constitutional goal of reconciliation that is reflected in s. 35 of the Constitution."[129] It is too early yet to ascertain whether the decision will give rise to policies similar to those generated by the Court's *Calder* decision almost exactly forty years earlier.

TREATY RIGHTS UNDER THE HISTORICAL NUMBERED TREATIES
Introduction

The *Royal Proclamation of 1763*[130] anticipated that lands might be ceded to the Crown. In the case of the numbered treaties, commissioners met with Indians for this purpose.[131] The Supreme Court confirms that the objective of the historical numbered treaties "was to facilitate the settlement of the West."[132] The Crown had asserted sovereignty and was in the course of exercising control by enabling a transcontinental railway and opening the lands to settlement and consequential development pursuant to the federal *Dominion Lands Act* and other statutes and regulations. An era in which lands that had seen fur trade with canoes and York boats for over a century following contact between Indians and Europeans, during which time a distinct Métis population had evolved, was about to change irrevocably to an era of migration on a scale previously unseen in this region of the world. It was reasonable that land uses associated with settlement were likely to be inconsistent in some cases with the Aboriginal avocations of hunting, fishing, and trapping. Indians were advised of the Crown's intent and were invited to enter into treaties that documented their consent to the opening up of lands in this way. Aboriginal rights and title were ceded—extinguished—in return for rights documented in the treaties and referred to here as Treaty rights. The Court confirms in *R. v. Horse* that "The ultimate objective of this treaty was for the Government to obtain ownership of the lands it covered and to open the surrendered lands to settlement."[133]

Avocations of Hunting, Fishing, and Trapping

The numbered treaties therefore extinguish Aboriginal rights and title of Indian signatories in return for treaty commitments. Those most often engaged by project development are Treaty rights described as the avocations of hunting, fishing, and trapping. The Court comments in its decision in *Côté* that "a substantive ... right will normally include the incidental right to teach such a practice, custom and tradition to a younger generation."[134] The Court confirms in *R. v. Marshall; R. v. Bernard* that Treaty rights "are not frozen in time" such that the traditional avocations of hunting, fishing, and trapping can be carried out in modern ways that are reasonably incidental to the avocation.[135] What is "reasonably incidental" is determined on a case-by-case basis using an objective test. Would "a reasonable person, fully apprised of the relevant manner of hunting or fishing, consider the activity in question reasonably related to the act of hunting or fishing?"[136]

Limitations Inherent to Hunting, Fishing, and Trapping

The terms of the numbered treaties themselves establish limitations inherent to the Treaty rights to hunt, fish, and trap. Writing in 1998 in regard to Treaty 8, the Supreme Court notes that

> The Treaty, however, imposed two limitations on the right to hunt. First, there was a geographic limitation. The right to hunt could be exercised "throughout the tract surrendered ... saving and excepting such tracts as may be required or taken up from time to time for settlement, mining, lumbering, trading or other purposes." Second, the right could be limited by [federal] government regulations passed for conservation purposes.[137]

The Natural Resource Transfer Agreements of 1930

Until 1930, the federal Crown held administration and control of Crown lands, including mines and minerals, in the lands that now comprise the Prairie provinces.[138] Administration and control of Crown lands were transferred to Alberta, Saskatchewan, and Manitoba in 1930 pursuant to a constitutional amendment embodied in the *Natural Resource Transfer Agreements* [NRTAs] concluded with each province and given force and effect by the *Constitution Act, 1930*. The NRTAs comprise a constitutional document and an additional source of constitutional protection for hunting, fishing, and trapping under the numbered treaties.

Source of Constitutional Status

Regarding the avocations of hunting, fishing, and trapping in the numbered treaties, the NRTAs provide that,

> In order to secure to the Indians of the Province the continuance of the supply of game and fish for their support and subsistence, Canada agrees that the laws respecting game in force in the Province from time to time shall apply to the Indians within the boundaries thereof, provided, however, that the said Indians

shall have the right, which the Province hereby assures to them, of hunting, trapping and fishing game and fish for food at all seasons of the year on all unoccupied Crown lands and on any other lands to which the said Indians may have a right of access.[139]

Purpose

The Supreme Court defines the purpose of this article in the NRTAs. In *Moosehunter v. The Queen,* the Court states that "The reason or purpose underlying paragraph 12 was to secure to the Indians a supply of game and fish for their support and subsistence and clearly to permit hunting, trapping and fishing for food at all seasons of the year on all unoccupied Crown lands and lands to which the Indians had access."[140] In *R. v. Horseman,* the Court states that "...of equal importance was the desire to re-state and reassure to the treaty Indians the continued enjoyment of the right to hunt and fish for food."[141] In *R. v. Blais,* the Court indicates that "[t]he purpose ... of the NRTA is to ensure respect for the Crown's obligations to 'Indians' with respect to hunting rights. It was enacted to protect the hunting rights of the beneficiaries of Indian treaties and the *Indian Act* in the context of the transfer of Crown land to the provinces."[142] Common to all of these cases is affirmation that the NRTAs give constitutional protection as a sign of respect for the treaty obligations.

Merger and Consolidation

The NRTAs also caused what is described as merger and consolidation to the constitutional protection afforded to hunting, fishing, and trapping under the numbered treaties. First, the treaty avocations of hunting, fishing, and trapping are expanded beyond the boundaries of the treaty itself and extend throughout the Prairie provinces. Second, any commercial aspect of these avocations is extinguished.[143] Third, these avocations, which under the treaty itself could be regulated only by federal law, can be regulated by provincial game laws provided that they have a conservation purpose.[144]

Limitation on Provincial Powers

The effect of the NRTAs on the exercise of provincial legislative power as it may apply to the rights of Indians under the numbered treaties was discussed by the Supreme Court in *Frank v. The Queen* at page 100,[145] *The Queen v. Sutherland et al.,*[146] *Moosehunter v. The Queen* at page 285,[147] *R. v. Horse,*[148] *R. v. Horseman* at pages 931–32,[149] *R. v. Badger* at paragraph 45,[150] and in regard to Métis in *R. v. Blais.*[151] The

NRTAs impose constitutional obligations on the provinces in regard to the Treaty rights of hunting, fishing, and trapping and therefore limit provincial legislative powers as they apply to Indians. The effective result is described in *R. v. Horseman* and followed in *R. v. Badger*:

> [A]n Indian of the Province is free to hunt or trap game in such numbers, at such times of the year, by such means or methods and with such contrivances, as he may wish, provided he is doing so in order to obtain food for his own use and on unoccupied Crown lands or other lands to which he may have a right of access. The Court notes in R. v. Badger that "the 'right of access' in the NRTA does not refer to a general right of access but, rather, it is limited to a right of *access for the purposes of hunting*."[152]

If hunting is absolutely prohibited by provincial legislation in a provincial park or game reserve, then that prohibition would apply to Indians since there is no right of access. However, if limited hunting is allowed, such as during open season, then Indians may hunt year round for food regardless of the close season. This right to hunt for food does not extend to threatened or endangered species for which there is a ban on hunting, fishing, or trapping, in order to preserve the species.

Access to Private Lands

The Court notes in *R. v. Horse* that, for private lands, Treaty 6 affords no right of access to occupied private land except with the consent of the owner of the land. This rationale applies to all of the numbered treaties in the absence of specific treaty language to the contrary. For private lands, therefore, numbered treaty rights to pursue the avocations of hunting, fishing, and trapping do not normally apply and the constitutional protections afforded by the NRTAs do not normally operate. As the Court notes in *Mikisew Cree*, again with regard to Treaty 8, the numbered treaties were "designed to open up the Canadian west and northwest to settlement and development" and therefore Treaty 8 rights to hunt, fish, and trap are excluded from lands taken up.[153]

But how does a person know when lands are privately owned or otherwise taken up? In many cases, this is not necessarily evident to those on the ground.[154] The Court addressed this issue in *R. v. Badger*, applying the concept of "visible, incompatible land use." Although such use needs to be determined in the context of each case, it is entirely consistent with a contextual analysis, and the Court considers this standard "neither unduly vague nor unworkable."[155]

Reserves and Treaty Land Entitlement

The treaties promised the creation and protection of reserves, a land base for Indians. The Crown created reserves throughout the prairies over many years, but, in the result, cases of insufficient allocation of reserve land arose. Grievances today are addressed through federal-provincial cooperation reflecting the need to accumulate Crown land, including mines and minerals, and transfer it from provincial control to federal control, in order to satisfy outstanding obligations.

In 1992, Saskatchewan and Canada concluded a *Treaty Land Entitlement [TLE] Framework Agreement*[156] under which, over time, a series of individual *Treaty Land Entitlement Agreements* with individual First Nations have been concluded. The Legislative Assembly of Saskatchewan enacted the *Treaty Land Entitlement Implementation Act*,[157] which defines the interests of Saskatchewan, if any, in reserves created under the *TLE Framework Agreement*. The legislature also concluded an *Agreement* amending the Saskatchewan *Natural Resource Transfer Agreement*, given effect by *An Act to Confirm an Agreement between the Government of Canada and the Government of Saskatchewan Varying the Saskatchewan Natural Resources Transfer Agreements*, in order to address the provincial obligation to set aside treaty lands so that it was consistent with the obligations undertaken in the *TLE Framework Agreement*.[158] Parliament enacted corresponding legislation, the *Saskatchewan Treaty Land Entitlement Act (1993)*,[159] ratifying the amendment to the *NRTA* for Saskatchewan and creating the Treaty Land Entitlement (Saskatchewan) Fund for money contributed by both levels of government under the *Framework Agreement*. Manitoba concluded a *Treaty Land Entitlement Master Agreement* in 1997.[160] Treaty land entitlement claims in Alberta are managed through the federal Specific Claims Process[161] and are individually settled with the assistance of Alberta.[162]

Fundamental Principles of Environmental Assessment and Regulatory Review

The protection of the environment has become one of the major challenges of our time. To respond to this challenge, governments and international organizations have been engaged in the creation of a wide variety of legislative schemes and administrative structures.

—*Friends of the Oldman River Society v. Canada (Minister of Transport)*, [1992] 1 S.C.R. 3.

SUSTAINABLE DEVELOPMENT AND THE COSTS OF FAILURE

In this chapter, I describe environmental assessment and regulatory review processes with reference to the essential functions that they perform rather than to the many specific forms that they take. Although the actual procedures can vary under differing legislative regimes, the underlying functions of planning, approval, and control remain constant.

A blogger in the *Harvard Business Review*, offering unproven opinion on underlying causes of the BP's Deepwater Horizon disaster in the Gulf of Mexico in 2010, points out the potential for harm where planning, approval, and control functions are not robust: "It should come as no surprise that the current oil spill happened not in Norway, but in a jurisdiction where regulatory oversight of deep-sea drilling was relatively weak."[1] The final report of the commission established to inquire into the oil spill affirms this observation, concluding that a weak regulatory oversight system needed improvement:

> To assure human safety and environmental protection, regulatory oversight of leasing, energy exploration, and production require reforms even beyond those significant reforms already initiated since the *Deepwater Horizon* disaster. Fundamental reform will be needed in both the structure of those in charge of regulatory oversight and their internal decision making process to ensure their political autonomy, technical expertise, and their full consideration of environmental protection concerns.[2]

The costs of failure in environmental assessment/regulatory review or regulatory oversight can be controversial, economically, socially, and environmentally damaging, and politically unacceptable. At their best, therefore, industry and governments have a common interest in ensuring that sustainability of development is assessed and implemented through robust environmental assessment/regulatory review, approval, and regulatory oversight processes.[3]

Qualities that make up a robust regulatory system are summarized in *Road to Improvement*, a report prepared by a former chair of the Alberta Energy Resources Conservation Board, in regard to regulatory bodies in the Northwest Territories.[4] *Road to Improvement* describes the objectives of a model regulatory system as being understandable and neutral; enjoying a clear mandate exercised with an open, transparent, and fair process that is timely, consistent, and predictable; and being accountable for its decision-making process. The tribunal must have adequate funding to ensure a certain level of education and training for the regulatory body to perform its duties, including proper orientation, continuing education, and upgrading of skills. Where there are multiple regulatory bodies in relation to the same matter, tribunals must coordinate their actions to avoid duplication and ensure timeliness. And the tribunal can establish rules and ensure that they are enforced.[5] These principles are applied in studies and learning materials distributed through regulatory associations such as the Council of Canadian Administrative Tribunals[6] or the Society of Ontario Adjudicators and Regulators.[7]

In Canada, the purpose of robust environmental assessment/regulatory review and subsequent regulatory oversight is to contribute to sustainable development. Many statutes adopt the term "sustainable development" as a goal or objective. The term is derived from the "Brundtland Report."[8] Its meaning is most frequently said to be development that meets the needs of the present without compromising the ability of future generations to meet their own needs. It is natural to include Aboriginal communities in the scope of the term "future generations." It follows that there is a natural relationship between Aboriginal consultation and the law of environmental assessment and regulatory review.

THE FUNCTIONS OF ENVIRONMENTAL ASSESSMENT AND REGULATORY REVIEW

Parliament and legislatures enact laws requiring proponents of projects to obtain project approval and also licences, permits, or other forms of regulatory approval in relation to project development. These are primary legal mechanisms through which governments seek to control potentially adverse environmental effects of projects undertaken within their jurisdictions or to ensure the social and economic benefits of such projects. All are usually subject to conditions. Project approval therefore does not confer a right to operate regardless of environmental impact or benefit, but an obligation to operate within constraints and parameters imposed by conditions of approval.[9] These conditions usually include an obligation to comply with law as it may exist from time to time in the future. Conditions of approval themselves, as well as laws, may change from time to time after project approval, in order to respond to changing conditions and technologies.

In many instances, responsibility for these planning, approval, or control functions is delegated by the legislative branch of government to a tribunal with expertise in the subject matter. Such tribunals are created by legislation and empowered by that legislation to make plan, approve, or control projects with regard to the specific mandate conferred by the enabling legislation. In some cases, the decisions of such tribunals are subject to cabinet, ministerial, or other forms of approval before having any legal effect.[10]

DIVISION OF POWERS IN CANADA'S FEDERAL DEMOCRACY

Environmental assessment law developed rapidly in the last quarter of the twentieth century.[11] Today all jurisdictions in Canada have a form of environmental assessment legislation. The leading case from the Supreme Court of Canada dealing with environmental assessment is *Friends of the Oldman River Society v. Canada (Minister of Transport)*.[12] That case established three fundamental points: (1) that environmental assessment is a process of decision making; (2) that the environment includes the biophysical and human spheres; and (3) that legislative power in regard to the environment with the division of powers in sections 91 and 92 of the *Constitution Act, 1867* is shared between the federal and provincial governments. On the last principle, two recent judgments of the Court—*MiningWatch Canada v. Canada (Fisheries and Oceans)*[13] and *Quebec (Attorney General) v. Moses*[14]—point toward cooperative federalism as a preferred mechanism for addressing the overlap of constitutional responsibility in regard to environmental assessment.

Environmental assessment is a process of decision making. Its purposes are described in *Friends of the Oldman River Society*, where the Court states:

> Environmental impact assessment is, in its simplest form, a planning tool that is now generally regarded as an integral component of sound decision-making. Its fundamental purpose is summarized by R. Cotton and D. P. Emond in "Environmental Impact Assessment," in J. Swaigen, ed., *Environmental Rights in Canada* (1981), 245, at p. 247:
>
>> The basic concepts behind environmental assessment are simply stated: (1) early identification and evaluation of all potential environmental consequences of a proposed undertaking; (2) decision making that both guarantees the adequacy of this process and reconciles, to the greatest extent possible, the proponent's development desires with environmental protection and preservation.
>
> As a planning tool it has both an information-gathering and a decision-making component which provide the decision maker with an objective basis for granting or denying approval for a proposed development.... In short, environmental impact assessment is simply descriptive of a process of decision-making.[15]

Although the Court was considering a federal regulation in this case, since repealed, these principles transcend the particulars of the case and are valid in all cases of environmental assessment.

The Commissioner of the Environment and Sustainable Development, an office of the Auditor General of Canada, writes that "[i]dentifying the potential environmental effects of a project *before it proceeds* is critical to anticipating, preventing, and reducing environmental damages" (emphasis added). He continues:

> Conducting environmental assessment early in the planning and proposal stages of a project is important so that the analysis can be of practical use to decision makers and mitigation measures can be incorporated into the project plans. Failure to predict and mitigate adverse environmental effects before carrying out a project can lead to significant environmental degradation and increased economic costs.
>
> Effective, timely, and meaningful public consultation can help ensure that public concerns and values are considered during the environmental assessment process.[16]

The Supreme Court confirms that environmental assessment is not limited to the biophysical environment of flora and fauna but must also include the human environment of economy and social well-being. Citing the "Brundtland Report"[17] as support, the Court states:

> I cannot accept that the concept of environmental quality is confined to the biophysical environment alone; such an interpretation is unduly myopic and contrary to the generally held view that the "environment" is a diffuse subject matter; see *R. v. Crown Zellerbach Canada Ltd.*, [1988] 1 S.C.R. 401. The point was made by the Canadian Council of Resource and Environment Ministers, following the "Brundtland Report" of the World Commission on Environment and Development, in the *Report of the National Task Force on Environment and Economy*, September 24, 1987, at p. 2:
>
> > Our recommendations reflect the principles that we hold in common with the World Commission on Environment and Development... . These include the fundamental belief that environmental and economic planning cannot proceed in separate spheres. Long-term economic growth depends on a healthy environment. It also affects the environment in many ways. Ensuring environmentally sound and sustainable economic development requires the technology and wealth that is generated by continued economic growth.

Economic and environmental planning and management
must therefore be integrated.

Surely the potential consequences for a community's livelihood,
health and other social matters from environmental change are
integral to decision-making on matters affecting environmental
quality, subject, of course, to the constitutional imperatives, an
issue I will address later.[18]

The consequence for a federal nation such as Canada, in which the
"environment" as a matter is not enumerated in the division of powers,
is that "[i]t must be recognized that the environment is not an independent matter of legislation under the *Constitution Act, 1867* and that
it is a constitutionally abstruse matter which does not comfortably fit
within the existing division of powers without considerable overlap
and uncertainty."[19]

As a planning tool, environmental assessment is advisory (that is,
it informs subsequent decision making). The Court describes "what is
involved" as "essentially an information gathering process in furtherance
of a decision-making function" such that "the recommendations made
at the conclusion of the information gathering stage are not binding on
the decision maker." The Court finds that it is "not particularly helpful"
to characterize any particular project as either "a 'provincial project'
or an undertaking 'primarily subject to provincial regulation.'"[20] It
is not helpful to suggest, therefore, that a level of government with
a regulatory power in relation to a project may not consider the full
range of environmental effects of that project before exercising that
regulatory power. Rather,

What is important is to determine whether either level of government may legislate. One may legislate in regard to provincial
aspects, the other federal aspects. Although local projects will
generally fall within provincial responsibility, federal participation will be required if the project impinges on an area of federal
jurisdiction, as is the case here.[21]

Where both levels of government have legislative power (for example,
approval, permitting, or licencing authority) in relation to the same
project or aspects of that project, then they may validly consider the full
range of potential environmental effects of that project when considering
whether to exercise their respective legislative powers. This is necessarily incidental to the exercise of legislative power in each case because

assessment of environmental effects is not capable of being divided into watertight compartments allocated to the federal or provincial government exclusively. "To suggest otherwise"—as the Court states in *Friends of the Oldman River Society*—"would lead to the most astonishing results, and it defies reason to assert that Parliament is constitutionally barred from weighing the broad environmental repercussions, including socio-economic concerns, when legislating with respect to decisions of this nature."[22] There is, therefore, broad constitutional capacity for effective planning in both levels of government. But regardless of the breadth of that constitutional capacity, legislation may limit or define the scope of the inquiry delegated to a tribunal or to any particular branch of government during environmental assessment and regulatory review. This is evident in the *Canadian Environmental Assessment Act, 2012*, where the environmental effects that are to be the focus of federal environmental assessment are specifically listed in section 5.[23]

Environmental assessment informs regulatory decision making and blends into it. Such assessment identifies the environmental effects of a project with regard to the implementation of mitigation measures. That is a planning exercise, and there is little sense in considering the significance of potential environmental effects separately from measures that might mitigate those adverse effects.[24] The transition from a planning exercise to a regulatory oversight occurs with regard to the actual implementation of mitigation measures. Mitigation measures that are significant to the assessment of adverse environmental effects need to be implemented by being made conditions of regulatory approval. At that point, the constitutional capacity of each level of government to implement mitigations becomes significant, because environmental assessment has fulfilled its advisory capacity and a regulatory decision is being made. At that point, a planning function becomes a regulatory decision, and the constitutional capacity of each level of government to actually implement mitigations becomes significant.

COOPERATIVE FEDERALISM AND REDUCTION OF DUPLICATION OF PROCESS

Overlap of federal and provincial jurisdictions in regard to project development is *ordinary* in Canada's federal system. This was articulated most recently in *NIL/TU,O Child and Family Services Society v. B.C. Government and Service Employees' Union*:[25]

> [42] Today's constitutional landscape is painted with the brush of co-operative federalism (*Husky Oil Operations Ltd. v. Minister of National Revenue*, [1995] 3 S.C.R. 453, at para. 162,

per Iacobucci J.; *Multiple Access Ltd. v. McCutcheon*, [1982] 2 S.C.R. 161; *Reference re Firearms Act*, 2000 SCC 31, [2000] 1 S.C.R. 783; *Kitkatla Band v. British Columbia (Minister of Small Business, Tourism and Culture)*, 2002 SCC 31, [2002] 2 S.C.R. 146; *Fédération des producteurs de volailles du Québec v. Pelland*, 2005 SCC 20, [2005] 1 S.C.R. 292; *Canadian Western Bank*, at paras. 21–24; *Consolidated Fastfrate*, at paras. 29–30). A cooperative approach accepts the inevitability of overlap between the exercise of federal and provincial competencies.

Since responsibility for the environment is shared between the federal and provincial governments, cooperative federalism is necessary to ensure the efficient operation of process at each level.

When different levels of government have environmental assessment/regulatory review responsibilities in regard to the same project, there is the prospect of duplicative environmental assessment and regulatory process. The law promotes reduction of such duplication. The objective of minimization of duplication of process finds expression in statute law as well as judicial pronouncement. The validity of this objective was recognized with approval by the Federal Court of Appeal[26] and the Supreme Court of Canada.[27]

Parliament has used a joint review panel (JRP) as one vehicle to reduce duplication and to overcome difficulties of overlap arising from the divided responsibility for the environment, although reliance upon equivalent provincial process via substitution is also now anticipated.[28] A JRP is a single tribunal established by two or more governments, boards, or agencies to discharge the statutory environmental assessment obligations required of all. The legitimacy of the JRP as a vehicle for the reduction of duplication and overlap arising from shared responsibility for the environment was confirmed in *Lavoie v. Canada (Minister of the Environment)*: "It is well recognized in Canadian constitutional law that one of the ways to overcome difficulties of divided jurisdiction is through federal–provincial cooperation and, in this respect, the techniques are well-known: cooperation without delegation, delegation, federal–provincial agreements, and joint panels."[29]

The Canadian Council of the Ministers of the Environment[30] concluded a *Canada-Wide Accord on Environmental Harmonization*[31] with three objectives: enhancing environmental protection, promoting sustainable development, and achieving greater effectiveness, efficiency, accountability, predictability, and clarity of environmental management for issues of Canada-wide interest. The ministers have also concluded a *Sub-Agreement on Environmental Assessment*.[32] It calls for joint

environmental assessment processes as a means of reducing duplication and overlap while ensuring the highest level of environmental
protection consistent with the legislation and policies of both levels of
government. Its preamble states:

> Environmental assessment provides a means to integrate envi-
> ronmental factors into project planning and decision-making. It
> involves the preparation of an environmental assessment report by
> a proponent and the review and critical evaluation of that report
> and other input. It is a public process to provide information
> about the environmental effects of a proposed project to assist
> decision-making by proponents and by governments.

The *Sub-Agreement* applies "when more than one Party must make
a decision or issue an approval which must by law be preceded by an
environmental assessment." It calls for "one assessment for a proposed
project, which will meet the information requirements of all Parties
making decisions on the basis of the assessment." Individual harmonization accords have been concluded between Canada and the provinces.[33]

Harmonization has been applied in regard to major projects across
Canada and can take several forms including: environmental assessment undertaken by each level of government based on a single set of
information provided by the project proponent; or the creation of joint
panels that conduct public hearings before issuing a report assessing the
significance of adverse environmental effects and then recommending
mitigations to reduce or eliminate those effects; or use of substitution
mechanisms where the process of one level of government is accepted by
the other as substantially equivalent to its own. In any case, mitigations
identified in the harmonized process are to be implemented by each
level of government according to its respective legislative competence
and powers.

In 1991, Saskatchewan and Canada structured the first joint
provincial-federal public review of its kind in Saskatchewan for five
uranium-mining proposals then under consideration for northern
Saskatchewan.[34] Since then, numerous joint review panels have been
convened across Canada. Newfoundland and Labrador convened joint
panels with Canada for the Terra Nova Offshore Oil Development
Project[35] and the Voisey's Bay Mine and Mill Project.[36] Nova Scotia
convened a joint panel for the Sydney Tar Ponds and Coke Ovens Sites
Remediation Project.[37] Quebec convened a joint review panel for the
Lake Kénogami Watershed Flood Control Project,[38] the Lachine Canal Decontamination Project,[39] the Romaine Hydroelectric Complex

Project,[40] the Rabaska Project—Implementation of an LNG Terminal and Related Infrastructure,[41] the Eastmain-1-A and Rupert Diversion Project,[42] and the Cacouna Energy LNG Terminal Project.[43] In Ontario, a federal-provincial joint review panel has been appointed in relation to the Marathon Platinum Group Metals and Copper Mine Project.[44] Alberta convened joint review panels for the EnCana Shallow Gas Infill Development Project in the Suffield National Wildlife Area;[45] Glacier Power Limited Dunvegan Hydroelectric Project at Fairview;[46] Kearl Oil Sands Project—Mine Development;[47] Muskeg River Mine Expansion—Albian Oil Sands Project;[48] Cheviot Coal Mine Project;[49] Highwood Storage and Diversion Plan;[50] Horizon Oil Sands Project;[51] Jackpine Oil Sands Project;[52] and Little Bow Project/Highwood Diversion Plan.[53] British Columbia convened a joint panel for the Kemess North Gold–Copper Mine.[54]

Legislation may provide for environmental assessment or regulatory review by a tribunal. Utilities are frequently the subject of regulation by tribunals. The British Columbia Utilities Commission was considered in *Rio Tinto*, and other examples are the Alberta Utilities Commission, the Ontario Energy Board, and the Quebec Régie de l'énergie. Prominent federal tribunals are the National Energy Board and the Canada Nuclear Safety Commission. Tribunals have also been created under modern land claim agreements.

The principle of harmonization may be applied through environmental assessment and regulatory review by a tribunal. Alberta, for example, has long relied on a tribunal for environmental protection in regard to oil and gas development.[55] The Energy Resources Conservation Board has concluded Memoranda of Understanding with Alberta government departments to clarify roles and responsibilities in regard to projects where the tribunal and the departments may have applicable responsibilities.[56] The British Columbia Utilities Commission and the British Columbia Environmental Assessment Office have concluded a Memorandum of Understanding that expresses how their overlapping processes with regard to the same project will be harmonized.[57] The rationale is expressed in the Commission's website:

> BC Utilities Commission (BCUC) and the BC Environmental Assessment Office (BCEAO) have signed a Memorandum of Understanding to coordinate their processes, where possible, in order to promote the efficient and effective regulation of public utilities. In many cases a utility will require both a Certificate of Public Convenience and Necessity and an Environmental Assessment

Certificate resulting in potential overlap between the processes conducted by the BCUC and BCEAO.[58]

There are several examples of joint panels that reflect harmonization of overlapping federal planning processes (as opposed to overlapping provincial processes or overlapping federal and provincial processes). A joint federal panel of this kind was established to examine the proposal by Ontario Power to develop a new nuclear power plant.[59] A similar joint federal panel has been convened for the deep geologic repository project by Ontario Power Generation Inc. within the Municipality of Kincardine.[60]

THE ROLE OF INDUSTRY IN SUSTAINABLE DEVELOPMENT

It is no small matter to marshal financing and contractual arrangements necessary to support a major project. Industry, required to conduct both public and Aboriginal consultation in advance of an application for environmental assessment and regulatory review, has developed expertise in liaison with Aboriginal communities. Industry is often interested in cooperating with Aboriginal groups to distribute the economic and social benefits of its project within the Aboriginal community.[61] There are, therefore, also corporate commitments to the causes of reconciliation espoused in the law of Aboriginal consultation.

This reality is recognized in the *State of the Debate* report issued by the National Round Table on the Environment and the Economy.[62] Created by industry, the National Round Table on the Environment and the Economy "established the Aboriginal Communities and Non-renewable Resource Development Program to examine the key issues affecting the sustainability of Aboriginal communities involved with, or impacted by, mineral, oil and gas exploration in Canada's north." The report indicates that

> Industry has a key role to play in the development of capacity within Aboriginal communities. Companies are currently involved in a range of capacity-building initiatives, from basic literacy and pre-employment training to specialized skills development programs. In many cases, these initiatives are undertaken on a project-by-project basis, primarily through the requirement for benefits plans under oil and gas legislation and through the negotiation of impact and benefits agreements as well as socio-economic agreements for mining projects.[63]

Although the report was written in regard to conditions north of sixtieth parallel, Aboriginal consultation and, where necessary, accommodation have extended dialogue about impact and benefit agreements nationally. Industry can lead in regard to these discussions.

International best practices recommend that these planning processes (1) proceed and inform project development, (2) be inherently consultative and (3) be integrated so that all information in relation to project development informs project approval and implementation decisions.

The World Bank imposes environmental assessment as part of its planning process "to ensure that development options under consideration are environmentally sound and sustainable and that any environmental consequences are recognized early and taken into account in project design."[64] The World Bank itself identifies the world-wide trend toward environmental assessment as a fundamental component of sound decision making:

> As concern has grown worldwide about environmental degradation and the threat it poses to human wellbeing and economic development, many industrial and developing nations, as well as donor agencies, have incorporated [environmental assessment] procedures into their decision-making. Bank [environmental assessments] emphasize identifying environmental issues early in the project cycle, designing environmental improvements into projects, and avoiding, mitigating, or compensating for adverse impacts.[65]

Indeed, the World Bank describes environmental assessment as "an essential tool for integrating environmental and social concerns into development policies, programs and projects by providing the minimum requirements that all Bank-supported operations must meet."[66]

The International Council on Mining and Metals (ICMM) publishes a health impact assessment as an aspect of project planning in regard to mining. Health impact assessment informs project approval decision making. The ICMM recognizes that a mining project will have both positive and negative impacts and that approval decisions should strive to be informed by both to achieve an informed and balanced understanding associated with sustainable development:

> The purpose of [health impact assessment] is to support and add value to the decision-making process on whether, and in what way, a policy, plan, program or project goes ahead. It does so by providing a systematic analysis of the potential community

health impacts as well as developing options for maximizing the positive health impacts, minimizing the negative impacts and enhancing health equity/reducing health inequalities.[67]

In this sense, health is broadly defined to include not just physical health but mental and economic health as well. The ICMM notes that "[a]ccess to jobs, income, goods and services can enhance mental health and wellbeing and reduce stress. Having a sense of control over one's life is crucial for mental wellbeing, so mining and metals projects can improve mental health by reducing poverty, increasing self esteem and empowering local communities...." Moreover, "the stimulus that a mining and metals project can bring to a local economy can help to strengthen and deepen social ties by increasing the prosperity of the community and providing resources for people to take on a wider range of social and community activities."[68] The ICMM further notes that "assessment and management of community health, safety and wellbeing impacts [are] increasingly considered part of the risk management and social responsibility of mining and metals operators" because "[a] proactive approach to preventing ill health and maximizing health and wellbeing benefits can improve the financial performance of a project and parent company."[69]

The Organization for Economic Co-operation and Development, which includes Canada, has published a paper suggesting that project planning and decision making should incorporate cost/benefit analysis. Such analysis here is defined as "an indispensible tool for policy design and decision making" in which "benefits are defined as increases in human wellbeing (utility) and costs are defined as reductions in human wellbeing." In this model, project approval decision making is informed by a form of assessment whether "its social benefits exceed its social costs."[70]

The International Association of Oil and Gas Producers also recognizes "the importance of social and environmental assessment in all aspects of project planning and implementation." It speaks of environmental assessment as a consultative process:

Social and environmental assessment (SEA) is a formal, consultative process that can help address social and environmental issues. ... SEA is intended to integrate environmental and social considerations into project planning and implementation in a cost effective manner. It is an integral part of project management and engineering for all operations from seismic to decommissioning. The SEA process is iterative, and it occurs throughout the life-cycle of the project from the early planning through to decommissioning.

Consultation is a key element of SEA. Consultation provides a means to identify interested stakeholders, their issues, concerns, needs, ideas and values as well as areas of mutual interest in and political conflict with the goals and objectives of the company's activities. If consultation is started early and performed well, it can identify key issues that will allow project design and other changes to be made at the beginning of the process, and thus be less costly than if done later. Effective, sustained consultation can help establish and maintain good relationships and positive attitudes among stakeholders towards the company's activities and projects over the short and long term.

Social and environmental assessment can be beneficial to the project schedule and cost by increasing public support, anticipating problems and aiding in regulatory compliance. Key benefits of integrated social and environmental assessment include protection of the environment and communities, improved project planning, better and more cost effective mitigation, increased public support and reduced conflict. SEA is considered an element of responsible environmental management both within the industry and externally.[71]

The benefits of consultation to both business and to communities are identified by the International Petroleum Industry Environment Conservation Association (IPIECA) in its publication *Guide to Social Impact Assessment in the Oil and Gas Industry*.[72] Benefits to business include use of the consultative process as "an effective risk management tool" that can inform and encourage timely decisions on projects and "influence project design and improve the quality of decision making." The IPIECA makes a positive link here between consultation and changes in project design in the planning stage of a project. Benefits to communities are described as:

- access to the company to express its views/concerns and suggestions and involvement in the decision-making processes as a result of effective consultation;

- identification of opportunities for economic development through the supply of goods and services by local stakeholders;

- contribution to local capacity building in infrastructure, services and environmental protection;

- increase in human capacity building through the transfer of best practices;

- social investment to meet both local and project needs;

- support for traditional industries alongside development of the project;

- protection of cultural resources for the communities; and

- inclusion for local communities through better understanding of both the positive and the negative effects of the project or operation.

The IPIECA recognizes that project assessment can take different forms and names and encourages integration. Whether described as social impact assessment, health impact assessment, environmental impact assessment, environmental and social impact assessment, or strategic impact assessment, integration leads to better decision making: "[a] number of different impact assessments can be needed for the same activity. Therefore, it makes sense to integrate the studies. ... In all instances, the results of such impact assessments need to be integrated to optimise project / operations planning." The IPIECA also recognizes that this is a consultative process that can inform project planning and design. Indeed, early consultation is described as "critical" to ensure that the information derived from the consultation process is considered in project design and planning.

IMPACT AND BENEFIT AGREEMENTS

The Canadian Business Ethics Research Network[73] maintains an Impact and Benefit Agreement (IBA) Research Network. The website for the network defines impact and benefit agreements as follows: "Most simply put, these negotiated, private agreements serve to document in a contractual form the benefits that a local community can expect from the development of a local resource in exchange for its support and cooperation."[74] The analysis of impact and benefit agreements in Canada is limited due to the generally private and confidential nature of bilateral or multilateral agreements.[75]

The National Aboriginal Health Organization held a roundtable in 2008 to discuss impact and benefit agreements in regard to Inuit communities and comments that "[i]n our conversations with Inuit observers we found general agreement that Inuit would benefit from a more open process in negotiating IBAS, to contribute to learning from community to community, and to strengthen the social and health provisions in each new agreement that is negotiated."[76] Another commentator suggests that impact and benefit agreements "recognize Aboriginal peoples' interests with the land and parallel more broadly with the corporate social responsibility phenomena" but that there can be challenges:

> Challenges facing IBAS include their confidential nature and their relationship to conventional environmental assessment (EA). IBAS go beyond the regulatory and advisory EA processes and often find themselves in conflict due to overlapping objectives and blurred boundaries. IBAS can perpetuate injustices if benefits are not equally distributed to the community or if monitoring and follow-up on behalf of both parties are not continuous.[77]

Notwithstanding the challenges, impact and benefit agreements today form an important tool used by industry to achieve reconciliation of Aboriginal concerns and project development.

Development of the Law of Aboriginal Consultation by the Supreme Court of Canada

Reconciliation is not a final legal remedy in the usual sense. Rather, it is a process flowing from rights guaranteed by s. 35(1) of the *Constitution Act, 1982*. This process of reconciliation flows from the Crown's duty of honourable dealing toward Aboriginal peoples, which arises in turn from the Crown's assertion of sovereignty over an Aboriginal people and de facto control of land and resources that were formerly in the control of that people.

—*Haida Nation v. British Columbia (Minister of Forests)*, 2004 SCC 73, [2004] 3 S.C.R. 511 at paragraph 32.

A CONSTITUTIONAL DUTY OF A GENERATIVE ORDER

In 2004 and 2005, the Supreme Court introduces the law of Aboriginal consultation and, where necessary, accommodation into the existing matrix of Indian Aboriginal rights and Treaty rights, and Métis Aboriginal rights. Although the first cases originate in British Columbia,[1] the Court extends the law of consultation to the taking up of land under Treaty 8 in Alberta and then to modern treaties in a case involving the Yukon. That extension was consolidated in 2010 in another case originating from British Columbia. In this last of the five cases, the Court addresses the role of administrative tribunals in the assessment and conduct of Aboriginal consultation. Here the Court confirms that the duty to consult flows from the honour of the Crown and, though not a section 35 right, is nevertheless "a constitutional duty."

Rio Tinto defines the overarching purpose of the duty to consult by describing it as having a "generative constitutional order" that fosters reconciliation. The Court describes reconciliation as a dynamic and ongoing matter "that begins with the assertion of sovereignty and continues beyond formal claims resolution." That is, reconciliation continues *after* the conclusion of treaties:

> The duty seeks to provide protection to Aboriginal and treaty rights while furthering the goals of reconciliation between Aboriginal peoples and the Crown. Rather than pitting Aboriginal peoples against the Crown in the litigation process, the duty recognizes that both must work together to reconcile their interests. It also accommodates the reality that often Aboriginal peoples are involved in exploiting the resource. Shutting down development by court injunction may serve the interest of no one.[2]

This passage emphasizes cooperation in the ongoing relationships, processes and negotiations that the law of Aboriginal consultation prefers. This has important implications for remedies since courts prefer remedies that support interest-based cooperation, or negotiation, rather than position-based rigidity.

The duty to consult is, at its simplest, intended to ensure that Crown decision making regarding development of natural resources "respects Aboriginal interests in accordance with the honour of the Crown."[3] Although corollary to Aboriginal (or Treaty) rights, the duty to consult and, where necessary, accommodate is not itself an Aboriginal right or Treaty right recognized and affirmed by section 35 of the *Constitution Act, 1982*. It is, rather, an obligation owed to Aboriginal peoples by the Crown that is legally enforceable by Aboriginal peoples through remedies that "promote ongoing negotiations" rather than a halt to development.[4] Describing the duty to consult as having a generative constitutional order recognizes the special status of the historical relationship between the Crown and Aboriginal peoples and the special status that the duty to consult embodies. It underscores the significance of relationship building.

HAIDA NATION V. BRITISH COLUMBIA (MINISTER OF FORESTS)
Context

The case that recognizes the law of Aboriginal consultation and, where necessary, accommodation, is *Haida Nation v. British Columbia (Minister of Forests).*[5] The term used here is "recognizes" because the Court states that the duty originated prior to confederation and the constitution making which was associated with the creation of Canada as a self-governing Dominion.[6]

The Haida challenged the decision of a provincial minister under the provincial *Forest Act*, R.S.B.C. 1996 c. 157. The minister had approved the transfer of a tree farm licence from one forestry company to another. The licence authorized timber cutting on lands that were the subject to land claim negotiations with the Haida. The timber in question was cedar, an integral part of Haida culture. The Haida went to court to set aside the transfer of the licence. The case reached the Supreme Court in March of 2004, and Judgment was delivered in November 2004.

The Supreme Court describes the issue before it in paragraph 6 of its judgment, in language that references the context of the case as regards British Columbia, asserted but as yet unproven land claims of the Haida people, and the BC Treaty Process: "[W]hat duty if any does the government owe the Haida people? More concretely, is the government required to *consult* with them about decisions to harvest the forests and to *accommodate* their concerns about what if any forest in Block 6 should be harvested before they have proven their title to land and their Aboriginal rights?" The Court refers to the treaty process in Canada, stating that "Many bands reconciled their claims with the sovereignty of the Crown through negotiated treaties"[7] and that "Treaties serve to reconcile pre-existing Aboriginal sovereignty with assumed Crown sovereignty, and to define Aboriginal rights guaranteed by s. 35 of the *Constitution Act, 1982*."[8] Noting that many Aboriginal peoples in British Columbia had yet to conclude a treaty, the Court states in paragraph 25 with regard to the asserted Aboriginal rights of the Haida that

> The potential rights embedded in these claims are protected by s. 35 of the *Constitution Act, 1982*. The honour of the Crown requires that these rights be determined, recognized and respected. This, in turn, requires the Crown, acting honourably, to participate in processes of negotiation. While this process continues, the honour of the Crown may require it to consult and, where indicated, accommodate Aboriginal interests.

In the Court's view, the process of consultation and, where necessary, accommodation "preserves the Aboriginal interest pending claims resolution and fosters a relationship between the parties that makes possible negotiations."[9] The Court discusses the source of the duty, when the duty arises, the scope and content of the duty, whether the duty extends to third parties, and remedies. Each is discussed here.

The Honour of the Crown Is the Source of the Duty to Consult

Regarding the source of the duty, the Court states that it is the honour of the Crown that is corollary to section 35 of the *Constitution Act, 1982*. The Court uses the specific term "corollary" in regard to the duty, implying that the duty is not itself a section 35 right[10] but may nevertheless be legally enforceable. The Court's description of the honour of the Crown was further articulated in *Manitoba Metis Federation v. Canada (Attorney General)*.[11]

The Duty Arises When the Crown Contemplates Conduct That May Adversely Affect Aboriginal or Treaty Rights

Regarding when the duty arises in the context of claims in British Columbia, the Court states that "the duty arises when the Crown has knowledge, real or constructive, of the potential existence of the Aboriginal right or title and contemplates conduct that might adversely affect it."[12]

The Scope of the Duty Varies with the Context

Regarding the scope and content of the duty triggered in the context of claims in British Columbia, the Court states that they will vary with the circumstances and that tribunals and courts can assist. The variance stems from difficulty in assessing an asserted Aboriginal right because of absence of proof or definition of the claim.

The Court makes the analogy to a spectrum, without limitation to any particular course of action in any particular case. At one end of the spectrum, where "the claim to title is weak, the Aboriginal right limited, or the potential for infringement minor," the Crown need only "give notice, disclose information, and discuss any issues raised in response to the notice." At the other end of the spectrum, "where a strong *prima facie* case for the claim is established, the right and potential infringement is of high significance to the Aboriginal peoples, and the risk of non-compensable damage is high," the Crown would offer "the opportunity to make submissions for consideration, formal participation in the decision-making process, and provision of written reasons to show that Aboriginal concerns were considered and to reveal the impact they had on the decision."[13]

Accommodation May Be Required, Especially Where Potential Adverse Effects Are Significant

In terms of accommodation, the Court notes that the

> effect of good faith consultation may be to reveal a duty to accommodate. Where a strong *prima facie* case exists for the claim, and the consequences of the government's proposed decision may adversely affect it in a significant way, addressing the Aboriginal concerns may require taking steps to avoid irreparable harm or to minimize the effects of infringement, pending final resolution of the underlying claim.[14]

The Crown May Delegate Procedural Aspects of the Duty to Third Parties

As to whether third parties such as Weyerhauser owe a duty to consult, the Court answered in the negative, noting, however, that procedural aspects of the duty can be delegated to industry proponents "seeking a particular development; this is not infrequently done in environmental assessments."[15]

A Breach of the Duty to Consult Does Not Necessarily Invalidate Past Events

By way of remedy, the Court merely varied the order issued by the British Columbia Court of Appeal, clarifying that the Crown's obligation to consult did not extend to Weyerhaeuser. This did not invalidate the transfer of the tree licence.

To appreciate the restraint showed by the courts, it is necessary to examine the appellate judgments in British Columbia. The British Columbia Court of Appeal had declared that there was a legally enforceable duty to consult owed by British Columbia to the Haida.[16] The Court of Appeal notes that it does not necessarily follow that past events are invalid even if consultation is found to have been inadequate.[17] In the result, it adopts the "least disruptive order" (declaratory relief short of invalidating the tree farm licence) available in the circumstances:

> The aim of the remedy should be to protect the interests of all parties pending the final determination of the nature and scope of aboriginal title and aboriginal rights. Once that final decision is made, and perhaps in the same proceedings, a final determina-

tion can be made of the quality and extent of any *prima facie* infringement of the aboriginal title and aboriginal rights that may have occurred before that determination, including, particularly, over the period when the Crown and Weyerhaeuser were in possession of sufficient facts that they ought to have known of the probability that infringements were occurring. When the decisions are made about infringement then further decisions about justification can be made.[18]

The Court's restraint in remedy clothes the judgment with sensitivity to interests of third parties as well as potential judicial resolution of a land claim in British Columbia. The Haida obtained a declaration with significant implications for future relationships with the Crown but did not succeed in setting aside the tree farm licence on the basis of an asserted Aboriginal right or title.

TAKU RIVER TLINGIT FIRST NATION V. BRITISH COLUMBIA (PROJECT ASSESSMENT DIRECTOR)
Context

The Supreme Court's judgment in *Taku River Tlingit First Nation v. British Columbia (Project Assessment Director)*[19] was pronounced the same day as the judgment in *Haida Nation*. While *Haida Nation* is directed to recognition of a duty to consult and, where necessary, accommodate, *Taku River* is directed to the contours of the duty—including its limits. The opening paragraph of the judgment describes the issue as "the limits of the Crown's duty to consult with and accommodate Aboriginal peoples when making decisions that may adversely affect as yet unproven Aboriginal rights and title claims."

Taku River involves the reopening of a mine. The lands on which the mine was to operate were also the subject of a land claim by the Taku River Tlingit First Nation (TRTFN) that was the subject of negotiation in the BC Treaty Process. The Court attaches the duty to consult to the project approval decision, including conditions of approval: "It follows that the honour of the Crown required it to consult and if indicated accommodate the TRTFN in making the decision whether to grant project approval to Redfern, and on what terms."[20]

The project approval decision was informed by a three-year environmental assessment process that preceded it. The environmental assessment was conducted under provincial legislation that, according to the Court, "sets out a process of information gathering and consultation" that includes First Nations potentially affected by the proposed project.[21] The Taku River Tlingit First Nation was given financial assistance for involvement in the environmental assessment process and was involved "with the exception of a period of time from February to August of 1995, when they opted out of the process, wishing instead to address the issue through treaty talks and development of a land use policy."[22] The First Nation was not satisfied with the resulting approval decision or its conditions.

Consultation in the Environmental Assessment Stage of Project Development May Be Satisfactory

The Court accepts that the environmental assessment process was sufficient to satisfy the obligations of the duty to consult. The Court states that British Columbia "was not required to develop special consultation measures to address TRTFN's concerns, outside of the process provided for by the *Environmental Assessment Act*, R.S.B.C. 1996, c. 119 [rep. 2002, c. 43, s. 58], which specifically set out a scheme that required consultation with affected Aboriginal peoples."[23] Under the BC legislation as it then was, a multistakeholder group described as the Project Committee was "the primary engine driving the assessment process."[24] Its functions include those common to all environmental assessments: assessment of the potential effects of the project, and the prevention or mitigation of adverse effects. This is reaffirmed in the Court's subsequent decision in *Beckman v. Little Salmon/Carmacks First Nation*, in which the Court states the *ratio decidendi* of its judgment in *Taku River*: "In *Taku River Tlingit First Nation v. British Columbia (Project Assessment Director)*, 2004 SCC 74, [2004] 3 S.C.R. 550, the Court held that participation in a forum created for other purposes may nevertheless satisfy the duty to consult if *in substance* an appropriate level of consultation is provided."[25]

The Court also recognizes the project development cycle. It notes that through the environmental assessment process, the Crown had turned its mind to consultation and accommodation on matters that were appropriate at that early stage of the project. "Project approval," the Court states, "is simply one stage in the process by which a development moves forward."[26] The Court approves the view that other processes were appropriate venues for some of the outstanding First Nation concerns, including regulatory decisions after project approval, treaty negotiations, and land use planning venues.[27]

Societal Interests Weigh in the Balance of Accommodation

The Court affirms that accommodation requires balancing of Aboriginal concerns with other societal concerns: "where consultation is meaningful," it stated, "there is no ultimate duty to reach agreement. Rather, accommodation requires that Aboriginal concerns be balanced reasonably with the potential impact of the particular decision on those concerns and with competing societal concerns. Compromise is inherent to the reconciliation process."[28]

MIKISEW CREE FIRST NATION V. CANADA (MINISTER OF CANADIAN HERITAGE)
Context

The Court extends the duty to consult to Treaty 8 of the historical numbered treaties in *Mikisew Cree First Nation v. Canada (Minister of Canadian Heritage)*.[29] The opening paragraph gives glimpse of the essential fact, described as indifference, that motivated the result.[30] The indifference in this instance was that of Parks Canada officials conducting an environmental assessment for a proposed winter road project that would cross a reserve of the Mikisew Cree without speaking directly to the band about the potential intrusion onto reserve property. The Court finds that the planning process for this project was not executed with sufficient sensitivity, though it could have been.

In 1986, the Mikisew had concluded a *Treaty Land Entitlement Agreement*. It included the creation of a small Indian reserve within Wood Buffalo National Park. The *Canada National Parks Act* was amended to exclude the new reserve from the boundary of the park.[31] The reserve was located astride an abandoned logging road running through the park. A developer, which included Aboriginal interests, proposed to build a winter road through the park to enhance regional transportation. To minimize environmental impact the winter road was proposed to run along the route of the old logging road—and therefore through the new reserve. The environmental assessment was conducted at the lowest screening level by government officials in Parks Canada. Parks Canada provided an opportunity for public consultation on the draft of the environmental assessment report. Although there was opportunity for public comment, there was no evidence of earlier direct discussions with the Mikisew Cree about it—even though the road was proposed to run through their reserve. The band received notice through the public consultation and, after a delay, announced opposition to the project. Parks Canada officials then altered the route of the road to run (at its eastern terminus) along and contiguous to the boundary of the new reserve. A senior Park official apologized after the minister had approved the project, including the adjustment of the proposed route.[32] The Mikisew initiated a judicial review, alleging inadequate consultation, and the case reached the Supreme Court of Canada.

Indifference

The Court was not pleased with what it viewed as Crown indifference regarding the route of the road through the reserve or the subsequent road realignment. The Court states at paragraph 3 that "The government did not think it necessary to engage in consultation directly with the Mikisew before making this decision. After the Mikisew protested, the winter road alignment was changed to track the boundary of the Peace Point reserve instead of running through it, again without consultation with the Mikisew." Not surprisingly, the Court concludes that "[i]n this case, the relationship was not properly managed. Adequate consultation in advance of the Minister's approval did not take place. The government's approach did not advance the process of reconciliation but undermined it."

The Court offers some suggestions on how the Crown should have acted, stating that engagement with the Mikisew about the project on reserve land "ought to have included the provision of information about the project addressing what the Crown knew to be Mikisew interests and what the Crown anticipated might be the potential adverse impact on those interests. The Crown was required to solicit and to listen carefully to the Mikisew concerns, and to attempt to minimize adverse impacts on the Mikisew hunting, fishing and trapping rights."[33]

The Court's concern about the apparent indifference regarding alignment of the proposed winter road route through the reserve is apparent. Although the Court discusses consultation about the impacts of the winter road on hunting, fishing, and trapping, it is the indifference with regard to road alignment that is most injurious. Without reference to how further accommodations might have been identified in regard to hunting, fishing, and trapping, the Court refers to how accommodation might have affected the road realignment had meaningful consultation been conducted: "[t]here could ... be changes in the road alignment or construction that would go a long way towards satisfying the Mikisew objections."[34] The injurious nature of the routing of the winter road through a reserve without any direct communication with the First Nation, followed by a unilateral decision to change the route to a position outside of but contiguous to the reserve, is confirmed twice in the Court's 2010 decision in *Beckman v. Little Salmon/Carmacks First Nation*. There the Court cites *Mikisew Cree* for the proposition that "some accommodation was possible through a rerouting of the proposed winter road" and also states that the dispute in *Mikisew Cree* was "over the route of a winter road."[35]

Accommodations in regard to hunting, fishing, and trapping, the constitutionally protected rights under Treaty 8, were addressed through the mitigations identified in the environmental assessment process and incorporated as conditions of approval of the project.[36] The road, which was not built in the result, would have been subject to mitigations intended to minimize environmental impacts, and the decision to build the road was reversible if unforeseen impacts arose. The case turned on Crown indifference during the planning process to the routing of the road through an Indian reserve and not the significance of the environmental impacts of the project on Treaty rights to hunt, fish, or trap.

Constitutional Considerations

The Court's judgment in *Mikisew Cree* attaches the duty to consult to the taking up of land under the provisions of Treaty 8.[37] The Court also confirms that Aboriginal rights and titles were surrendered and extinguished by Treaty 8:

> 31 I agree with Rothstein J.A. that not every subsequent "taking up" by the Crown constituted an infringement of Treaty 8 that must be justified according to the test set out in *Sparrow*. In *Sparrow*, it will be remembered, the federal government's fisheries regulations infringed the aboriginal fishing right, and had to be strictly justified. This is not the same situation as we have here, where the aboriginal rights have been surrendered and extinguished, and the Treaty 8 rights are expressly limited to lands not "required or taken up *from time to time* for settlement, mining, lumbering, trading or other purposes" (emphasis added). The language of the treaty could not be clearer in foreshadowing change. Nevertheless the Crown was and is expected to manage the change honourably.[38] [emphasis in the original]

The Court states that both "historical context and the inevitable tensions underlying implementation of Treaty 8 demand a *process* by which lands may be transferred from the one category (where the First Nations retain rights to hunt, fish and trap) to the other category (where they do not)." At paragraph 43 of the *Mikisew Cree* Judgment the Court notes that its earlier Judgment in *Badger* "did not (as it did not need to) discuss the process by which 'from time to time' land would be 'taken up' and thereby excluded from the exercise of those rights."

The Court therefore makes a constitutional pronouncement, qualifying *Badger*'s identification of "two inherent limitations on Indian hunting, fishing and trapping rights under Treaty 8 (geographical limits and specific forms of government regulation) by a third, namely the Crown's right to take up lands under the treaty, which itself is subject to its duty to consult and, if appropriate, accommodate First Nations' interests before reducing the area over which their members may continue to pursue their hunting, trapping and fishing rights." The Court then describes the nature of the Crown obligation, and its limitations:

> [T]he Crown is nevertheless under an obligation to inform itself of the impact its project will have on the exercise by the Mikisew of their hunting and trapping rights, and to communicate its findings to the Mikisew. The Crown must then attempt to deal with the Mikisew "in good faith, and with the intention of substantially addressing" Mikisew concerns (*Delgamuukw*, at para. 168). This does not mean that whenever a government proposes to do anything in the Treaty 8 surrendered lands it must consult with all signatory First Nations, no matter how remote or unsubstantial the impact. The duty to consult is, as stated in *Haida Nation*, triggered at a low threshold, but adverse impact is a matter of degree, as is the extent of the Crown's duty.[39]

A Procedural Obligation

The duty to consult is then described as a procedural obligation owed by the Crown ("its *procedural* obligations") distinct from the obligation to justify a substantive breach of a Treaty right. The ability to take up land is described as an inherent limitation on the Indian hunting, fishing, and trapping rights under Treaty 8 and is subject to a procedural safeguard: that is, "the duty to consult and, if appropriate, accommodate First Nations' interests before reducing the area over which their members may continue to pursue their hunting, trapping and fishing rights."

Traditional Territories

The Court's decision in *Badger* redefines the boundaries of the Treaty right to hunt for food through recognition of merger and consolidation. In *Mikisew Cree*, the Court refers to another form of geographic expression. It defines the duty to consult in relation to a geographic area comprising "traditional lands." It then defines traditional lands, writing that the potential impact of the project on a Treaty 8 right "is not ascertained on a treaty-wide basis (all 840,000 square kilometres of it) but in relation to the territories over which a First Nation traditionally hunted, fished and trapped, and continues to do so today." The Court also states, in *obiter dicta*, that "a potential action for treaty infringement, including the demand for a *Sparrow* justification, would be a legitimate First Nation response" in a time when there was "no meaningful right to hunt" remaining "over *its* traditional territories."[40]

Reciprocal Obligations Within the Duty to Consult

The Court places an obligation on First Nations to inform the Crown of its concerns. The Crown is obliged to communicate with the First Nation and "to listen carefully to the Mikisew concerns, and to attempt to minimize adverse impacts on the Mikisew hunting, fishing and trapping rights."[41] The First Nation has some reciprocal onus "to carry their end of the consultation, to make their concerns known, to respond to the government's attempt to meet their concerns and suggestions, and to try to reach some mutually satisfactory solution."[42]

BECKMAN V. LITTLE SALMON/CARMACKS FIRST NATION
Context

Beckman v. Little Salmon/Carmacks First Nation[43] involved judicial consideration of the *Little Salmon/Carmacks First Nation Final Agreement*[44] concluded following the *Umbrella Final Agreement between the Government of Canada, the Council for Yukon Indians, and the Government of the Yukon.*[45] The Supreme Court decision again speaks of the significance of the treaty-making process, and recognizes the significance of the tribunals which the process creates:

> [8] Historically, treaties were the means by which the Crown sought to reconcile the Aboriginal inhabitants of what is now Canada to the assertion of European sovereignty over the territories traditionally occupied by First Nations. The objective was not only to build alliances with First Nations but to keep the peace and to open up the major part of those territories to colonization and settlement. No treaties were signed with the Yukon First Nations until modern times.

> [9] Unlike their historical counterparts, the modern comprehensive treaty is the product of lengthy negotiations between well-resourced and sophisticated parties. The negotiation costs to Yukon First Nations of their various treaties, financed by the federal government through reimbursable loans, were enormous. The [Little Salmon/Carmacks First Nation] share alone exceeded seven million dollars. Under the Yukon treaties, the Yukon First Nations surrendered their Aboriginal rights in almost 484,000 square kilometres, roughly the size of Spain, in exchange for defined treaty rights in respect of land tenure and a quantum of settlement land (41,595 square kilometres), access to Crown lands, fish and wildlife harvesting, heritage resources, financial compen-

sation, and participation in the management of public resources. To this end, the [Little Salmon/Carmacks First Nation] Treaty creates important institutions of self-government and authorities such as the Yukon Environmental and Socio-economic Assessment Board and the Carmacks Renewable Resources Council, whose members are jointly nominated by the First Nation and the territorial government.

"Consultation" was a defined term in the *Agreement*, which imposed numerous obligations regarding consultation throughout its detailed text. The Yukon Government considered the *Agreement* a complete code in terms of its obligations to conduct Aboriginal consultation and, where necessary, accommodation.

A dispute arose over a decision regarding a transfer of land from the Crown for agricultural use. The transfer was approved following a review process established by policy, including review by a Land Application Review Committee on which the Little Salmon/Carmacks First Nation had representation. This policy-based apparatus was in operation because, as the Supreme Court notes, "at the time the Director dealt with the application, the treaty implementation provision contemplated in Chapter 12 had itself not yet been implemented."[46] Chapter 12 defined a development assessment process of planning and approval. Implementation of Chapter 12 was dependent on the enactment of "development assessment legislation."[47]

When that Committee sat to review the application for transfer, it was aware that the First Nation opposed the application, could not attend the meeting of the Committee, and had not asked for deferral or expressed concern about the meeting proceeding in its absence. The Committee recommended the application to the minister, who approved it without further notice to the First Nation or the individual who had traplines in the vicinity. The First Nation, and the individual trapper, sought ministerial reconsideration; when that was turned down on technical grounds, it brought judicial review of the minister's decision.

The case reached the Supreme Court of Canada, where the majority found that the treaty was not intended to be a complete code for consultation and that the procedural gap arising from the fact that Chapter 12 had not yet been implemented made it appropriate to rely on the general duty to consult as a framework within which to resolve the dispute. The Court went on to find that the obligations of consultation had been met by the administrative process in place.

Administrative Law Principles Are Relevant to the Duty to Consult

The Court affirms that administrative law is relevant to the duty to consult. It follows that administrative law principles embodied in environmental assessment and regulatory review process are relevant to the duty. The Court specifically rejects the argument that there is "a bright line" between the duty to consult and administrative law principles such as procedural fairness.

> [46] The link between constitutional doctrine and administrative law remedies was already noted in *Haida Nation*, at the outset of our Court's duty to consult jurisprudence:
>
>> In all cases, the honour of the Crown requires that the Crown act with good faith to provide meaningful consultation appropriate to the circumstances. In discharging this duty, regard may be had to the procedural safeguards of natural justice *mandated by administrative law*. [Emphasis added; para. 41.]
>
> The relevant "procedural safeguards" mandated by administrative law include not only natural justice but the broader notion of procedural fairness. ...
>
> [47] ... Administrative law is flexible enough to give full weight to the constitutional interests of the First Nation. Moreover, the impact of an administrative decision on the interest of an Aboriginal community, whether or not that interest is entrenched in a s. 35 right, would be relevant as a matter of procedural fairness, just as the impact of a decision on any other community or individual (including Larry Paulsen) may be relevant.

Relevance of Obligations Owed to Project Proponents

The Court's reference to Mr. Paulsen touches on the obligation of the Crown, and of tribunals, to balance competing interests when making decisions. The Court also states that a relevant contextual consideration is the impact of a decision on other persons interested in the decision, including to project proponents.

> [35] I believe the existence of Larry Paulsen's stake in this situation is of considerable importance. Unlike *Mikisew Cree*, which involved a dispute between the Federal government and

the Mikisew Cree First Nation over the route of a winter road, Mr. Paulsen made his application as an ordinary citizen who was entitled to a government decision reached with procedural fairness within a reasonable time.

The director, in this instance, was charged with weighing respective interests, taking Yukon agricultural policy into consideration, and giving the concerns of First Nations full and fair consideration. The majority concludes: "It seems the Director was simply not content to put Mr. Paulsen's interest on the back burner while the government and the First Nation attempted to work out some transitional rough spots in their relationship. He was entitled to proceed as he did."[48]

RIO TINTO ALCAN INC. V. CARRIER SEKANI TRIBAL COUNCIL
Context

In *Rio Tinto,* the Supreme Court discusses the role of the British Columbia Utilities Commission in the duty to consult. The Court ultimately upholds the decision of the Commission, which maintained that its decision to approve an *Electricity Purchase Agreement* would have no impact on the asserted Aboriginal rights of the Carrier Sekani and that a duty to consult was not triggered.

Kemano Hydro Facilities and the Electricity Purchase Agreement

Between 1950 and 1954, Alcan Inc. constructed the Kemano Hydro-electric Generating Station and the Nechako Reservoir.[49] The reservoir was formed by the construction of the Kinney Dam on the Nechako River. From the reservoir, water flows through the Generating Station into the Kemano River. Electrical power from the Generating Station flows through transmission lines to an aluminum smelter at Kitimat, British Columbia. Until 1961, Alcan used the power generated for its aluminum smelter at Kitimat,[50] and for local uses in the Kitimat region. In 1961, the Province of British Columbia began to purchase surplus electricity for broader local distribution, including the municipalities of Terrace and Prince Rupert. In 1979, BC Hydro upgraded its transmission capacity such that surplus power could be sold to the BC Hydro grid. In 1990, this arrangement was formalized through the conclusion of a *Long Term Energy Purchase Agreement.* In 2007 Alcan and BC Hydro concluded a new *Electricity Purchase Agreement* (the 2007 EPA). Under it, BC Hydro would obtain from Alcan all of the power from the Kemano system not otherwise required for the smelter at Kitimat.

The British Columbia Utilities Commission

BC Hydro asked the British Columbia Utilities Commission to approve the 2007 EPA. In this context, the Crown through BC Hydro was the project proponent. The *Utilities Commission Act*[51] confers on the Commission the power to consider whether an energy supply contract is in the public interest and sets out criteria for the determination of whether a matter is in the public interest.[52] The *Act* also confers on the Commission the power to approve the proposed contract or to declare the contract unenforceable either in whole or in part and to make such other order as the Commission considers advisable in the circumstances. No subsequent approval of the Lieutenant Governor in Council is required. In the context of the approval of the 2007 EPA, the Commission was both the regulatory review and the approving entity.

The Commission is a quasi-judicial tribunal, operating under rules of procedure in accordance with principles of administrative law.[53] Upon receipt of the application, the Commission held a series of procedural conferences to allow interested parties to register, determine the scope of the proceeding, and fix a timetable for regulatory review filings leading to a public hearing. The Haisla Nation was the only Aboriginal party to the Commission proceedings during the procedural conferences, and it did not ask the Commission to assess the adequacy and accommodation afforded to the Haisla Nation by BC Hydro on the 2007 EPA. The Commission therefore issued a Scoping Order[54] stating that the issue before the Commission was limited to determining the cost effectiveness of the 2007 EPA, and that the duty of the Crown to consult and, if necessary, accommodate First Nations was not within the scope of the proceeding.

Shortly after the Scoping Order was issued, the Carrier Sekani Tribal Council obtained status as intervenor in the Commission proceedings, on the condition that it comply with the existing schedule for public hearings. At the outset of the public hearings, the Council requested by way of motion a reconsideration of the Scoping Order with respect to the duty to consult.[55]

The Commission reconsidered the Scoping Order through a two-phase reconsideration procedure. Under Phase 1, the Commission considered whether the Carrier Sekani Tribal Council had established a *prima facie* case for reconsideration. The Commission concluded that the Council had established a *prima facie* case for reconsideration of a single question. The question was whether the approval of the EPA by the Commission without assessment of Crown consultation would be an error of law going to jurisdiction (absent consent from all other affected First Nations).[56] The Commission therefore fixed a timetable for consideration of the merits of the motion for reconsideration on that question. In Phase II, the Commission assumed as correct the Carrier Sekani Tribal Council assertions that its members hold Aboriginal rights to and title over areas affected by the Kemano operations, that operation of the Nechako Reservoir (including diversion of the waters of the Nechako River) had significant adverse effects on these rights and title, and that the Carrier Sekani had never been consulted on or accommodated for this infringement. The Commission also concluded, as a fact, that the 2007 EPA would not affect the Carrier Sekani. Based upon these assumptions and this finding, the tribunal stated a question of law: "Assuming there has been a historical, continuing infringement of aboriginal title and rights and assuming there has been no consultation or accommodation with [Carrier Sekani Tribal Council] on either the historical, continuing infringement or the 2007 EPA, would it be a jurisdictional error for the Commission to accept the 2007 EPA?"[57]

The Commission's reasons on this question are reproduced in Section 8 of its decision to approve the EPA.[58] The Commission reasoned that "acceptance of the 2007 EPA is not a jurisdictional error because a duty to consult does not arise by acceptance of the 2007 EPA and because a failure of the duty of consultation on the historical, continuing infringement can not be relevant to acceptance of the 2007 EPA where there are no new physical impacts."[59]

The Commission went on in section 8 of its decision to address what it described as "procedural issues." Here the Commission responded to a Carrier Sekani Tribal Council objection to the effect that the Commission Scoping Order should have considered impacts on Aboriginal rights and title as a matter necessarily within the public interest as set out in the *Utilities Commission Act* and, in effect, that the Commission had an independent duty to consult, or an independent duty to assess the adequacy of Crown consultation, regardless of the submissions made or not made at the time of the Scoping Order. The Commission rejected this submission. The rejection relied on a National Energy Board decision[60] for the propositions that First Nations are under an obligation to raise issues in a timely way and that, in considering the rights of First Nations to procedural fairness, the Commission must balance these rights with those of others, including the right of an applicant to have the application heard in a timely way. The Commission held that it was not a jurisdictional error to exclude from the scope of the proceeding an assessment of the adequacy of Crown consultation because the Carrier Sekani Tribal Council had not sought intervenor status at the time that the Scoping Order was issued, and the issue had not been raised by the Haisla. The Commission also held that, as a quasi-judicial body, it was not under an independent duty to consult.

Appendix D of the Commission's decision to approve the application contains the determination that there were no new physical impacts from the 2007 EPA.[61] The Commission finds as a fact that the 2007 EPA would not have any impact on the volume, timing, or source of water flows into the Nechako River, would not change the volume of water to be released into the Kemano River, and would cause an imperceptible change in water level in the Nechako Reservoir, which would not affect water flows other than timing of release of water into the Kemano River. In reaching this conclusion, the Commission rejects a further argument of the Carrier Sekani Tribal Council that the duty to consult was triggered because the 2007 EPA provided for a Joint Operating Committee, which effected a change in the management structure for the reservoir. The Commission accepts the evidence of Alcan and BC Hydro that "the role of the Joint Operating Committee is limited to information exchange and does not change the operating responsibility for the reservoir."[62]

The Commission's finds that the 2007 EPA was in the public interest.[63] Approval is embodied in the Commission's order that the 2007 EPA was an energy supply contract pursuant to section 71 of the *Utilities Commission Act*. The order was overturned by the British Columbia Court of Appeal,[64] and the Supreme Court of Canada granted leave to appeal.

The Supreme Court of Canada

Rio Tinto reflects a development context in which the Crown is a proponent[65] and the Utilities Commission provides final project approval. The BC Utilities Commission had a statutory mandate to consider whether the project was in the public interest and in that exercise could make findings of fact and law. That, at a minimum, allowed it to assess the impacts of the project on the asserted Aboriginal rights of the Carrier Sekani. It did not authorize the Commission to conduct Crown consultation. Since the 2007 EPA had no effect on asserted Aboriginal rights, no duty to consult applied. Had the duty to consult been triggered by the 2007 EPA, the Crown should have conducted Aboriginal consultation, and the Commission would have assessed the adequacy of that consultation in the course of its proceedings before making a final approval decision.

The Constitutional Nature of the Law of Aboriginal Consultation

The Court confirms that the duty to consult and accommodate has a constitutional character grounded in the honour of the Crown and corollary to section 35 of the *Constitution Act, 1982*. The Court describes "[c]onsultation itself" as "a distinct and often complex constitutional process."[66] The process is owed by the Crown in certain circumstances, and the process may be served by tribunals. The Court adopts Brian Slattery's description of the duty as embodying "a 'generative' constitutional order."[67] That generative function is described by the Court in the language of Dwight Newman: "to recognize that actions affecting unproven Aboriginal title or rights or treaty rights can have irreversible effects that are not in keeping with the honour of the Crown."[68]

The Court itself describes the function as one of balancing: "to protect Aboriginal rights and to preserve the future use of the resources claimed by Aboriginal peoples while balancing countervailing Crown interests."[69] The centre of the balance can be said to be its preventative purpose with regard to irreversible harm: "Consultation centres on how the resource is to be developed in a way that prevents irreversible harm to existing Aboriginal interests."[70] Prevention avoids the creation of circumstances "where the resource has long since been altered and the present government conduct or decision does not have any further impact on the resource."[71] Or it may be directed to "organizational or power-structure changes"[72] that affect either "the Crown's future ability to deal honourably with Aboriginal interests"[73] or "its ability to exercise decision making ... consistent with the honour of the Crown."[74] In any case, consultation is a constitutional obligation that "must be met" where the test for the duty to consult is met.[75]

Historical Impacts Do Not Trigger the Duty to Consult

The Supreme Court concludes that the 2007 EPA had to have some adverse impact upon the Carrier Sekani Tribal Council before a duty to consult was triggered: "The claimant must show a causal relationship between the proposed government conduct or decision and a potential for adverse impacts on pending Aboriginal claims or rights. Past wrongs, including previous breaches of the duty to consult, do not suffice."[76] This was so regardless of the scale or extent of historical impacts or ongoing adverse effects of the Kemano Project on the Carrier Sekani Tribal Council. In defining adverse impacts, the Court stated that they are *not* an adverse effect on a First Nation's future negotiating position[77] or an underlying or continuing breach.[78] The Commission's finding that the 2007 EPA had no adverse impact was a reviewable by a court and was a reasonable finding on a mixed question of fact and law. The Commission was therefore correct in law to hold that it did not need to assess the adequacy of Crown consultation before approving the EPA by making a section 71 determination.

A duty to consult arises in relation to a contemporary Crown decision. Establishing that the contemplated and contemporary Crown conduct might adversely affect an actual or asserted Aboriginal right or title "requires demonstration of a causal connection between the proposed Crown conduct and a potential adverse impact on an Aboriginal claim or right." The Court found it necessary to expressly disagree with the broader approach to the scope of Aboriginal consultation advocated by the Carrier Sekani:

> [52] The respondent's submissions are based on a broader view of the duty to consult. It argues that even if the 2007 EPA will have no impact on the Nechako River water levels, the Nechako fisheries or the management of the contested resource, the duty to consult may be triggered because the 2007 EPA is part of a larger hydro-electric project which continues to impact its rights. The effect of this proposition is that if the Crown proposes an action, however limited, that relates to a project that impacts Aboriginal claims or rights, a fresh duty to consult arises. The current government action or decision, however inconsequential, becomes the hook that secures and reels in the constitutional duty to consult on the entire resource.

> [53] I cannot accept this view of the duty to consult. *Haida Nation* negates such a broad approach. It grounded the duty to consult in the need to preserve Aboriginal rights and claims pending resolution. It confines the duty to consult to adverse impacts flowing from the specific Crown proposal at issue—not to larger adverse impacts of the project of which it is a part. The subject of the consultation is the impact on the claimed rights of the *current* decision under consideration.

If the duty is to function to protect the future exercise of asserted rights, pending claims resolution, then it is forward looking and prospective. The emphasis is not on consultation about, and accommodation of, past infringements. For these, other remedies are appropriate. The emphasis is on the protection of future exercise of claimed rights (as in this BC case) or on Treaty rights. If the Crown is, as the Court requires, "to take contested or established Aboriginal rights into account *before* making a decision that may have an adverse impact on them,"[79] then it may consider the impact of the contemporary decision on the future exercise of asserted rights with regard to the placement of that impact within cumulative effects of other decisions on that future exercise. This does not convert the consultation and accommodation process into a dialogue about the entire history of the management of a resource. Rather, it allows the consultation process to appreciate cumulative impacts in a manner that is consistent with how such impacts are typically be assessed in a mature environmental assessment/regulatory review process.

A Duty to Consult Is Not Limited to Physical Impacts of Crown Conduct

The Court took the opportunity to state the "test" for Aboriginal consultation in three elements: (1) the Crown's knowledge, actual or constructive, of a potential Aboriginal claim or right; (2) contemplated Crown conduct; and (3) the potential that the contemplated conduct may adversely affect an Aboriginal claim or right. In terms of the third element, the Court looked at the 2007 EPA in two ways, stating that "a duty to consult may arise not only with respect to specific physical impacts, but with respect to high-level managerial or policy decisions that may potentially affect the future exploitation of a resource to the detriment of Aboriginal claimants."[80]

The Court therefore considers whether the Commission had properly considered (1) whether there was any new physical impact arising from the 2007 EPA on the Nechako River and its fishery and hence upon the future exercise of asserted Aboriginal rights and title by the Carrier Sekani Tribal Council, and (2) whether the 2007 EPA might bring about organizational, policy, or managerial changes that might adversely affect the future exercise of the asserted rights of the Carrier Sekani.

The Court characterizes these two questions as mixed questions of fact and law falling within the statutory jurisdiction of the Utilities Commission to determine and reviewable by a Court on a standard of reasonableness. In considering whether the conclusion of the tribunal was reasonable, the Supreme Court examines the evidence before the Commission and the Commission's reasoning based upon that evidence. The Court concludes that "[i]t has not been established that the Commission acted unreasonably in arriving at these conclusions."[81]

The Role of the Commission in the BC Treaty Process

The Court dismissed the general proposition that a power to consider questions of law was sufficient to enable a tribunal to accept a delegation of the power to conduct Crown consultation. Here the remedial powers of a tribunal are also material.[82] The Court did not find that the legislature had given the British Columbia Utilities Commission the capacity to engage in what it described as "interim resource consultations" with the Carrier Sekani "pending the final settlement of claims."[83] The Court's decision evidently appreciates the breadth and complexity that such a responsibility would place upon the Utilities Commission of a province where asserted Aboriginal rights and titles are negotiated in a six-stage process defined in the BC Treaty Process.

Case Studies Involving Aboriginal Consultation and the National Energy Board of Canada

THE NATIONAL ENERGY BOARD

The National Energy Board (NEB) is an independent tribunal exercising quasi-judicial functions pursuant to the *National Energy Board Act*[1] and other legislation.[2] Its statutory responsibilities include the regulatory review and oversight of interprovincial and international pipelines and power lines, traffic tolls and tariffs on pipelines within its jurisdiction, energy export from and import to Canada, frontier oil and gas development in some circumstances, technical and administrative assistance to the Northern Pipeline Agency,[3] and preparation of energy studies and research.

Although its responsibilities are not limited to interprovincial pipeline development, such development illustrates the significance of its role in project development. Today the NEB's regulatory review function necessitates the preparation of a report setting out its recommendation whether a Certificate of Public Convenience and Necessity should or should not be issued for all or part of a project, the reasons for that conclusion, and the terms and conditions it would attach to the Certificate were one to be issued.[4] In the current legislative scheme the NEB report is advisory only, and the Governor in Council has sole responsibility for making project approval, or denial, decisions. The legislative scheme in force at the time of the case studies was slightly different in that the NEB had the authority to deny an application.

Issuance of a certificate following approval by the Governor in Council allows a pipeline proponent to "arrange financing, mobilize labour and materials, and construct facilities."[5] When the National Energy Board was created in 1959, the existing pipeline system in Canada already "rivaled the railways as a major transportation artery."[6] In 2008, the Canadian pipeline transportation system regulated by the NEB carried some $127 billion worth of products to markets in Canada and the United States.[7] Today the Enbridge component of this system "is the largest crude oil pipeline in the world and the primary transporter of crude oil from western Canada to markets in eastern Canada and the U.S. Midwest."[8]

EVOLUTION OF NEB POLICIES REGARDING CONSULTATION WITH ABORIGINAL PEOPLES IN THE COURSE OF PROJECT DEVELOPMENT

The initial position of the National Energy Board reflects its understanding that Aboriginal consultation was rooted in the law of fiduciary obligation owed by the Crown to Aboriginal peoples. This position evolved when the Supreme Court clarified that the law of Aboriginal consultation flowed from the honour of the Crown, and not from fiduciary obligation. In that evolution, the NEB moves away from the position that it would require evidence of Crown consultation to be filed with it and toward its contemporary position that its own process is capable of appreciating Aboriginal concerns regarding the social, economic and environmental considerations integral to its decisions.

The initial product of this considered thought was a Memorandum of Guidance dated March 4, 2002, on the subject of consultation with Aboriginal peoples.[9] At that time, two and a half years *before* the decision of the Supreme Court in *Haida Nation*, the NEB considered that the Crown owed a fiduciary obligation to Aboriginal peoples when a government decision or action interferes with Aboriginal rights or Treaty rights. Such a fiduciary obligation typically required Crown consultation with the affected Aboriginal peoples. In its memorandum, the NEB addressed the question of whether it owed a fiduciary obligation to consult with Aboriginal peoples where the issuance of a certificate could be said to interfere with Aboriginal rights or Treaty rights. The NEB took the position that imposing such a fiduciary obligation upon the Board was not consistent with its statutory mandate as an independent tribunal. Nevertheless, the NEB recognized that its decisions had to be consistent with constitutional obligations. The 2002 Memorandum of Guidance therefore asserted that the NEB had an obligation to determine whether there had been adequate Crown consultation before making a decision that could interfere with an Aboriginal right or Treaty right. The result was that, in addition to the obligations of proponent consultation with Aboriginal peoples, it would require applicants to provide evidence that there had been adequate Crown consultation where section 35 rights may be adversely impacted by an NEB decision. The Board then issued a direction on April 3, 2002, regarding information required with an application filed with the Board.[10] This listed the information that proponents were to gather and present with their Application for a Certificate of Public Convenience and Necessity, where a project had the potential to affect Aboriginal rights or Treaty rights. The list primarily set out details of consultation conducted directly by a proponent with Aboriginal peoples but also added a final item regarding the details of Crown consultation of which the proponent was aware.

This early Memorandum of Guidance was withdrawn with evolution of the law following issuance of the Supreme Court decisions in *Haida Nation* and *Taku River*. With the *Haida Nation* judgment in 2004, it was clear that the honour of the Crown, not fiduciary obligation, was the foundation of the law of Aboriginal consultation. In 2005, the NEB issued a replacement memorandum entitled *Implications of Supreme Court of Canada Decisions on the NEB's Memorandum of Guidance on Consultation with Aboriginal People*.[11] Here the NEB clarified that it would ensure that Aboriginal peoples had opportunities to express their views about projects before the NEB through the NEB Aboriginal Engagement program[12] and by requiring applicants to gather and provide information on project impacts on Aboriginal peoples to standards described in the NEB Filing Manual[13] and through additional measures such as the NEB may require in any specific case.

In July 2008, the NEB published a further memorandum entitled *Consideration of Aboriginal Concerns in National Energy Board Decisions*.[14] It described, in plain English, why the NEB did not itself conduct Aboriginal consultation and how it nevertheless considered Aboriginal concerns. On the first question, the NEB explained that, as a quasi-judicial and independent tribunal, it was obliged to consider evidence via the record of proceedings and could not engage in one-on-one discussions with any interested parties outside the hearing process. On the second question, the NEB explained how it took steps to ensure that it had sufficient evidence before making its decision, including evidence on the impacts that the proposed project may have on Aboriginal peoples. This consisted of requiring an applicant to consult with Aboriginal peoples before and after an application was filed and inviting Aboriginal peoples to participate directly in the NEB proceedings after an application was filed. The NEB Filing Manual required the proponent of a project to contact potentially affected Aboriginal communities well before an application was filed with the Board; to gather and present to the NEB information regarding its consultation, concerns expressed by Aboriginal peoples, and whether and how such concerns were addressed by the applicant; and to analyze the potential impacts of the project on the exercise of traditional practices such as hunting, fishing, trapping, and gathering. The NEB reserved the rights to review the information for completeness and to require a proponent to file additional evidence.

CASE STUDY 1: THE MACKENZIE GAS PROJECT
The Berger Inquiry

The Mackenzie Gas Project anticipates exploitation of natural gas in the arctic region of Canada and transmission of that gas via a pipeline running along the length of the Mackenzie River Valley in the Northwest Territories—essentially from the Arctic Ocean to Alberta—where it would connect with an existing pipeline system. Such a pipeline was first proposed in the late 1960s and early 1970s, and Thomas Berger received an appointment to conduct a public inquiry into the environmental, social, and economic impacts of the project. The Berger Inquiry issued a final report[15] after several years of public hearings in the Northwest Territories, including televised portions that introduced the metropolitan south to Aboriginal peoples of that northern region in a way not possible before the widespread use of that immediate visual technology. In that report, the development of gas resources in the Canadian arctic was seen as inevitable. A recommendation was made, however, that such development should not occur until Aboriginal land claims in the region had been settled.[16] The first proposal for such a pipeline never resulted in commercial development, but the enduring legacy of this work has been as catalyst in the development of Aboriginal law through the conclusion of land claims. As will be seen, this has implications for the environmental assessment and regulatory review of a second initiative to develop a Mackenzie Gas Project in the first decade of the twenty-first century.

Modern Treaties and New Tribunals

After the final report of the Berger Inquiry, and following upon the decision of the Supreme Court of Canada in *Calder*, a comprehensive land claims policy was developed by Canada. Comprehensive land claims were filed by many First Nations "north of 60," including but not limited to those in the Mackenzie Valley. Canada initiated comprehensive claims negotiations with Aboriginal peoples who filed comprehensive claims accepted for negotiation. Constitutional amendment in 1982 affirmed that any agreements that might be concluded would have the status of modern treaties within section 35 of the *Constitution Act, 1982*. Agreements were concluded with the Inuvialuit, the Gwich'in and the Sahtu Dene and Métis. These agreements created constitutionally protected institutions of different kinds with responsibility for, *inter alia*, environmental assessment, land use planning, and regulatory decision making. Through these institutions, the Aboriginal signatories to the modern treaties had a say in governance of activity within their settlement areas. The *Mackenzie Valley Resource Management Act* was enacted by Parliament to structure the regulatory apparatus in the Northwest Territories to facilitate the work of these new institutions.[17]

The Deh Cho (an umbrella collection of over a dozen separate communities in the Northwest Territories) asserted exclusive jurisdiction in their land claim area even though they had not yet finalized a land claim agreement.[18] Canada was negotiating with the Deh Cho, in a negotiation referred to as the Deh Cho Process,[19] but that did not give rise to a final settlement of the Deh Cho comprehensive claim. An *Interim Measures Agreement* was concluded through the Deh Cho Process, and it conferred on the Deh Cho the opportunity to nominate a representative for appointment to the Mackenzie Valley Environmental Impact Review Board, the primary tribunal under the *Mackenzie Valley Resource Management Act*.[20]

A Renewed Project Proposal in a New Era

In 2000, Imperial Oil Resources, Gulf Canada Resources Limited, Shell Canada Limited, and Mobil Canada announced that they had entered into an agreement to study the feasibility of developing Mackenzie Delta gas. An equity interest in the Project would ultimately be taken by the Aboriginal Pipeline Group, initially representing Inuvialuit, Sahtu, and Gwich'in interests.[21] This second proposal for a Mackenzie Gas Project[22] would involve exploiting gas fields in the Mackenzie River Delta through a gathering system and then shipping the gas to markets through a pipeline running along the length of the Mackenzie River and into Alberta at a point where it would connect with the existing gas pipeline system there. A lineal project of this dimension, over 1,000 kilometres in length and billions of dollars in cost, would span the legal regimes established by the settlement agreements with the Inuvialuit, Gwich'in, and Sahtu, the lands claimed by the Deh Cho, and (upon entry into Alberta) touch on the legal regime of Treaty 8.

Reducing Duplication of the Regulatory Process

Governments and industry sponsored a series of "regulatory roadmaps" to better define the permitting and tribunal obligations that such a project would face. Readers interested in the details are invited to read the regulatory roadmaps.[23] The complexity of the process was described by the chairman of the National Energy Board in a later presentation to the Standing Senate Committee on Energy, the Environment and Natural Resources: "Land claim settlements north of 60, which are certainly seen as positive by all players, have also produced a complex array of assessment and regulatory bodies. Each has important work to do, but to a proponent seeking approval to construct a pipeline down the Valley, the review process must look daunting."[24]

The tribunals with a public hearing process in regard to such a project, in whole and in part, consisted of the National Energy Board, Mackenzie Valley Environmental Impact Review Board,[25] Mackenzie Valley Land and Water Board,[26] Northwest Territories Water Board,[27] Government of the Northwest Territories, Environmental Impact Screening Committee[28] and Environmental Impact Review Board[29] for the Inuvialuit Settlement Region, Inuvialuit Settlement Region Land Administration,[30] Inuvialuit Game Council,[31] Sahtu Land and Water Board,[32] and Gwich'in Land and Water Board.[33]

To coordinate their respective planning processes, the chairs of the tribunals with public hearing processes began periodic meetings to discuss the interaction of their respective enabling legislation.[34] The Deh Cho of the Northwest Territories, but not the Dene Tha' of Alberta, were invited to participate as an observer in the discussions. And, in describing how the chairs approached that task, the chairman of the NEB began with the "important assumption" that the chairs would "work within the existing legal framework."[35]

The chairs saw themselves engaged in the business of good government: that is, reducing duplication of process under existing legislation to achieve a single assessment process that would meet the regulatory obligations of all the tribunals engaged.

The chair of the National Energy Board described how it became necessary in this exercise of coordinating complex regulatory structures to separate the environmental impact assessment (EIA) from the regulatory review processes:

> Initially, efforts were made to combine the public hearing aspects of the EIA and regulatory processes. However, this would have resulted in a large and unwieldy panel, and to address this, the Agencies agreed that the EIA and regulatory hearing processes

should be separate. This will also allow the EIA panel to proceed in a less formal manner that will be more responsive to local needs and expectations.[36]

This resulted in separation of the environmental assessment process from the regulatory review process for the project. The two would proceed in a separate but parallel and coordinated manner.

In the end, a joint review panel (JRP) and the National Energy Board conducted parallel environmental assessment and regulatory review proceedings, respectively. When the JRP issued its report, the NEB continued with its process, receiving final argument on whether to adopt the JRP recommendations as conditions of a Certificate of Public Convenience and Necessity under section 52 of the *National Energy Board Act* (as it then was).

The JRP discharged functions of environmental assessment under a *Joint Panel Agreement*. The National Energy Board discharged functions of regulatory review under the *National Energy Board Act*[37] and the *Canada Oil and Gas Operations Act*.[38] Normally, the NEB conducts an environmental assessment in a manner that is fully integrated with, and indistinguishable from, its regulatory process. In the case of the Mackenzie Gas Project, the NEB would rely on the JRP for the environmental assessment, appointing one of its members to the JRP who, in time, would submit the JRP report to the NEB as the NEB environmental assessment. Since environmental impact is essential to the assessment of public interest under the NEB regulatory process, NEB proceedings would begin at the same time as JRP proceedings but last longer. The JRP would issue its report on the environmental effects of the project, and how they would be mitigated; the NEB would then continue its public hearing proceedings with particular reference to integration of the JRP report into the public interest test under section 52 of the *National Energy Board Act* (as it then was).

Creation of a single joint review panel for the Mackenzie Gas Project was possible because the need for cooperative measures was well accepted in law and reflected in the land claim agreements and the enabling or applicable legislation. The *Mackenzie Valley Resource Management Act*, which established the tribunals provided for in the *Comprehensive Claims Agreements* with the Gwich'in and Sahtu, allowed for the use of joint review panels as vehicles for the coordination and reduction of duplication in environmental assessment or regulatory process. Section 141(2)(a) of the *Mackenzie Valley Resource Management Act* authorized the Mackenzie Valley Environmental Impact Review Board to enter into an agreement with the federal Minister of the

Environment for the creation of a JRP under section 40 of the *Canadian Environmental Assessment Act*. The *Inuvialuit Final Agreement* also provides for joint panel reviews in the interests of coordination and reduction of duplication.[39] Section 11 of the *Inuvialuit Final Agreement* establishes an environmental impact screening and review process and creates a Screening Committee with environmental assessment functions within the Inuvialuit Settlement Region. Section 11(15) of the *Inuvialuit Final Agreement* allows the Screening Committee to refer a project to any other body conducting an environmental assessment of that project. A joint review panel was also authorized by sections 40 and 41 of the *Canadian Environmental Assessment Act* (CEAA) then in force. The CEAA authorized the Minister of the Environment to enter into an agreement for a JRP with any "jurisdiction" referred to in section 40(1), paragraphs (a) to (d), of CEAA inclusive. These jurisdictions were (1) a federal authority; (2) a provincial government; (3) any body with environmental assessment responsibility established pursuant to an act of Parliament or a legislature; and (4) any body with environmental assessment responsibility established pursuant to a land claims agreement referred to in section 35 of the *Constitution Act, 1982*. In this case, the bodies referred to in section 40(1)(d) of CEAA include the boards created under the *Inuvialuit Final Agreement*, the *Gwich'in Comprehensive Land Claim Settlement Agreement*, and the *Sahtu and Dene Land Claim Settlement Agreement*.[40]

In 2002, the chairs finalized the *Cooperation Plan for the Environmental Impact Assessment and Regulatory Review of a Northern Gas Pipeline Project through the Northwest Territories (Cooperation Plan)*.[41] The *Cooperation Plan* conceptually divided the entire environmental assessment/regulatory review process into four stages: preparation, which included completion of various agreements necessary to give legal effect to the joint review panel; provision of information from the project proponents; conduct of the environmental assessment of the joint review panel coordinated with the regulatory hearing of the National Energy Board; and then, assuming project approval, completion of other regulatory processes by other regulatory agencies (with or without an obligatory public hearing process according to their respective enabling legislation).

In April 2003, to assist this harmonization work being conducted by the chairs, the project proponents provided a preliminary information package giving general information on the project.[42] At this moment, still very early in the commercial and planning stages of the project, the southern terminus of the pipeline was anticipated to be either a few metres south of the Alberta–Northwest Territories border or a point farther south of the border where the pipeline could connect to existing infrastructure owned by TransCanada Pipeline through its subsidiary Nova Gas Transmission Limited.[43] If the former, then a connecting pipeline and associated pumping stations and other works would need to be constructed inside Alberta by a third party, who would need to obtain regulatory approval from the Alberta Energy Resources Conservation Board as a separate project outside the harmonized framework developed for the Mackenzie Gas Project. If the latter, then the pipeline in Alberta would be part of the Mackenzie Gas Project financial structure and regulated by the National Energy Board within the harmonized framework. Although an application for the connecting facilities was made to the Alberta Energy Resources Conservation Board by Nova Gas Transmission Limited in 2006,[44] jurisdiction over the entire trans-Canada gas pipeline system in Alberta was assumed by the NEB in 2009 before the Energy Resources Conservation Board concluded its process.[45]

A regulators' agreement was concluded on April 22, 2004, by agencies with statutory responsibilities relating to the Mackenzie Gas Project.[46] The regulators' agreement expressed a commitment, by these agencies, to (1) coordinate public hearings, (2) use the environmental assessment conducted by a joint review panel in order to "eliminate unnecessary duplication in review of environmental issues in the regulatory hearings," (3) develop consistent standards for rules of procedure, and (4) create a secretariat to provide centralized services for the efficient running of public hearings (including translation and recording, transportation and accommodation, technical support to the parties to the agreement, and a centralized Internet-accessible, public registry system).

In July 2004, an *Agreement for the Environmental Impact Review of the Mackenzie Gas Project* was concluded.[47] It provided the terms of reference for the JRP. The terms of reference of the panel were drafted specifically to emphasize Aboriginal interests. The JRP mandate was defined in a schedule to the JRP agreement. The term "impact on the environment" was defined to mean "any change to present or future wildlife harvesting" and "any change to the social or cultural environment or to heritage resources." The JRP was specifically mandated to "have regard to the protection of the existing and future social, cultural and economic well-being of residents and communities" when considering factors of the environmental assessment listed in Annex 2 to the schedule of the JRP agreement, including "[t]he impact of the Project on the environment ... and any cumulative impact that is likely to result from the Project in combination with other projects or activities that have been or will be carried out" and "[t]he capacity of renewable resources that are likely to be significantly affected by the Project to meet existing and future needs." Additional factors were defined for the Inuvialuit Settlement Region. With regard to traditional knowledge, the joint review panel was charged with "best efforts to promote and facilitate the contribution of traditional knowledge to the environmental impact review." The JRP was to identify, evaluate, and report on the potential impacts of the project on the physical, biological, and human environments and to carry out specific responsibilities under the *Inuvialuit Final Agreement*, including an estimation of the potential liability of the proponent, determined on a worst case scenario basis and taking into consideration the balance between economic factors, including the ability of the proponent to pay, and environmental factors, as referred to in paragraph 13(11)(b) of the *Inuvialuit Final Agreement*.

To allay concerns regarding project splitting arising from a commercial decision of the project proponents taken in 2003,[48] the terms of reference were drafted to require the JRP to consider both the Mackenzie Gas Project and the connecting pipeline and facilities in northwestern Alberta, together with the cumulative effects of other developments.

In August of 2004 the JRP itself came into existence when its members were appointed by the Minister of the Environment. The joint review panel was constituted pursuant to the *Canadian Environmental Assessment Act,* the *Mackenzie Valley Resource Management Act*, and the *Inuvialuit Final Agreement.* The JRP subsequently issued its procedural rules.[49] The rules afford full rights of procedural fairness to intervenors, including Aboriginal intervenors, the ability to issue information requests to any party, to call evidence, cross-examine witnesses of other parties, make motions or seek directions, make oral and written submissions, and receive reasons.

On November 24, 2004, the National Energy Board in turn issued a Hearing Order for its proceedings.[50] It described the NEB process and procedures and defined the issues that the NEB would consider. They were set out in Appendix I to the Hearing Order and included the appropriateness of the proponent's public consultation program, including the adequacy of Aboriginal consultation. The National Energy Board had its own rules in relation to its regulatory process, with comparable powers and provisions with similar effect: that is, the conferral of full rights of procedural fairness on intervenors.[51]

In summary, this project would not barrel ahead without consideration of Aboriginal concerns. The processes of both the JRP and the NEB were designed to be sensitive to Aboriginal interests. Aboriginal engagement in the JRP and NEB processes was encouraged. The Canadian Environmental Assessment Agency administered a participant funding program that supported Aboriginal and public participation in the JRP process.[52] The Agency, and the Mackenzie Valley Environmental Impact Review Board, allocated a further fund "to assist the public to prepare for and participate in technical conferences and/or provide technical analysis to the Joint Review Panel on the adequacy of the Environmental Impact Statement (EIS)." The proponent also provided direct funding to individual groups in aid of its consultation program. The Department of Indian and Northern Affairs also provided funding in some circumstances.[53]

Litigation with the Deh Cho

On September 16, 2004, the Deh Cho initiated in Federal Court a challenge to the decision of the Minister of the Environment to appoint a JRP.[54] A similar action was also commenced in the Northwest Territories Supreme Court.[55] The Deh Cho Process discussions came to a halt at approximately this time. The Deh Cho claimed that the Crown had discriminated against the Deh Cho, breached fiduciary obligations toward the Deh Cho, and breached the section 35 rights of the Deh Cho, on the basis that the Deh Cho were entitled to participate in the planning and preparation of the Mackenzie Gas Project from 2000, when Imperial Oil announced that it would conduct a feasibility study, to 2004, when the Minister of the Environment decided to appoint a JRP, as if the Deh Cho had concluded a land claim agreement. The Deh Cho disputed that they had participated in this process through the Deh Cho nominee to the Mackenzie Valley Environmental Impact Review Board as provided for in the *Interim Measures Agreement*. The Crown ultimately appointed an envoy who negotiated a settlement with the Deh Cho.[56] The settlement addressed the impasse on the Deh Cho Process, as well as the dispute over Deh Cho participation in planning for the Mackenzie Gas Project.

Environmental Assessment and Regulatory Review Begin

In October 2004, the project proponents filed a formal application for regulatory approval of the Mackenzie Gas Project under the *National Energy Board Act* and the *Canada Oil and Gas Operations Act* together with an Environmental Impact Statement (EIS).[57] At that time, the project proponents made it clear that a decision to construct the project had not been made. The final decision to proceed with construction would depend on obtaining the necessary regulatory approvals—then anticipated by the proponents to be completed in 2006—and assessing any conditions attached to those approvals as well as several other factors, such as natural gas markets and project costs.

Filing of the applications and the EIS initiated the environmental assessment process of the JRP and the separate but parallel regulatory review process of the NEB. The JRP and NEB processes proceeded in a parallel and coordinated manner from October 2004 to December 2009 (when the JRP report was issued) and December 2010 (when the NEB report was issued). In 2004, when the EIS was filed, both the JRP and the NEB conducted a technical review of the EIS. The review consisted of identifying deficiencies in the EIS and considering a supplementary EIS filed by the project proponents in response to the deficiencies.[58] Public hearings by the JRP and NEB, conducted separately, began in early 2006.

Litigation with the Dene Tha'

On May 17, 2005, in the midst of the technical review, the Dene Tha' First Nation initiated a judicial review in Federal Court alleging failure by various federal ministers to comply with constitutional and fiduciary duties under section 35 of the *Constitution Act, 1982*, "to consult and accommodate the Aboriginal and Treaty rights of the Dene Tha' First Nation in respect of the environmental and regulatory review of the Mackenzie Gas Project."[59] The Dene Tha' First Nation is a Treaty 8 signatory that asserts traditional land uses (as well as unextinguished Aboriginal rights and titles) in a large area of northwestern Alberta, northeastern British Columbia, and the southern portion of the Northwest Territories. Unlike the Inuvialuit, the Sahtu, or the Gwich'in, the Dene Tha' had no tribunals with governance functions of planning, approval, or control in relation to the Mackenzie Gas Project. Unlike the Deh Cho, the Dene Tha' had never filed a comprehensive land claim (even though their traditional lands overlapped with the land claim area of the Deh Cho in the southern Northwest Territories) or concluded an *Interim Measures Agreement* that conferred an opportunity for participation in the tribunals created by the *Mackenzie Valley Resource Management Act*. In the judicial review application, the Dene Tha' claimed nevertheless to have lost the opportunity for input into the design of the environmental and regulatory review process for the Mackenzie Gas Project and to have lost the opportunity of *membership* in the joint review panel. The relief sought included a request that the environmental review process being undertaken by the JRP be stopped in mid-course until it was "revised to allow the Dene Tha' to have a meaningful and effective role in the process."[60] The Dene Tha' also presented the Court with the settlement agreement concluded with the Deh Cho, making that a public document via the Federal Court Registry. The Deh Cho settlement agreement was likely obtained from the Deh Cho website, where it had been posted for a period of time.

The judicial review application was case managed, and the Federal Court dismissed an application to stay the judicial review application on the basis that "[t]he subject matter of the Dene Tha's judicial review, being the creation of the processes for the review of the Mackenzie Gas Project, is largely completed. It is a discreet [sic] issue separate from what may be the outcome of those reviews. Therefore, it is a matter which can be dealt with without disrupting the existing and future proceedings."[61] The Dene Tha', actively participating in both the JRP and the NEB proceedings, nevertheless sought to delay them on the basis that Crown consultation with them had been inadequate. The NEB[62] and the JRP[63] both demurred. The JRP indicated that assessment of the adequacy of Aboriginal consultation was beyond its jurisdiction. The NEB pointed out that assessment of the adequacy of Aboriginal consultation was one of the issues defined in its Hearing Order for the Mackenzie Gas Project[64] and invited the Dene Tha' to participate further in the NEB process and to "submit evidence and make argument without the need of any further Order from the NEB."

The Dene Tha' then won from the Federal Court a judgment holding that Crown consultation had not been adequate in regard to the development of the environmental assessment and regulatory review process from 2000 to 2004.[65] This time period was before the Court's decision in *Haida Nation*. The Court was aware of the "north of 60" application of the *Mackenzie Gas Project Impacts Act*, was sympathetic to the Dene Tha' desire for recognition of Aboriginal rights in the Northwest Territories overlapping with the Deh Cho claim area,[66] and was sympathetic to the Dene Tha' desire for settlement similar to the "generous" settlement agreement concluded with the Deh Cho.[67] The Court therefore granted the Dene Tha' request for relief in the nature of "a 'stick,' an incentive, to goad the Crown."[68] The applicant had requested that the JRP hearing process be stayed pending further order of the Court. Notwithstanding the Court's earlier commitment that the judicial review would not disrupt the ongoing processes, and notwithstanding judicial pronouncement favouring restraint and balance in the exercise of relief in cases involving the honour of the Crown, the Court decided to issue interim relief staying that portion of the JRP proceedings in any way related to any aspect of the lands used by the Dene Tha' for traditional purposes and directing a "remedies hearing" after which it would issue final orders.[69]

Prior to the remedies hearing, Canada appointed an envoy to negotiate a settlement with the Dene Tha'.[70] Settlement was concluded, and the Federal Court proceedings were terminated without a remedies hearing. The Dene Tha' also withdrew their opposition to the Mackenzie

Gas Project and terminated their participation in the public hearing process of the JRP.

Pursuant to that settlement, and notwithstanding the absence of a live issue between the parties, Canada appealed to the Federal Court of Appeal to seek clarification of the law of Aboriginal consultation as it applied in the circumstances. The Federal Court of Appeal, dismissing the Crown appeal, did not agree with every conclusion of the Federal Court and specifically disagreed with the proposition "that adequate consultation in relation to an asserted Aboriginal right cannot be achieved unless the person or agency representing the Crown is empowered to determine the validity of the right."[71] Characterizing the Federal Court judgment as unique to the Mackenzie Gas Project, the Court of Appeal upheld the retrospective application of the law of Aboriginal consultation as stated by the Supreme Court in *Haida Nation* to the factual events prior to the *Haida* judgment. The Court of Appeal stated that, "[o]nce Justice Phelan found, as he was entitled to do, that the obligation to consult arose in relation to the development of the environmental and regulatory process, and that there had been no consultation at all in that regard, he was bound to conclude that the Ministers had not fulfilled their duty." No further application for leave to appeal to the Supreme Court was filed. The Supreme Court subsequently cited the litigation, without discussion or analysis, in regard to its general proposition that "the duty to consult extends to strategic, higher level decisions that may have an impact on Aboriginal claims and rights."[72]

Report of the Joint Review Panel

The JRP for the Mackenzie Gas Project issued its report in December 2009.[73] The report contained 176 recommendations to mitigate potential adverse impacts of the project. These recommendations were directed to the Government of Canada, the National Energy Board, proponents, the Government of the Northwest Territories, and the Government of Alberta. Regarding impact and benefit agreements, the panel commented that the privacy of such agreements prevented the panel from taking them into account in its deliberations.[74]

In terms of the socio-economic impacts of the project, the JRP report stated that "resources far beyond those currently available to the [Government of the Northwest Territories] and communities would be required to address the combination of potential Project impacts and the existing conditions of social well-being."[75] In this respect, the report considered the *Mackenzie Gas Project Impacts Act,* noting that the *Settlement Agreement* with the Dene Tha' was to provide a similar mitigation capacity applicable to the Dene Tha' should the Project proceed.[76]

In January 2007, with a similar objective, the Government of the Northwest Territories executed a *Socio-Economic Agreement* with the proponents of the Mackenzie Gas Project.[77] The JRP report also considered that.[78]

Parliament enacted in 2006 the *Mackenzie Gas Project Impacts Act,*[79] which created the Corporation for the Mitigation of Mackenzie Gas Project Impacts. The Minister of Finance was authorized to pay to the corporation $500 million, though payment could only be made on the recommendation of the Minister of Indian Affairs and Northern Development, who could only make such a recommendation if the project was not terminated and if the minister was of the opinion that progress was being made on the project. The corporation was authorized to make contributions to regional organizations in the Northwest Territories to mitigate existing or anticipated socio-economic impacts on communities arising from the Mackenzie Gas Project. The *Act* came into force in 2006, at a time when it was initially anticipated that the JRP and NEB processes would be concluding.

Section 137 of the *Mackenzie Valley Resource Management Act* imposed a unique Consult to Modify Process.[80] Pursuant to this process, the Government of Canada and the NEB were to consult with the JRP respecting the recommendations that they proposed to adopt with modifications or reject.

In May 2010, the Governments of Canada and the Northwest Territories issued an interim response to the JRP report. The response signaled an intention to accept, or to accept with some modifications, 87 of the 115 recommendations within their respective jurisdictions, to take no position on sixty recommendations directed to the National Energy Board and one recommendation directed to the Government of Alberta, and not to accept twenty-eight recommendations. The Governments stated that, of these final twenty-eight recommendations, twenty-one were outside the scope of the JRP's mandate. Regarding socio-economic issues, the governments expressed confidence that future initiatives conditional upon the project being completed would provide capacity to Aboriginal groups necessary to meet changing conditions:

> The Governments of Canada and the Northwest Territories are of the opinion that the *Mackenzie Gas Project Impacts Act* (MGPIA) along with the Mackenzie Gas Project Socio-Economic Agreement will be able to mitigate most, if not all, of the socio-economic impacts arising from the MGP. The MGPIA, which was

adopted in 2006 by the Government of Canada, set aside up to $500 million for projects that mitigate the existing or anticipated socio-economic impacts on communities in the Northwest Territories arising from the MGP. The Government of the Northwest Territories and the Proponents signed the Mackenzie Gas Project Socio-Economic Agreement (SEA) in January 2008. The SEA establishes a socio-economic monitoring program, including reporting mechanisms and an NWT Oil and Gas Socio-Economic Advisory Board. The role of the Advisory Board is to ensure that the Project related effects are monitored and that mitigation measures are adapted to meet changing elements.[81]

The National Energy Board engaged in the Consult to Modify Process.[82] On March 9, 2010, the NEB released draft conditions that could be appended to a Certificate of Public Convenience and Necessity, if issued.[83] Final argument before the NEB proceeded in April 2010, and parties were invited to make submissions on the proposed conditions.

The Consult to Modify Process between governments and the JRP was prolonged due to uncertainty over the nature of the process and whether it would be confidential.[84] After concluding additional Aboriginal consultation, the governments asserted that they had reached an agreement with the JRP to allow the Consult to Modify Process to move to conclusion.[85] On October 4, 2010, the JRP responded to the government's interim response, rejecting the government proposals.[86]

The governments' final response to the JRP report was issued in November 2010.[87] It provided a detailed list of each JRP recommendation, and of the response to it. The final response noted that many of the recommendations directed to the NEB were incorporated as proposed conditions for a Certificate of Public Convenience and Necessity under section 52 of the *National Energy Board Act*.

Review of the Regulatory Systems across the North

An environmental assessment and regulatory review process lasting more than five consecutive years was heavily criticized.[88] Canada responded by appointing a special representative to set out recommendations to the Minister of Indian and Northern Affairs for improving the regulatory regime in the North. The report noted the complexity of the regulatory regimes established by the land claims agreements, past and pending, and made two basic recommendations:

Option 1 outlines a fundamental restructuring that would require the agreement of all parties to amend the comprehensive land claim agreements and the *Mackenzie Valley Resource Management Act ... .*

Option 2 outlines a less extensive restructuring which may require some amendments to the *Mackenzie Valley Resource Management Act.*[89]

The Government of the Northwest Territories responded to the recommendations in March 2009.[90] The Chief of the Deh Cho First Nations was quoted as stating that "[t]he ... [federal] report looks like an attempt to make resource development a lot easier. ... It doesn't really support what we're trying to do."[91] The Government of Canada established the Northern Project Management Office in September 2009 "as a core program within the Canadian Northern Economic Development Agency (CanNor), to coordinate federal regulatory work in the territories and help ensure review and approval processes proceed smoothly on northern resource development projects."[92]

Reasons for Decision of the National Energy Board

On December 16, 2010, the National Energy Board released its Reasons for Decision regarding the Mackenzie Gas Project.[93] The NEB recommended the issuance of a Certificate of Public Convenience and Necessity, with conditions. The NEB could not issue a certificate without approval of the Governor in Council. On December 20, 2011, the NEB issued Orders DP-01-2010, DP-02-2010, and DP-03-2010 pursuant to section 5.1 of the *Canada Oil and Gas Operations Act.*[94] These were not effective until approval of the Governor in Council was received.

The National Energy Board Reasons for Decision point out how Aboriginal consultation by the proponent, and Aboriginal engagement in the JRP and NEB processes, demonstrably resulted in modifications to the project and contributed to the NEB conclusion regarding the issuance of a Certificate of Public Convenience and Necessity for the project. As for Aboriginal consultation, the NEB report described the proponent's consultation program for the Mackenzie Gathering System and Mackenzie Valley Pipeline, and for the development fields, consultation with government, participation by parties in the JRP hearing process, participation by parties in the NEB hearing process, and consideration of Aboriginal concerns through either accommodation by the proponent or by NEB response to additional concerns raised in its hearing process.

The NEB referred to Aboriginal engagement in the environmental assessment and regulatory process throughout the life cycle of the project, and not to a separate track of Aboriginal consultation by the Crown. Speaking generally of how Aboriginal peoples were consulted, the NEB stated that "One of our important responsibilities is to make sure the companies consult thoroughly and properly with all affected parties. We heard directly from people in our 58 days of public hearings and also through the Joint Review Panel Report."[95] Although the NEB cited Aboriginal consultation by the Crown, it did not seem to inform the NEB decision but was said to have taken place because "[t]he federal government addressed its obligations to Aboriginal people under Section 35 of the Constitution in a separate Crown consultation process."[96] The NEB cited Crown consultation but did not assess its adequacy even though some Aboriginal groups continued to assert in final argument in April 2010 that Crown consultation had been inadequate. Instead, the NEB emphasized engagement by Aboriginal persons in consultation by the proponent and in the JRP and NEB processes:

> We rely on those with an interest in a project to participate in our hearing process, so that we can hear directly from them and consider their views and concerns. We also encourage all those who might be affected by a project to engage early in the project planning and assessment stages with proponents, so that they may work collaboratively to address any interests.[97]

Regarding Aboriginal consultation by the Proponent, and responsiveness to Aboriginal concerns, the NEB stated that

> Local and regional concerns led to more than a dozen significant changes in the planned route. Smaller alterations in locations and plans were also made. Some of the changes were made on the basis of Aboriginal people's traditional knowledge of the land. For example, the community of Tulita requested that the Great Bear River compressor station be located further away from the culturally significant Bear Rock. It was moved eight kilometres south, across the Great Bear River. The companies said they could not make some of the requested changes due to cost, safety or technical reasons. In these situations, the companies said they looked for other ways to reduce the impacts. For example, where the route could not avoid crossing traditional camping or hunting areas, the construction schedule was changed to address some of the concerns.[98]

Examples of changes to the project arising from consultation by the proponent were listed in Table 9.1 of the National Energy Board Report.[99]

The NEB concluded that Aboriginal consultation was effective to address Aboriginal concerns, either through accommodations from the proponent or from additional conditions imposed by the NEB through its certificate:

> Throughout its hearing process, the National Energy Board requires an applicant to consult with Aboriginal groups in order to determine their concerns, and to attempt to address them to the extent possible. If there are concerns that remain unaddressed after consultation, the National Energy Board can impose conditions to address them. In our hearing, we considered the concerns of Aboriginal people when making our decision, and our conditions address these concerns. With the Proponents' measures and commitments, and the requirements contained in our conditions, we believe the concerns raised by parties and Aboriginal groups have been or will be adequately addressed, and identified impacts will be effectively mitigated.[100]

This was, in the Board's view, consistent with section 35 of the *Constitution Act, 1982.*

The Board's decision emphasized the ongoing nature of NEB regulatory oversight during the life cycle of a project:

> Inspections and monitoring activities by the National Energy Board include:
>
> - verifying compliance with, and assessing the effectiveness of, mitigation measures, conditions, and environmental protection plans;
>
> - verifying compliance with the appropriate standards and regulations; and
>
> - monitoring construction and operations, including verifying construction progress reports.
>
> If inspectors find that the company is not meeting the conditions or the regulations, the National Energy Board takes action to enforce them.

The National Energy Board enforces safety and environmental commitments and requirements. If we find a company is not meeting its commitments and requirements we immediately ask the company to voluntarily correct the situation. If a situation cannot be corrected immediately, or if additional information is required from a company, the National Energy Board's Inspection Officers may ask for a written assurance of voluntary compliance from the company. The company must later confirm that compliance was achieved.[101]

With regard to integration of Aboriginal concerns into this ongoing process, the NEB stated that it expects the proponent "to continue their discussions with those who will be affected by their project as the regulatory process unfolds, and during the construction and operation phases of their project," and that "all interested and affected parties may contact us at any time regarding the Proponents' activities, and we would give appropriate consideration to any submission as it is received."[102]

Project Approval and Ongoing Regulatory Review Process

In March 2011, the Governor in Council approved the Mackenzie Gas Project. This took the form of an Order in Council pursuant to section 52 of the *National Energy Board Act,* as it then was, approving the issuance by the National Energy Board of Certificate of Public Convenience and Necessity GC-116,[103] a further Order in Council pursuant to subsection 5.1(4) of the *Canada Oil and Gas Operations Act* consenting to the approval by the National Energy Board of Part I of the Development Plan for the Parsons Lake gas field,[104] and a third Order in Council pursuant to subsection 5.1(4) of the *Canada Oil and Gas Operations Act* consenting to the approval by the National Energy Board of Part I of the Development Plan for the Taglu gas field.[105]

As of January 2012, it is uncertain whether the Mackenzie Gas Project will proceed. The NEB required the proponents to file updated cost estimates and report on their decision to build the pipeline by the end of 2013. Actual construction must begin by the end of 2015 for the NEB decision, if approved by the Governor in Council, to remain valid.[106] Appointments to the Corporation for the Mitigation of Mackenzie Gas Project Impacts remained unfilled as of the date of publication of this book.[107]

CASE STUDY 2: THE ALBERTA CLIPPER, KEYSTONE, AND SOUTHERN LIGHTS INTERPROVINCIAL PIPELINES

Three Interprovincial Pipeline Projects

Early in the twenty-first century, industry applied to the National Energy Board for Certificates of Public Convenience and Necessity for three oil pipeline projects that would expand the capacity of Canada's oil pipeline system: Enbridge proposed the Alberta Clipper[108] and Southern Lights[109] Pipeline Projects; TransCanada Pipelines proposed the Keystone Pipeline Project.[110] These projects became the subject matter of litigation regarding Aboriginal consultation. There was separate litigation at the Federal Court and Federal Court of Appeal levels. These cases all consider the integration of Aboriginal concerns into the NEB's environmental assessment and regulatory review process and subsequent Governor in Council approval of the issuance of a Certificate of Public Convenience and Necessity by the NEB, and they all involve the post-*Haida* practices of the NEB regarding the integration of Aboriginal concerns into its process.[111]

Federal Court considered the capacity of the Governor in Council to rely on the NEB process when approving the issuance of a Certificate of Public Convenience and Necessity. The Federal Court judgment was not appealed.[112] The Federal Court of Appeal considered the capacity of the National Energy Board to issue a Certificate without first examining and commenting on the adequacy of Aboriginal consultation and, where necessary, accommodation by the Crown. The Federal Court of Appeal litigation reached the Supreme Court of Canada via applications for leave to appeal, all of which were dismissed on December 2, 2010, shortly after the Court's decision in *Rio Tinto*.[113]

The resulting judgments in the pipeline litigation cases collectively support the proposition that the NEB process (which, of course, includes the proponent's Aboriginal consultation and accommodation) is capable of assessing the significance of project impacts on Treaty rights having regard to the implementation of mitigation measures. Where the NEB reasonably concludes that project impacts on Treaty rights are not likely to be significant having regard to the accommodations of the proponent and the conditions of approval to be attached to the Certificate of Public Convenience and Necessity by the NEB itself, the Governor in Council may rely upon the NEB process to fully discharge the duty to consult. In summary, a project approval decision of the Governor in Council may occur in a context where the NEB did not assess the adequacy of Crown consultation. The inherently consultative nature of the regulatory review process, including the Aboriginal consultation by the Proponent, and the measures identified there to mitigate project impacts on Treaty rights, can be sufficient of themselves for the purposes of fulfillment of the Crown's duty to consult.

In analyzing these litigation cases, I adopt a three-step approach. First, I discuss the NEB processes in the three pipeline cases. Second, I examine the Federal Court judicial review of the decision of the Governor in Council to approve the issuance of a certificate. Third, I discuss appeals to the Federal Court of Appeal from the NEB's issuance of a certificate without necessity of assessing the adequacy of Crown consultation during the regulatory review process, and the decision of the Supreme Court to dismiss leave to appeal from the decision of the Federal Court of Appeal.

An Integrated Environmental Assessment and Regulatory Review Process for the Three Pipeline Projects

Proponents sought separate Certificates of Public Convenience and Necessity from the NEB in regard to the Alberta Clipper Pipeline Project, Keystone Pipeline Project, and the Southern Lights Pipeline Project. The NEB conducted a separate process for each project. Each is described here in a way that merges the common aspects to emphasize Aboriginal engagement.

The NEB process for each proceeding illustrates integrated environmental assessment under the *Canadian Environmental Assessment Act* (*CEAA*) as it then was, and regulatory review under the *National Energy Board Act* as it then was. The NEB applied its normal regulatory review process to each application, which ultimately led to a determination of that the projects were each in the public interest. The NEB regulatory process under the legislation as it then existed included environmental assessment under *CEAA*. That is, for each project, a *CEAA* environmental assessment was conducted by the NEB. [114] Those interested in the comments of responsible and federal authorities during the screening process may examine the documentation in the Environmental Screening Report folder located in the NEB's public registry for each project. [115]

Aboriginal Engagement by the Proponents and Aboriginal Participation in the NEB Public Hearing Process

The National Energy Board Filing Manual obligated the proponents to conduct Aboriginal consultation as a condition of making application for NEB regulatory review. The proponents described their Aboriginal engagement in each of their applications. [116] Dozens of Aboriginal groups were involved, given the lineal extent of the three projects.

Some of the Aboriginal groups contacted by the proponents went on to participate in the NEB environmental assessment/regulatory review process. For the Alberta Clipper Pipeline Project, fourteen Aboriginal groups participated as intervenors in the NEB process, though six ultimately withdrew from it. Some of those who withdrew did so because they concluded impact and benefit agreements with the project proponent regarding project-specific concerns and issues. Ten of the Aboriginal intervenors filed evidence, three presented witnesses, and the same three presented final argument. In regard to the Keystone Pipeline Project, the Standing Buffalo Dakota First Nation participated as an intervenor. The Dakota Nations of Manitoba (Birdtail Sioux First Nation, Canupawakpa Dakota First Nation, Dakota Plains First Nation, Dakota Tipi First Nation, Sioux Valley Dakota Nation) made arguments.

The National Energy Board Reasons for Decision in regard to the Keystone Pipeline Project are representative of NEB views of how Aboriginal participants were engaged in the NEB regulatory review process. These reasons outline how the NEB regulatory review process is itself inherently consultative:

> Once an application is filed, all interested parties, including Aboriginal persons, have the opportunity to participate in the Board's processes to make their views known so they can be factored into the decision-making. With respect to the Keystone Project, the Board notes that Standing Buffalo and the Dakota Nations of Manitoba took the opportunity to participate in the proceedings and the Board undertook efforts to facilitate their participation. The Board agreed to late filings by Standing Buffalo and the Elders had an opportunity to provide oral testimony in their own language at the hearing. In addition, the Board held two hearing days in Regina to facilitate the participation of Standing Buffalo and was prepared to consider hearing time in Winnipeg for the benefit of the Dakota Nations of Manitoba. The Board notes it undertook to ensure it understood the concerns of Standing Buffalo by hearing the testimony of the Elders, making an Information Request and asking questions at the hearing.

> The Board is satisfied that Standing Buffalo and the Dakota Nations of Manitoba were provided with an opportunity to participate fully in its process and to bring to the Board's attention all their concerns. The hearing process provided all parties with a forum in which they could receive further information, were

able to question and challenge the evidence put forward by the parties, and present their own views and concerns with respect to the Keystone Project. Standing Buffalo and the Dakota Nations of Manitoba had the opportunity to present evidence, including any evidence of potential infringement the Project could have on their rights and interests. The Dakota Nations of Manitoba did not provide evidence at the hearing.[117]

For the Southern Lights Pipeline Project, the Standing Buffalo Dakota First Nation filed an application for intervenor status and then sought a preliminary ruling on two issues. The NEB responded by directing that the preliminary issues be addressed by way of a Notice of Motion.[118] The Standing Buffalo motion in the Southern Lights Pipeline Project presented the NEB with jurisdictional issues: whether the NEB had jurisdiction to consider the applications filed by the applicant without first determining (1) whether Standing Buffalo had a credible land claim in the lands which the project was to cross; (2) the scope of the Crown's duty to consult in respect of that claim; and (3) that the Crown had satisfied its duty to consult.[119]

After hearing argument, the NEB dismissed the Standing Buffalo motion, with reasons. The NEB articulated that it would not require the participation of a Crown representative to discuss the Standing Buffalo claim and to describe Crown consultation. The NEB reasoned that it was not in a position to assess the Standing Buffalo claim or whether the legal obligations of federal and provincial government departments, including the adequacy of Aboriginal consultation, had been met. In most if not all instances, federal and provincial departments would not exercise their regulatory functions until after NEB approval, and it was for the courts (rather than the NEB) to assess the adequacy of consultation in regard to these future actions.

The NEB reasons dismissing the Standing Buffalo motion explain how the Board's environmental assessment function is integrated into its regulatory review function and is responsive to potential project impacts on Aboriginal interests:

The Board weighs the overall public good a project may create against its potential negative aspects, including any negative impacts on Aboriginal interests, and makes its decisions in accordance with the public interest. As part of the decision-making process, it takes into consideration the potential environmental and social impacts and the potential for mitigation of those impacts. Mitigation measures proposed by an applicant or interested parties may be as varied as, for example, implementing a heritage resources contingency plan, re-routing a pipeline or adjusting the proposed construction schedule. The Board's mandate allows it to respond to potential impacts of a project on Aboriginal interests in a variety of ways, including accepting the impact in light of the benefits associated with the project, imposing conditions on the approval of the application to minimize the impact or denying the Application.[120]

The NEB reasons also explain how the NEB Filing Manual requires project proponents to obtain and report on Aboriginal concerns regarding a project, and how the NEB "frequently requested additional information from applicants about potential impacts of a project on Aboriginal people and mitigation options."[121] Furthermore, the NEB invites Aboriginal people to participate in the NEB hearing process to make the NEB aware of their concerns, and, to the extent consistent with its legal obligations within the rules of natural justice and procedural fairness, the NEB adopts "a fair and flexible process so as to allow Aboriginal people to provide their views and evidence to the Board."[122] In the circumstances, the Board emphasized the full participation of Standing Buffalo in the NEB hearing process for the Southern Lights Pipeline Project and how the Board was satisfied that it had the evidence it required to assess the project impacts on Standing Buffalo and to determine whether the project was in the public interest.

The Board addressed project impacts on Aboriginal interests in its Reasons for Decision for each Project.[123] Common was a finding that the evidence of project-specific impacts on Treaty rights was very general in nature and that the project proponent had addressed these interests. Regarding the evidence of current Aboriginal uses of land for hunting, fishing, and trapping within the rights-of-way occupied by the projects, the NEB found in each case that, though there were allegations of such use, actual evidence was lacking. The project facilities were largely to be buried and were primarily located on private and disturbed lands currently used for agricultural purposes. With regard to these facts, the NEB thought that potential impacts of the projects on traditional uses within the rights-of-way were minimal and that each project was in the public interest.

The Governor in Council subsequently approved the issuance of a Certificate of Public Convenience and Necessity for each project.[124] The NEB then issued the certificates. Litigation challenges took several forms.

*Judicial Review in Federal Court of the Decision
of the Governor in Council to Approve the Issuance of
Certificates of Public Convenience and Necessity*

In *Brokenhead Ojibway First Nation v. Canada (Attorney General)*, seven Treaty 1 First Nations filed a judicial review applications seeking declaratory and other prerogative relief in connection with the Governor in Council (GIC) decisions to approve the issuance by the National Energy Board of Certificates of Public Convenience and Necessity for the Keystone Pipeline Project, Southern Lights Pipeline Project, and Alberta Clipper Pipeline Project:

> [6] On the recommendation of the NEB the GIC issued Order in Council No. P.C. 2007-1786 dated November 22, 2007 approving the issuance of a Certificate of Public Convenience and Necessity authorizing the construction and operation of the Keystone Project. This is the decision which is the subject of the Applicants' claim for relief in T-225-08.

> [13] On the recommendation of the NEB the GIC issued Order in Council Nos. P.C. 2008-856 and P.C. 2008-857, both dated May 8, 2008, approving the issuance of Certificates of Public Convenience and Necessity authorizing the construction and operation respectively of the Southern Lights Project and the Alberta Clipper Project. These are the decisions which are the subject of the Applicants' claims for relief in T-921-08 and in T-925-08.[125]

The seven First Nations applicants had not participated in all of the NEB hearings but had corresponded with the executive branch of the Government of Canada seeking consultation and expressing concern about the potential for the projects to adversely affect outstanding claims to treaty land entitlement. The executive did not respond to this correspondence.

Evidence filed with the Federal Court in the subsequent judicial review contained similar qualities to those referenced by the NEB. Federal Court findings with regard to most project impacts emphasize how concerns about impacts were capable of being addressed through the environmental assessment/regulatory review process:

> [30] Except for the issue of their unresolved land claims in southern Manitoba that evidence fails to identify any interference with a specific or tangible interest that was not capable of

being resolved within the regulatory process. Even to the extent that cultural, environmental and traditional land use issues were raised in the evidence, they were not linked specifically to the projects themselves. This is not surprising because the evidence was clear that the Pipeline Projects were constructed on land that had been previously exploited and which was almost all held under private ownership. For example, the evidence is clear that the Alberta Clipper and Southern Lights projects will have negligible, if any, impact upon the Treaty One First Nations outstanding land claims in southern Manitoba. The Southern Lights Pipeline uses the same corridor as the Alberta Clipper Pipeline. Both are constructed within or contiguous to existing pipeline rights-of-way which run almost entirely over private and previously disturbed land. With the exception of 700 meters of pipeline corridor crossing the Swan Lake Reserve (with that Band's consent) the Aboriginal representatives consulted by Enbridge indicated that the affected lands were not the subject of any land claim or the site of any traditional activity.

[31]   Although Enbridge and the NEB did receive representations from Aboriginal leaders about specific impacts upon known and unidentified archaeological, sacred, historical, and paleontological sites, the record indicates that those concerns were considered and accommodated including, in one instance, the relocation of the right-of-way to protect a burial ground. The level of engagement between Enbridge and Aboriginal communities and Band Councils (including the Treaty One First Nations) was, in fact, extensive and quite thorough. The NEB findings in relation to the Aboriginal concerns raised before it are reasonably supported by the record before me and the Treaty One First Nations have not argued otherwise except to say that they do not necessarily agree.

The Federal Court dismissed the applications, stating that "[t]here must be some unresolved non-negligible impact arising from such a development to engage the Crown's duty to consult" and held that "no meaningful linkage" between approval of the project and Aboriginal concern "is apparent on the evidence before me."

The Court adopted the NEB rationale for the capacity of the NEB regulatory process, including environmental assessment, to address Aboriginal concerns:

[42]   I am satisfied that the process of consultation and accommodation employed by the NEB was sufficient to address the specific concerns of Aboriginal communities potentially affected by the Pipeline Projects including the Treaty One First Nations. The fact that the Treaty One First Nations may not have availed themselves fully of the opportunity to be heard before the NEB does not justify the demand for a separate or discrete consultation with the Crown. To the extent that regulatory procedures are readily accessible to Aboriginal communities to address their concerns about development projects like these, there is a responsibility to use them. First Nations cannot complain about a failure by the Crown to consult where they have failed to avail themselves of reasonable avenues for seeking relief. That is so because the consultation process is reciprocal and cannot be frustrated by the refusal of either party to meet or participate: see *Ahousaht v. Canada*, 2008 FCA 212, [2008] F.C.J. NO. 946 at paras. 52-53. This presupposes, of course, that available regulatory processes are accessible, adequate and provide First Nations an opportunity to participate in a meaningful way.

[43]   It cannot be seriously disputed that the Pipeline Projects have been built on rights-of-way that are not legally or practically available for the settlement of any outstanding land claims in southern Manitoba. Even the Treaty One First Nations acknowledge that the additional lands they claim were intended to be taken from those lands not already taken up by settlement and immigration....[126]

The Court then concluded by stating:

[45]   ...There is no evidence before me or, more importantly that was before the NEB or the GIC, to prove that the Pipeline Projects would be likely to interfere with traditional Aboriginal land use or would represent a meaningful interference with the future settlement of outstanding land claims in southern Manitoba. To the extent that any duty to consult was engaged, it was fulfilled by the notices that were provided to the Treaty One First Nations and to other Aboriginal communities in the context of the NEB proceedings and by the opportunities that were afforded there for consultation and accommodation.[127]

In its view, the Crown had a duty to consult in this case, but it was met by reliance on the existing NEB process. The Court stated that the environmental assessment/regulatory review process was one means by which the Crown could be satisfied that Aboriginal concerns had been heard and accommodated:

> [25]   In determining whether and to what extent the Crown has a duty to consult with Aboriginal peoples about projects or transactions that may affect their interests, the Crown may fairly consider the opportunities for Aboriginal consultation that are available within the existing processes for regulatory or environmental review: *Hupacasath First Nation v. British Columbia*, 2005 BCSC 1712, 51 B.C.L.R. (4th) 133 at para. 272. Those review processes may be sufficient to address Aboriginal concerns, subject always to the Crown's overriding duty to consider their adequacy in any particular situation. This is not a delegation of the Crown's duty to consult but only one means by which the Crown may be satisfied that Aboriginal concerns have been heard and, where appropriate, accommodated: see *Haida*, above, at para. 53 and *Taku*, above, at para. 40.

Appeals to the Federal Court of Appeal from the NEB's Issuance of a Certificate of Public Convenience and Necessity

Decisions of the NEB may be the subject of appeal to the Federal Court of Appeal by virtue of section 22 of the *National Energy Board Act*. Four appeals were filed from the NEB decisions to issue Certificates of Public Convenience and Necessity in regard to the three pipeline projects. These four appeals were all heard together. Judgment in *Standing Buffalo Dakota First Nation v. Enbridge Pipelines Inc.* was rendered on October 23, 2009.[128] The Federal Court of Appeal dismissed all of the appeals.

In paragraph 2 of its judgment, the Court of Appeal defined the issue before it as

> whether, before making its decisions in relation to those applications, the NEB was required to determine whether by virtue of the decision in *Haida Nation v. British Columbia (Minister of Forests)*, [2004] 3 S.C.R. 511, 2004 SCC 73, the Crown, which was not a party to those applications or a participant in the hearings, was under a duty to consult the appellants with respect to potential adverse impacts of the proposed projects on the appellants and if it was, whether that duty had been adequately discharged.

In resolving this question, the Court of Appeal accepted that the appellants were asserting that the NEB had to conduct a full *Haida Nation* analysis before the NEB could decide whether to grant the requested certificates.

The Court of Appeal defined the *Haida Nation* analysis as (1) whether the Crown was subject to a *Haida Nation* duty to consult the appellants in regard to the projects and (2), if so, whether the NEB was required to determine the scope of that duty and whether the Crown discharged it. In approaching this argument, the Court of Appeal also accepted that the NEB had not conducted any *Haida Nation* analysis at all:

> [25] Nowhere in the Decisions did the NEB make any finding that the Crown was or was not subject to a *Haida* duty. In other words, the NEB did not determine the existence of a *Haida* duty. It follows, in my view, that submissions with respect to the scope of such a duty, and whether or not the Crown has fulfilled it, need not be considered in these appeals. If I were to conclude that the NEB erred in not undertaking the initial step in the *Haida* analysis, I would remit the entire *Haida* analysis to the NEB for its consideration.

> [26] I would also add that because the NEB did not undertake the *Haida* analysis prior to making the Decisions, in my view, it follows that the Decisions cannot be taken as encompassing any conclusions with respect to whether the consultations that were undertaken by the proponents of the Projects were, or were not, capable of discharging, or sufficient to discharge, any *Haida* consultation duty that the Crown may have in respect of the Projects.

The Court of Appeal emphasized the roles of the proponents and the NEB itself in the regulatory review process undertaken by the NEB:

> [40] The process focuses on the applicant, on whom the NEB imposes broad consultation obligations. The applicant must consult with Aboriginal groups, determine their concerns and attempt to address them, failing which the NEB can impose accommodative requirements. In my view, this process ensures that the applicant for the Project approval has due regard for existing Aboriginal rights that are recognized and affirmed in subsection 35(1) of the Constitution. And, in ensuring that the applicant respects

such Aboriginal rights, in my view, the NEB demonstrates that it is exercising its decision-making function in accordance with the dictates of subsection 35(1) of the Constitution.

The Court of Appeal spoke with approval regarding the capacity of such a process to allow for the hearing and addressing of Aboriginal concerns about a project:

[44]   That process provides a practical and efficient framework within which the Aboriginal group can request assurances with respect to the impact of the particular project on the matters of concern to it. While the Aboriginal group is free to determine the course of action it wishes to pursue, it would be unfortunate if the opportunity afforded by the NEB process to have Aboriginal concerns dealt with in a direct and non-abstract manner was not exploited.

The Court of Appeal accepted that the NEB did not have to consider the adequacy of Aboriginal consultation by the Crown before issuing a certificate in the circumstances presented. It went on to hold that Aboriginal persons were free to bring a challenge to the adequacy of Aboriginal consultation before a court.

The appellants had filed a Notice of Constitutional Question alleging that the *National Energy Board Act* infringed on the constitutional rights of the appellants under section 35 of the *Constitution Act, 1982* because it did not obligate the NEB to adhere to the protection afforded to existing Aboriginal and treaty rights of Aboriginal peoples of Canada. The Federal Court of Appeal was satisfied that the NEB process itself respected section 35 of the *Constitution Act, 1982* and therefore concluded that the appellants had not discharged "their burden [of proof] of establishing that the NEB Act or any portion of it has the effect of interfering with any Aboriginal or treaty rights they may possess."[129]

The Court of Appeal upheld the NEB view of its functions: that is, that the NEB itself was not under a duty to conduct Aboriginal consultation, relying on the findings of the Supreme Court that the NEB is a quasi-judicial body.[130]

Supreme Court of Canada Dismisses Applications for Leave to Appeal

The First Nations that filed the appeals sought leave to appeal to the Supreme Court of Canada from the decision of the Federal Court of Appeal. The Supreme Court put these applications for leave to appeal into abeyance pending its judgment in the *Rio Tinto* appeal, rendered on October 28, 2010.[131] On December 2, 2010, the Supreme Court dismissed all four applications for leave to appeal, with costs to the project proponents.[132] Although the dismissal of a leave application does not mean that the Supreme Court agrees with the decision of the Federal Court of Appeal, it does mean that the Federal Court of Appeal judgment remains good law.

CHAPTER SIX

Concluding Observations

"How is it all going to work out from a practical perspective?"

—Chief Justice of the Supreme Court of Canada questioning counsel during argument before the Court in *Rio Tinto Alcan Inc. et al. v. Carrier Sekani Tribal Council*, scc Docket 33132, May 21, 2010.[1]

A REASONED PARADIGM SUPPORTING INTEGRATION

One can easily see that the question above posed by the Chief Justice recognizes the complexities inherent in the overlap of Aboriginal rights and Treaty rights, Aboriginal consultation, and environmental assessment/regulatory review processes of tribunals in Canada. Asserted Aboriginal rights and title vary across Canada in jurisdictions where treaties have not been concluded. Modern treaties will vary regarding the rights negotiated. Historical treaties also vary in the rights they confer, according to the context of the era in and purpose for which they were concluded. Natural resource development occurs within this typically Canadian mosaic and may engage any or all of these variable rights, or asserted rights, depending on the geographic location of the project and its potential impacts or benefits. Large lineal projects may touch many of these regimes, as the Mackenzie Gas Project does.

Legislatures delegate environmental assessment and regulatory review responsibilities for such projects to tribunals. The precise function of a tribunal itself will depend on the specific mandate conferred on it by the legislative branches of governments in Canada. These tribunals will apply the principles of natural justice and procedural fairness to their proceedings, and the precise operation of natural justice and procedural fairness will vary in each instance.[2] Overlaid onto this, then, is the law of Aboriginal consultation. This is a Crown duty for which tribunals may have some role. How *is* all of this to work practically in regard to natural resource development in Canada?

If the dynamic is examined from a purposive perspective, it is apparent that in Canada today there can be overlapping uses of land and natural resources by Aboriginal peoples and the broader Canadian society. Project development may diminish or impact Aboriginal uses, at least until the conclusion of the life cycle of the project. Such a diminishment may, or may not, be a significant adverse impact on Aboriginal peoples, and may be temporary or more permanent. Yet project development may also offer Aboriginal peoples the opportunity to participate in the economy that the development represents. Aboriginal peoples may seek to participate in this economic activity and derive benefits associated with it—as they have since the time of first contact with Europeans—while always being protective of the ability to maintain and pursue activities and values integral to Aboriginal identity. Corporations are frequently supportive of this engagement.

The law mandates that Crown decision making related to project development and capable of adversely affecting Aboriginal rights or Treaty rights take account of Aboriginal concerns as a constitutional imperative. Crown decision making, then, needs to be informed by both Aboriginal consultation and also by environmental assessment or regulatory review. Tribunals themselves mandate Aboriginal consultation, and practical accommodations, by project proponents. The environmental assessment and regulatory review process of a tribunal can draw together all parties with a viewpoint on a particular development, including Aboriginal peoples, to inform decision making.

Aboriginal consultation and environmental assessment/regulatory review need not be separate or sequential. Environmental assessment can anticipate the adverse impact that a project approval may have on actual or asserted Aboriginal rights to conduct traditional activities, including hunting, fishing, and trapping. At a minimum, environmental assessment/regulatory review can contribute to reconciliation by serving to facilitate relationships between proponents and Aboriginal peoples.

It can itself engage in the relationship process by identifying measures that can mitigate adverse impacts. The adoption of such mitigations as conditions of regulatory approval is a form of accommodation that can protect and sustain the environment and traditional Aboriginal practices in that environment. Beyond traditional activities, Aboriginal peoples may have "broader concerns" that, while raised during environmental assessment and regulatory review of a particular project, are best addressed by other processes.[3]

The Supreme Court cautions that the process is not simply one of giving Aboriginal peoples "an opportunity to blow off steam" before project approval is given.[4] The language used in this passage resembles jurisprudence that describes procedural fairness in administrative law. Participation is meaningful participation. The Supreme Court discusses this in the context of a claim by Aboriginal persons in *Quebec (Attorney General) v. Canada (National Energy Board)*.[5]

> In general, included in the requirements of procedural fairness is the right to disclosure by the administrative decision-maker of sufficient information to permit meaningful participation in the hearing process: *In re Canadian Radio-Television Commission and in re London Cable TV Ltd.*, [1976] 2 F.C. 621 (C.A.), at pp. 624-25. The extent of the disclosure required to meet the dictates of natural justice will vary with the facts of the case, and in particular with the type of decision to be made, and the nature of the hearing to which the affected parties are entitled.

The Federal Court of Appeal case cited by the Supreme Court discusses the function of public consultation, in the context of public hearings by an independent regulatory body:

> To be such a public hearing, it would, in my view, have had to be arranged in such a way as to provide members of the public with a reasonable opportunity to know the subject-matter of the hearing, and what it involved from the point of view of the public, in sufficient time to decide whether or not to exercise their statutory right of presentation and to prepare themselves for the task of presentation if they decide to make a presentation. In other words, what the statute contemplates, in my view, is a meaningful hearing that would be calculated to aid the Commission, or its Executive Committee, to reach a conclusion that reflects a consideration of the public interest as well as a consideration of the private interest of the licensee; it does not contemplate a

public meeting at which members of the public are merely given an opportunity to "blow off steam."[6]

Since the tribunal process is required by law to be meaningful, integration of Aboriginal consultation into tribunal process should be capable of reasonably ensuring "that aboriginal peoples are provided with all necessary information in a timely way so that they have an opportunity to express their interests and concerns, and to ensure that their representations are seriously considered and, wherever possible, demonstrably integrated into the proposed plan of action."[7]

This book presents a reasoned paradigm supporting integration of Aboriginal consultation into the environmental assessment and regulatory review of projects by tribunals in order to inform Crown decision making and meet this legal obligation. The proposal here is that robust environmental assessment and regulatory review of projects comprise a reasonable process for gathering and assessing information on the significance of project impacts on Aboriginal peoples. Integration will foster potential for reconciliation in regard to a project to be served efficiently by project proponents, tribunals, the Crown, the courts, and Aboriginal peoples. Integration early in the planning stages of projects can foster effective and efficient dialogue and inform project decision making. This is a good beginning to relationship building early in the planning stages of project development.

The Supreme Court jurisprudence recognizing the law of Aboriginal consultation, while profound, nevertheless builds incrementally on existing law. In *Little Salmon/Carmacks,* the Court declines to draw "bright lines" between the duty to consult and administrative law principles and cites Lamer C.J. in *R. v. Van der Peet* for the principle that "aboriginal rights exist within the general legal system of Canada (para. 49)."[8] In the same case, the Court observes that section 35 of the *Constitution Act, 1982* protects and preserves constitutional space for Aboriginal peoples to be Aboriginal but that, "[a]t the same time, Aboriginal people do not, by reason of their Aboriginal heritage, cease to be citizens who fully participate with other Canadians in their collective governance."[9]

Throughout its decisions, the Court affirms that the duty to consult has the capacity to be integrated in a complementary way with robust environmental assessment and regulatory review processes carried out prior to project approval. Where the Court recognizes that such a process was not sufficiently robust, as it does in *Mikisew Cree,* it identifies a problem in the quality of the integration of Aboriginal concerns into the planning process rather than in the use of the planning process as a tool to assess Aboriginal concerns.

- In *Haida Nation*, the court notes that "[t]he Crown may delegate procedural aspects of consultation to industry proponents seeking a particular development; this is not infrequently done in environmental assessments."[10]

- In *Taku River*, the Court finds that, "[i]n this case, the process engaged in by the Province under the *Environmental Assessment Act* fulfilled the requirements of its duty" as they existed at that stage of the project development.[11] Future consultation was a material consideration in the adequacy of Aboriginal consultation in *Taku River*, in which the Court noted at paragraph 22 that final project approval contained measures designed to address both immediate and long-term concerns of the First Nation and would include further consultation.

- In *Mikisew Cree* the Court notes that Aboriginal consultation in that case was "an afterthought to a general public consultation"[12] and failed to be meaningful in the circumstances. The Court then goes on to describe a meaningful consultation in terms that correspond to a more robust planning process: "to solicit and to listen carefully to the Mikisew concerns, and to attempt to minimize adverse impacts on the Mikisew hunting, fishing and trapping rights." The Court also describes potential accommodations as "changes in the road alignment or construction that would go a long way towards satisfying the Mikisew objections."[13] Such accommodations correspond to mitigations imposed as conditions of regulatory approval following a more robust planning process than occurred in that case.

- In *Beckman*, the Court finds the environmental assessment/land use planning process of the committee sufficient to fulfill the duty to consult, even though the parties to a modern treaty intended to create a tribunal with a more formal environmental assessment process and obligation that "was ultimately carried into effect in the *Yukon Environmental and Socio-economic Assessment Act*, S.C. 2003, c. 7."[14]

There are some outstanding uncertainties in this paradigm, discussed below. What role should tribunals play in the assessment of any Crown consultation? Must a separate process of Crown Aboriginal consultation be finally completed prior to or during the planning stage of project development? Is Aboriginal consultation an exercise that transforms project planning into a search for recognition of asserted rights? Discussion of these is preceded by a reference to the Court's reliance on contextual analysis.

UNIVERSALISM, FORMALISM, AND THE IMPORTANCE OF CONTEXTUAL ANALYSIS

In *Haida Nation,* the Supreme Court adopts an approach to the duty to consult embedded in universalism rather than formalism.[15] Describing the duty to consult as a framework is fully consistent with universalism, which seeks "the broad, general principles underlying the imposition of responsibility" such that "broad considerations of policy are foremost." Formalism, on the other hand, places emphasis "on rules, precedent and categories." Formalism is "clear and predictable." Universalism "can be unpredictable" because "it can be difficult to find a rational way to limit" application of the universal principle.

In any given instance, the Supreme Court relies on contextual analysis to locate the balance between the two. Contextual analysis, a common element of Supreme Court jurisprudence, is seen in the Court's ruling in *Sparrow* regarding the justification process for infringement of section 35 rights: "We wish to emphasize the importance of context and a case by case approach to s. 35(1). Given the generality of the text of the constitutional provision, and especially in light of the complexities of aboriginal history, society and rights, the contours of a justificatory standard must be defined in the specific factual context of each case."[16] In *Haida Nation,* at paragraph 39, contextual analysis is then applied to the duty to consult: "The content of the duty to consult and accommodate varies with the circumstances." This is repeated in *Taku River* at paragraph 25[17] and then applied to the circumstances of Treaty 8 in *Mikisew Cree* at paragraph 63:

> The determination of the content of the duty to consult will, as *Haida* suggests, be governed by the context. ... Here, the most important contextual factor is that Treaty 8 provides a framework within which to manage the continuing changes in land use already foreseen in 1899 and expected, even now, to continue well into the future. In that context, consultation is key to

achievement of the overall objective of the modern law of treaty and aboriginal rights, namely reconciliation.[18]

Contextual analysis is brilliant in its conception, for it allows the law to be sufficiently flexible to fit the circumstances of each particular case. This is especially significant given the nuance inherent to appreciation of Aboriginal rights and Treaty rights. But it is also challenging, because it demands more than the simple application of rules rigidly embedded in legal precedent.

The approach adopted in this book does not advocate formalism. The approach recognizes that the Supreme Court itself attempts to foster reconciliation within an existing framework of democratic institutions. It is appropriate for tribunals created by democratic legislatures, or by land claim agreements with Aboriginal peoples, to perform their governance functions of planning and control of project development. The Supreme Court notes in *R. v. Sparrow* that "[t]he objective ... is not to undermine Parliament's ability and responsibility with respect to creating and administering overall conservation and management plans.... The objective is rather to guarantee that those plans treat aboriginal peoples in a way ensuring that their rights are taken seriously."[19]

In the planning stage of the tribunal process, during environmental assessment and regulatory review, tribunals may meaningfully gather and assess the impact of projects on Aboriginal rights and Treaty rights, and the Crown may rely on a robust tribunal process for this specialized purpose. This will enjoy the benefits set out in the Court's decision in *Douglas/Kwantlen Faculty Association v. Douglas College*,[20] discussed next.

THE DEVELOPING ROLE OF TRIBUNALS

Integration of Aboriginal consultation into the tribunal process is a logical extension of the Supreme Court jurisprudence involving the capacity of higher-level tribunals to consider constitutional issues. The Court notes in the jurisprudence cited as the *Cuddy Chicks* trilogy of cases[21] that there are benefits where higher-level tribunals are capable of addressing matters of a constitutional dimension:

> [A] tribunal at a higher level of the administrative scheme whose functions can be described as being more adjudicative in nature—that is, which frequently resolves questions of law or fact in accordance with legislative rules or regulations—is likely to be in a better position both to receive argument on, and to

resolve constitutional questions than a tribunal which is engaged primarily in fact finding.[22]

The Court identifies the essential benefits this would offer: "administrative tribunals have the skills, expertise and knowledge in a particular area which can with advantage be used to ensure the primacy of the Constitution. Their privileged situation as regards the appreciation of the relevant facts enables them to develop a functional approach to rights and freedoms as well as to general constitutional precepts."[23]

High-level tribunals charged with responsibility for environmental assessment and regulatory review of projects are well placed to assess project impacts on Aboriginal rights and Treaty rights and respond to those concerns within the ambits of their jurisdiction. The integration of administrative law, as delivered by tribunals, and constitutional law is the subject of a narrative description in the Supreme Court decision in *R. v. Conway*.[24] Although the Court was speaking of the integration of tribunals and constitutional law in regard to the *Canadian Charter of Rights and Freedoms*, there is no difference in principle between constitutional law in the *Charter* and constitutional law corollary to the honour of the Crown. *Conway* further integrates constitutional law into the administrative law regime conducted by high-level tribunals exercising delegated authority from a legislature or Parliament. The judgment in *Conway* was rendered on June 11, 2010. The Court's judgment in *Rio Tinto*[25] was delivered on October 28, 2010, and cites *Conway*.[26]

THE RELATIONSHIP OF TRIBUNALS TO THE CROWN

Legislative branches of government have created tribunals intended to operate at arm's length from the executive branches of government. The diagram introduced in the opening chapter is reproduced here (Figure 6) as a convenient reminder of the functions that a tribunal, or other entities of the Crown, may perform in the project development process.

Legislative branches of governments have created tribunals that are intended to operate at arms-length from the executive branches of government. By way of federal illustration, the *National Energy Board Act* confers on the Board all such powers, rights, and privileges as are vested in a superior court of record "with respect to the attendance, swearing and examination of witnesses, the production and inspection of documents, the enforcement of its orders, the entry on and inspection of property and other matters necessary or proper for the due exercise of its jurisdiction."[27] The *Act* also confers "full jurisdiction to hear and determine all matters, whether of law or of fact," in regard to matters falling within its statutory jurisdiction.[28] The Supreme Court describes the Board as "an independent decision-making body operating at arm's length from government."[29] The Board interprets its functions as precluding it from conducting consultation with Aboriginal peoples.[30]

By way of a provincial illustration, the legislative regime in Alberta provides a commissioner under the *Public Inquiries Act*[31] with certain powers akin to a Court of Record and immunities and privileges normally afforded a judge of the Court of Queen's Bench. In turn, the legislation creating the Energy Resources Conservation Board confers these powers and privileges on members of the Board.[32] The Government of Alberta "fully recognizes the importance of independence" of its energy regulators "as quasi-judicial, arms-length bodies."[33]

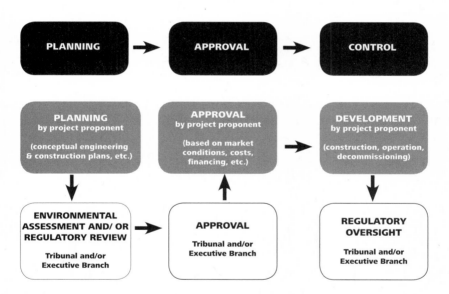

Figure 6. Functions that a Tribunal may perform in project development.

The Supreme Court respects the legislative decision to create tribunals that operate at arm's length from the executive, stating that "[t]he courts must be careful not to compromise the independence of quasi-judicial tribunals and decision-making agencies. ..."[34] In *Rio Tinto*, the Supreme Court observes that the British Columbia legislature had not given that Utilities Commission power "to engage in consultations in order to discharge the Crown's constitutional obligation to consult."[35] The Court makes the point that

Consultation itself is not a question of law, but a distinct constitutional process requiring powers to effect compromise and
do whatever is necessary to achieve reconciliation of divergent
Crown and Aboriginal interests. The Commission's power to
consider questions of law and matters relevant to the public interest does not empower it to itself engage in consultation with
Aboriginal groups.[36]

Legislatures have not, to this point in time, conferred on tribunals
conducting environmental assessment or regulatory review of projects
such power "to do whatever is necessary to achieve reconciliation of
divergent Crown and Aboriginal interests." Rather, these tribunals are
mandated to assess project impacts. They provide a lens through which
the Crown examines project impacts, including those on Aboriginal
rights and Treaty rights.

Whether the tribunal process is characterized as a delegated aspect
of Crown consultation or the distinct tool through which the Crown
consults may not be a substantive distinction. As long as Aboriginal
concerns about project impacts on rights are robustly considered in the
planning process of the tribunal, the matter of substance is the result
of the process.[37]

WHETHER TRIBUNALS MUST ASSESS THE ADEQUACY
OF CROWN CONSULTATION AT THE PLANNING
STAGE OF PROJECT DEVELOPMENT

The short answer to the question posed in the heading above is that
there is no duty to assess Crown consultation applicable to all tribunals in all circumstances. A tribunal may not have been delegated any
jurisdiction to conduct such an assessment from the legislative branch
of government. Or, where a tribunal may have received a jurisdiction
to consider the adequacy of Crown consultation, that tribunal may
also itself exercise an independent discretion whether to exercise that
jurisdiction. Contextual factors material to the exercise of the discretion may include (1) whether or not a tribunal exercises final project
approval functions, and (2) whether or not the exercise of a final project
approval by a tribunal is likely to enable significant impacts on actual
or asserted Aboriginal or Treaty rights. The NEB case studies are an
example of a tribunal that did not exercise final project approval function. The BC Utilities Commission in the *Rio Tinto* case is an example
of a tribunal that did exercise a final approval function. In taking into
account how to exercise such jurisdiction in any given case, the tribunal

should have regard to its specific functions in the project development process in the context of each legislative regime.

Crown reliance on a tribunal for planning and approval may be absolute or qualified. In an absolute government regulatory model, the Crown relies on the tribunal exclusively for project planning *and* approval. In a qualified government regulatory model, government or Crown entities other than, or in addition to, a tribunal may exercise planning, approval, or oversight functions.

Rio Tinto was an absolute reliance model. Its result is driven by the context in which the Crown was the proponent, and the tribunal exercised final approval authority. It is not a typical project development situation.

Qualified and distributed reliance models are far more common in the project development process described in this book. A corporation will typically be a proponent, and a tribunal will exercise one or both of planning and project approval functions. The contours of these functions will vary across legislative regimes and over time. The project itself may or may not impact actual or asserted Aboriginal or Treaty rights. Aboriginal interests may be reconciled with project development by the proponent, through impact benefit agreements, changes in project design, or other factors inherent in the planning stage of the project. The resulting intersections are far too nuanced to support a general rule of law requiring tribunals to assess the adequacy of Crown consultation in all cases.

Rio Tinto can be read, simplistically, as standing for the proposition that tribunals as a whole (rather than the BC Utilities Commission specifically considering an *Electricity Purchase Agreement*) may either assess consultation or conduct consultation (depending on the jurisdiction conferred in their enabling legislation). Such a binary reading is incorrect. Contextual analysis requires an appreciation of how Crown and tribunal planning, approval and control functions operate and intersect during project development in any given case.

Within weeks of the *Rio Tinto* decision, the Court dismissed an application for leave to appeal in the three pipeline cases discussed in the second case study. In these cases, the Federal Court of Appeal upheld decisions of the National Energy Board in which the Board had *declined* to assess the adequacy of the Crown's Aboriginal consultation in the circumstances before it both because *its own process* was adequate to assess project impacts on Aboriginal peoples and because Crown consultation would occur at later stages in the development cycle of the project and could be reviewed by a court. In that case, at least, the Crown exhibited an absolute reliance on the tribunal process to that point in the project development process; and this was upheld where the tribunal had reasonably concluded that the project was not likely to cause an adverse impact on Treaty rights.

This strongly suggests that a robust tribunal may reasonably conclude a project will not adversely impact actual or asserted Aboriginal or Treaty rights, and that the tribunal may then itself validly exercise final project approval authority. The Crown does not necessarily need to have, outside of that tribunal process in that context, a separate process of Crown consultation.

Where there is a power to assess, there is also the potential for the delegation of a discretion whether to exercise a power of assessment. Tribunals which have a power to assess Crown consultation and accommodation may also have an inherent power to determine whether to exercise that power. In contextual analysis, material factors which can influence the result are: (1) the tribunal's findings respecting project impacts on actual or asserted Aboriginal or Treaty rights, and (2) the tribunal's appreciation of the interaction of Crown functions with tribunal functions of planning and approval and control.

Contextual analysis of the pipeline decisions reveals a context with private proponents, a high-level tribunal (the National Energy Board) that did not have power for final project approval, and a tribunal process that was sensitive to Aboriginal concerns and identified minimal impacts on Treaty rights. Analysis of the *Rio Tinto* decision reveals quite a different context, one involving a Crown proponent and a high-level tribunal (the BC Utilities Commission) that had authority for final project approval.

A formalistic interpretation of *Rio Tinto* can introduce a logical fallacy: that is, if a tribunal *must* assess Crown consultation, including accommodation, then there *must* be a separate process of Crown consultation, and potentially also accommodation, for the tribunal to assess. This is false reasoning. The *ratio decidendi* of *Rio Tinto* is that the function of tribunals in regard to Aboriginal consultation depends on the jurisdiction conferred in their enabling legislation. The Court stated that the powers and functions of a tribunal will vary, "depending on what responsibilities the legislature has conferred on them."[38]

It is inherent, therefore, that the function of tribunals in regard to Aboriginal consultation is not necessarily limited to, or necessarily encompasses either of, the binary choices of conducting or assessing the adequacy of Crown consultation. That binary function is specific to the Court's discussion of the statutory responsibility of the British Columbia Utilities Commission in the context of the Commission's consideration of whether to approve an *Electricity Purchase Agreement* proposed by the Crown that may have an adverse impact on asserted Aboriginal rights.

The legislative branch of the government, with judicial oversight, will ultimately define the functions and capacities of tribunals regarding Aboriginal consultation. In the meantime, contextual analysis will illuminate the correct path forward in individual cases.

WHETHER CROWN CONSULTATION AND ACCOMMODATION IS A PRECONDITION TO PROJECT PLANNING

Of course, since the Crown is ultimately responsible for its legal duty to consult, Crown consultation can in any given case be undertaken prior to, during, or after well-established tribunal environmental assessment and regulatory review process in the project development process. It follows from this that a separate process of Crown consultation and accommodation may support tribunal process. Indeed, Crown planning or decision-making at many levels form the broadest context in which project planning occurs.

But a separate process of project-specific Crown consultation is not necessarily a precondition to effective project planning by a tribunal. The principles underlying integration proposed in this book support the proposition that the law anticipates the potential for, but does not require in all cases, a separate process of Crown consultation and accommodation as a precondition to project planning. Crown consultation outside of robust tribunal process could be premature, duplicative, and delaying of legitimate decision making authority of tribunals as delegated by the legislative branch of government. Most importantly, it may not be effective.

It may be premature because, as the case studies demonstrate, a project in the environmental assessment and regulatory review process is not at all in a definite form, and is subject to substantial change. Consultation taking place in the environmental assessment and regulatory process itself may drive changes in project design or mitigation that may address Aboriginal concerns.

It may be duplicative in that it will compel the Crown to create a parallel mechanism for gathering and assessing information about the project and its impacts on Aboriginal and Treaty rights, the very function that the tribunal is to carry out, in order to correctly *begin* to discharge the Crown obligation regarding consultation. This runs contrary to the spirit of harmonization that underlies an efficient environmental and regulatory review process.

It may be delaying because, if the Crown's Aboriginal consultation about project impacts and, where necessary, accommodation, is to precede tribunal process, then the tribunal must wait until the Crown consultation and, where necessary, accommodation is completed. This may involve waiting for the final conclusion of litigation challenges respecting the adequacy of the Crown's Aboriginal consultation.

Crown responsiveness may be most effective regarding accommodation, if required, once information on project impacts with regard to the implementation of mitigation measures by a proponent and the tribunal itself has been gathered, assessed, and presented by a quasi-judicial, independent tribunal. Indeed, Crown consultation that precedes environmental assessment/regulatory review will not be informed by changes to project design introduced during that planning process.

Tribunal and Crown decision making functions may interact in materially different ways. Where the tribunal makes project approval decisions, and its process is sufficiently robust so as to consider and accommodate project impacts on Aboriginal peoples, then the jurisprudence suggests that the tribunal may both plan and approve a project—provided that it reaches the conclusion that project impacts are not likely to be significant, and that there is a potential for meaningful consultation and accommodation of remaining Aboriginal concerns at later stages of the project development process. Where the Crown exercises project approval authority, and where this is preceded and informed by a tribunal's planning function, then a tribunal may well defer consideration of the adequacy of Crown consultation to later stages of the project planning process. Courts will ultimately exercise oversight of the whole, intervening though the lens of contextual and functional analysis in each case.

WHETHER ENVIRONMENTAL ASSESSMENT AND REGULATORY REVIEW PROCESS CAN RECOGNIZE ACTUAL OR ASSERTED ABORIGINAL RIGHTS OR TREATY RIGHTS

Where a treaty exists, environmental assessment and regulatory review can certainly accept the rights defined in it. "In the case of a treaty" the Court states in *Mikisew Cree* "the Crown, as a party, will always have notice of its contents. The question in each case will therefore be to determine the degree to which conduct contemplated by the Crown would adversely affect those rights...."[39] This is also so for actual Aboriginal rights or title.

In cases of asserted Aboriginal rights or title, and in cases where Aboriginal peoples do not accept the Crown's view of the scope of Treaty rights or actual Aboriginal rights, Aboriginal peoples may tender evidence of the rights said to be potentially affected by a proposed project. Does this transform a planning process into one of proof of rights?

Tribunals are in the business of planning for and controlling project impacts. A primary object of the exercise is protection of Aboriginal rights or Treaty rights. Critical thought suggests that it does not necessarily follow that a tribunal must, as a matter of law, recognize asserted rights in order to address them. The focus of a planning exercise is predictive. Modeling and assumptions form an integral component of it. Courts recognize that the tribunal process is intended to "provide decisions in a shorter amount of time and with less expense than the courts."[40] For the purposes of planning, tribunals may receive evidence of asserted Aboriginal rights and proceed to assume that some or all assertions of right exist in order to assess potential impacts. This respects both the assertion of the right by Aboriginal peoples, and the proper function of full judicial process in conclusive proof of constitutionally protected rights.

All of which is respectfully submitted
Edmonton, Alberta

Notes

PROLOGUE

1   *Haida Nation v. British Columbia (Minister of Forests)*, 2004 SCC 73, [2004] 3 S.C.R. 511 at para. 11, at http://scc.lexum.org/en/2004/2004scc73/2004scc73.html.

2   *Taku River Tlingit First Nation v. British Columbia (Project Assessment Director)*, [2004] 3 S.C.R. 550, 2004 SCC 74 at http://scc.lexum.org/en/2004/2004scc74/2004scc74.html.

3   *Mikisew Cree First Nation v. Canada (Minister of Canadian Heritage)*, 2005 SCC 69, [2005] 3 S.C.R. 388 at http://scc.lexum.org/en/2005/2005scc69/2005scc69.html.

4   *Beckman v. Little Salmon/Carmacks First Nation*, 2010 SCC 53, [2010] 3 S.C.R. 103 at http://scc.lexum.org/en/2010/2010scc53/2010scc53.html.

5   *Rio Tinto Alcan Inc. v. Carrier Sekani Tribal Council*, 2010 SCC 43, [2010] 2 S.C.R. 650 at http://scc.lexum.org/en/2010/2010scc43/2010scc43.html.

6   *Haida Nation v. British Columbia (Minister of Forests)*, 2004 SCC 73, [2004] 3 S.C.R. 511 at para. 42, at http://scc.lexum.org/en/2004/2004scc73/2004scc73.html.

CHAPTER ONE: RELATIONSHIPS IN THE PROJECT DEVELOPMENT PROCESS

1   *R. v. Conway*, 2010 SCC 22, [2010] 1 S.C.R. 765 at http://scc.lexum.org/en/2010/2010scc22/2010scc22.html.

2   Treaty 1 and 2 at http://www.aandc-aadnc.gc.ca/al/hts/tgu/pubs/t1-2/trty1-2-eng.asp; Treaty 3 at http://www.aandc-aadnc.gc.ca/al/hts/tgu/pubs/t3/trty3-eng.asp; Treaty 4 at http://www.aandc-aadnc.gc.ca/al/hts/tgu/pubs/t4/trty4-eng.asp; Treaty 5 at http://www.aandc-aadnc.gc.ca/al/hts/tgu/pubs/t5/trty5-eng.asp; Treaty 6 at http://www.aandc-aadnc.gc.ca/al/hts/tgu/pubs/t6/trty6-eng.asp; Treaty 7 at http://www.aandc-aadnc.gc.ca/al/hts/tgu/pubs/t7/trty7-eng.asp; Treaty 8 at http://www.aandc-aadnc.gc.ca/al/hts/tgu/pubs/t8/trty8-eng.asp#chp4; Treaty 10 at http://www.aandc-aadnc.gc.ca/al/hts/tgu/pubs/t10/trty10-eng.asp.

3   *Wolf v. The Queen*, [1975] 2 S.C.R. 107 at http://scc.lexum.org/en/1974/1975scr2-107/1975scr2-107.html.

4   The functions of the National Energy Board are described at http://www.neb-one. gc.ca/clf-nsi/rthnb/whwrndrgvrmnc/rrspnsblt-eng.html.

5   *Rio Tinto Alcan Inc. v. Carrier Sekani Tribal Council,* 2010 SCC 43, [2010] 2 S.C.R. 650 at para. 38, at http://scc.lexum.org/en/2010/2010scc43/2010scc43.html.

6   *Haida Nation v. British Columbia (Minister of Forests),* 2004 SCC 73, [2004] 3 S.C.R. 511 at para. 26, at http://scc.lexum.org/en/2004/2004scc73/2004scc73.html.

7   *Friends of the Oldman River Society v. Canada (Minister of Transport),* [1992] 1 S.C.R. 3 at 71, at http://scc.lexum.org/en/1992/1992scr1-3/1992scr1-3.html.

8   *Quebec (Attorney General) v. Canada (National Energy Board),* [1994] 1 S.C.R. 159 at http://scc.lexum.org/en/1994/1994scr1-159/1994scr1-159.html.

9   *Friends of the Oldman River Society v. Canada (Minister of Transport),* [1992] 1 S.C.R. 3 at para. 1, at http://scc.lexum.org/en/1992/1992scr1-3/1992scr1-3.html ("protection of the environment").

10 *Mikisew Cree First Nation v. Canada (Minister of Canadian Heritage),* [2005] 3 S.C.R. 388, 2005 SCC 69 at http://scc.lexum.org/en/2005/2005scc69/2005scc69.html ("reconciliation of aboriginal peoples and non-aboriginal peoples and their respective claims, interests and ambitions").

11 The United Nations University, RMIT University, and the United Nations Environment Programme jointly developed an educational resource on Environmental Impact Assessment (EIA), which is described as a tool to "aid decision making regarding the significant environmental consequences of projects, developments and programmes. EIA helps the stakeholders with the identification of the environmental, social and economic impacts of a proposed development before a decision … on whether or not to proceed" (http://eia.unu.edu/wiki/index.php/Main_Page).

12 Howard L. Brown, "Expanding the Effectiveness of the European Union's Environmental Impact Assessment Law," in *Boston College International and Comparative Law Review* 20, 2 (1997): 313–34 at 315.

13 *National Environmental Policy Act of 1969* at http://ceq.hss.doe.gov/nepa/regs/nepa/ nepaeqia.htm.

    For a description of NEPA, see United States Environmental Protection Agency, Basic Information, at http://www.epa.gov/compliance/basics/nepa.html.

14 European Commission, *Council Directive of 27 June 1985 on the Assessment of the Effects of Certain Public and Private Projects on the Environment* at http://ec.europa. eu/environment/eia/full-legal-text/85337.htm. This was judicially considered in *Regina v. London Borough of Bromley (Respondents) ex parte Barker* at http://www.parliament.the-stationery-office.co.uk/pa/ld200607/ldjudgmt/jd061206/barker-1.htm.

15 *Environmental Assessment and Review Process Guidelines Order,* Canada Gazette, Part II, Vol. 118, No. 14, 2794–2802. SOR/84-467. The *Order* can be obtained via the search engine of archived Canada Gazette editions at http://www.collectionscanada. gc.ca/databases/canada-gazette/001060-100.04-e.php.

16 *Canadian Environmental Assessment Act,* S.C. 1992 c. 37 at http://laws-lois.justice. gc.ca/eng/acts/C-15.2/, since repealed and replaced by the *Canadian Environmental Assessment Act, 2012* at http://laws-lois.justice.gc.ca/eng/acts/C-15.21/index.html.

17 For a list of federal and provincial regimes, see Maureen Carter-Whitney, *Environmental Regulation in Canada* (Toronto: LexisNexis, 2010).

18 Earle Gray, *Forty Years in the Public Interest: A History of the National Energy Board* (Vancouver: Douglas and McIntyre in cooperation with the National Energy Board, 2000).

19 David Breen, *Alberta's Petroleum Industry and the Conservation Board* (Edmonton: University of Alberta Press, 1993) at xvii: "Although it is a provincial agency, Alberta's Energy Resources Conservation Board is one of the most important regulatory bodies in Canada. Decisions of this agency have had profound consequences, often beyond Alberta." See also the discussion in Cecilia A. Low, *Energy and Utility Regulation in Alberta: Like Oil and Water?*, Canadian Institute of Resources Law Occasional Paper 25 at http://dspace.ucalgary.ca/bitstream/1880/47345/1/UtilityOP25w.pdf.

20 *Friends of the Oldman River Society v. Canada (Minister of Transport)*, [1992] 1 S.C.R. 3 at 71, at http://scc.lexum.org/decisia-scc-csc/scc-csc/scc-csc/en/item/829/index.do?r =AAAAAQAMb2xkbWFuIHJpdmVyyAAAAAAAAQ

21 *MiningWatch Canada v. Canada (Fisheries and Oceans)*, 2010 SCC 2, [2010] 1 S.C.R. 6 at para. 14, at http://scc.lexum.org/en/2010/2010scc2/2010scc2.html.

22 *Ontario (Attorney General) v. Fraser*, 2011 SCC 20 at http://scc.lexum.org\ en/2011/2011scc20/2011scc20.html.

23 *Canada (Attorney General) v. TeleZone Inc.*, 2010 SCC 62 at para. 18, at http://scc. lexum.org/en/2010/2010scc62/2010scc62.html.

24 Aboriginal consultation obligations imposed by the National Energy Board on proponents are outlined in the NEB Filing Manual at http://www.neb-one.gc.ca/clf-nsi/ rpblctn/ctsndrgltn/flngmnl/flngmnl-eng.html. Aboriginal consultation obligations imposed on project proponents prior to the Alberta Energy Resources Conservation Board procedure are outlined in Alberta Environment's *Standardized Terms of Reference* for *in situ* projects, oil sands mines, coal mines, and industrial plants at http:// environment.alberta.ca/01501.html. The role of industry in Aboriginal consultation is anticipated in *Haida Nation v. British Columbia (Minister of Forests)*, 2004 SCC 73, [2004] 3 S.C.R. 511 at para. 53, at http://scc.lexum.org/en/2004/2004scc73/2004scc73. html: "The Crown may delegate procedural aspects of consultation to industry proponents seeking a particular development; this is not infrequently done in environmental assessments."

25 Ontario Energy Board, *Aboriginal Consultation Policy*, EB-2007-0617, at http://www. ontarioenergyboard.ca/documents/cases/EB-2007-0617/acp_policy_20070618.PDF and list of filing requirements at http://www.ontarioenergyboard.ca/documents/cases/ EB-2007-0617/acp_filing-requirements_20070618.pdf:

> The Board has drawn upon the experience of the National Energy Board and its policy in this area in drafting these filing requirements. ... [T]he Board will require the proponent to demonstrate that it has conducted appropriate consultation and accommodation. ... [T]he Board will make a determination regarding the adequacy of the consultation undertaken and any proposed accommodation for Aboriginal concerns as part of its review of the application. If the Board determines that the consultations undertaken by the applicant were not sufficient, it may require further consultation and/or accommodation.

26 *Draft Aboriginal Consultation Guide for Preparing a Renewable Energy Approval (REA) Application* at http://www.ene.gov.on.ca/stdprodconsume/groups/lr/@ene/@ resources/documents/resource/stdprod_088440.pdf. These are described at http:// www.ebr.gov.on.ca/ERS-WEB-External/displaynoticecontent.do?noticeId=MTEzN DMw&statusId=MTY5OTgz&language=en.

27 *Ontario Regulation 359/09* at http://www.e-laws.gov.on.ca/html/regs/english/ elaws_regs_090359_e.htm#BK19.

28 See, for example, *MNDM Policy: Consultation and Arrangements with Aboriginal Communities at Early Exploration* at http://www.mndm.gov.on.ca/sites/default/files/ aboriginal_exploration_consultation_policy.pdf.

29 *Aboriginal Consultation and Accommodation: Updated Guidelines for Federal Officials to Fulfill the Duty to Consult—2011* at http://www.aadnc-aandc.gc.ca/ eng/1100100014664; *Memorandum of Understanding for the Cabinet Directive on Improving the Performance of the Regulatory System for Major Resource Projects* at http://www.mpmo-bggp.gc.ca/documents/pdf/directive-eng.pdf.

30 See, for example: *Treaty 8 Alberta Chiefs' Position Paper on Consultation* (September 30, 2010) at http://www.treaty8.ca/documents/FINAL%20TREATY%208%20 CONSULTATION%20PAPER%20SENT%20TO%20GOVERNMENT%20ET%20 AL.pdf.

31 Arthur Pape, "The Duty to Consult and Accommodate: A Judicial Innovation Intended to Promote Reconciliation," in *Aboriginal Law Since Delgamuukw*, edited by Maria Morellato (Toronto: Canada Law Book, 2009), at 325.

32 See, for example, the Royal Bank website at http://www.rbcroyalbank.com/commercial/aboriginal/r-comm.html: "By taking a direct role in the economic development of Aboriginal communities across Canada, businesses will not only ensure a better standard of living for Aboriginal Canadians, but will ensure long-term value for their own shareholders."

33 See, for example, *Report of the Federal Review Panel on the Prosperity Gold-Copper Mine Project* at http://www.ceaa.gc.ca/050/documents/46911/46911E.pdf. The *Provincial Assessment Report for the Prosperity Gold-Copper Mine Project*, prepared by the British Columbia Environmental Assessment Office, is at http://a100.gov.bc.ca/ appsdata/epic/documents/p6/d31889/1263503323535_111bf55585d2ae6168f90be26d0 49256ece101a1db1b1077333129c863464809.pdf. A discussion of the provincial and federal processes in regard to this specific project was prepared by the West Coast Environmental Law Association and is at http://wcel.org/resources/environmental-law-alert/lessons-prosperity-mine-environmental-assessment. A second example is located in the Kemess North Gold-Copper Mine Joint Review Panel (JRP) Report at http://www.ceaa.gc.ca/050/documents_staticpost/cearref_3394/24441E.pdf and in the Government of Canada's response to the report at http://www.ceaa.gc.ca/052/ document-html-eng.cfm?did=25797. In 2012 the British Columbia Minister of Environment, and Minister of Energy and Mines, acting on the recommendation of the Director of the British Columbia Environmental Assessment Office, refused to issue a Certificate for the Morrison Copper/Gold Project: http://a100.gov.bc.ca/appsdata/epic/ documents/p224/d34962/1349110217007_1ffodffc5745a57aff5cecf9e76f0725433a5b8 5003d9c2116bbf658733375a8.pdf. In November of 2012 the Governor in Council, in its first Decision Statement under the *Canadian Environmental Assessment Act, 2012*, concluded that the significant adverse environmental effects of EnCana's Shallow Gas Infill Development Project in the Suffield National Wildlife Area were not justified in the circumstances: http://www.ceaa-acee.gc.ca/050/document-eng.cfm?document=83796.

34 National Energy Board, Southern Lights Pipeline Project, Reasons for Decision OH-3-2007, 2.2.1 Board Jurisdiction and Process at https://www.neb-one.gc.ca/ll-eng/ livelink.exe/fetch/2000/90464/90552/441806/456607/499885/499563/A1D4Q5_-_Reasons_For_Decision.pdf?nodeid=499564&vernum=0.

35 The National Energy Board's Aboriginal Engagement Program is described at http:// www.neb-one.gc.ca/clf-nsi/archives/rpblctn/spchsndprsnttn/2007/rgltryprcss/rgltry-prcss-eng.html.

36 *Rio Tinto Alcan Inc. v. Carrier Sekani Tribal Council*, 2010 SCC 43, [2010] 2 S.C.R. 650 at para. 56, at http://scc.lexum.org/en/2010/2010scc43/2010scc43.html.

CHAPTER TWO: DEFINING ABORIGINAL RIGHTS AND TREATY RIGHTS

1   Map of historical treaties adapted from http://www.aadnc-aandc.gc.ca/DAM/DAM-INTER-HQ/STAGING/texte-text/htoc_1100100032308_eng.pdf. Map of modern treaties adapted from http://www.landclaimscoalition.ca/modern-treaties/.

2   Brian Slattery, "Understanding Aboriginal Rights," *Canadian Bar Review* 66.4 (1987): 727–28 at http://papers.ssrn.com/sol3/papers.cfm?abstract_id=1567571, http://www.cba.org/CBA/Canadian_Bar_Review/Main/ and http://www.cba.org/cba_barreview/Search.aspx?VolDate=12%2f01%2f1987.

3   Brian Slattery, "Making Sense of Aboriginal and Treaty Rights," *Canadian Bar Review* 79.2 (2000): 197 at http://www.cba.org/CBA/Canadian_Bar_Review/Main/ and http://www.cba.org/cba_barreview/Search.aspx?VolDate=07%2f01%2f2000.

4   Peter W. Hogg Q.C., "The Constitutional Basis of Aboriginal Rights," in *Aboriginal Law since Delgamuukw*, edited by Maria Morellato (Toronto: Canada Law Book, 2009) at 15.

5   *Manitoba Metis Federation Inc. v. Canada (Attorney General)*, 2013 SCC 14 at http://scc.lexum.org/decisia-scc-csc/scc-csc/scc-csc/en/item/12888/index.do

6   *R. v. Sparrow*, [1990] 1 S.C.R. 1075 at http://scc.lexum.org/en/1990/1990scr1-1075/1990scr1-1075.html.

7   *R. v. Van der Peet*, [1996] 2 S.C.R. 507 at para. 1, at http://scc.lexum.org/en/1996/1996scr2-507/1996scr2-507.html.

8   *R. v. Nikal*, [1996] 1 S.C.R. 1013 at http://scc.lexum.org/en/1996/1996scr1-1013/1996scr1-1013.html (from BC).

9   *R. v. Gladstone*, [1996] 2 S.C.R. 723 at http://scc.lexum.org/en/1996/1996scr2-723/1996scr2-723.html (from BC).

10 *R. v. Côté*, [1996] 3 S.C.R. 139 at http://scc.lexum.org/en/1996/1996scr3-139/1996scr3-139.html.

11 *R. v. Adams*, [1996] 3 S.C.R. 101 at http://csc.lexum.org/en/1996/1996scr3-101/1996scr3-101.html.

12 *Delgamuukw v. British Columbia*, [1997] 3 S.C.R. 1010 at http://scc.lexum.org/en/1997/1997scr3-1010/1997scr3-1010.html.

13 *R. v. Marshall*, [1999] 3 S.C.R. 456 at http://scc.lexum.org/en/1999/1999scr3-456/1999scr3-456.html.

14 *R. v. Sioui*, [1990] 1 S.C.R. 1025 at http://scc.lexum.org/en/1990/1990scr1-1025/1990scr1-1025.html.

15 *Mitchell v. M.N.R.*, 2001 SCC 33, [2001] 1 S.C.R. 911 at http://scc.lexum.org/en/2001/2001scc33/2001scc33.html.

16 *Kitkatla Band v. British Columbia (Minister of Small Business, Tourism and Culture)*, [2002] 2 S.C.R. 146, 2002 SCC 31 at http://scc.lexum.org/en/2002/2002scc31/2002scc31.html.

17 *R. v. Powley*, 2003 SCC 43, [2003] 2 S.C.R. 207 at http://scc.lexum.org/en/2003/2003scc43/2003scc43.html.

18 *R. v. Marshall; R. v. Bernard*, 2005 SCC 43, [2005] 2 S.C.R. 220 at http://scc.lexum.org/en/2005/2005scc43/2005scc43.html.

19 *R. v. Sappier; R. v. Gray*, 2006 SCC 54, [2006] 2 S.C.R. 686 at http://scc.lexum.org/en/2006/2006scc54/2006scc54.html.

20 *R. v. Morris,* 2006 SCC 59, [2006] 2 S.C.R. 915 at http://scc.lexum.org/en/2006/2006scc59/2006scc59.html.

21 *R. v. Kapp,* 2008 SCC 41, [2008] 2 S.C.R. 483 at http://scc.lexum.org/en/2008/2008scc41/2008scc41.html.

22 *R. v. Horse,* [1988] 1 S.C.R. 187 at http://scc.lexum.org/en/1988/1988scr1-187/1988scr1-187.html.

23 *R. v. Horseman,* [1990] 1 S.C.R. 901 at http://scc.lexum.org/en/1990/1990scr1-901/1990scr1-901.html.

24 *R. v. Badger,* [1996] 1 S.C.R. 771 at http://scc.lexum.org/en/1996/1996scr1-771/1996scr1-771.html.

25 *R. v. Sundown,* [1999] 1 S.C.R. 393 at http://scc.lexum.org/en/1999/1999scr1-393/1999scr1-393.html.

26 *R. v. Blais,* 2003 SCC 44, [2003] 2 S.C.R. 236 at http://scc.lexum.org/en/2003/2003scc44/2003scc44.html.

27 *Lovelace v. Ontario,* 2000 SCC 37, [2000] 1 S.C.R. 950 at http://scc.lexum.org/en/2000/2000scc37/2000scc37.html; *Corbiere v. Canada (Minister of Indian and Northern Affairs),* [1999] 2 S.C.R. 203 at http://scc.lexum.org/en/1999/1999scr2-203/1999scr2-203.html.

28 *Mitchell v. Peguis Indian Band,* [1990] 2 S.C.R. 85 at http://scc.lexum.org/en/1990/1990scr2-85/1990scr2-85.html.

29 *R. v. Lewis,* [1996] 1 S.C.R. 921 at http://scc.lexum.org/en/1996/1996scr1-921/1996scr1-921.html.

30 *Opetchesaht Indian Band v. Canada,* [1997] 2 S.C.R. 119 at http://scc.lexum.org/en/1997/1997scr2-119/1997scr2-119.html; *Blueberry River Indian Band v. Canada (Department of Indian Affairs and Northern Development),* [1995] 4 S.C.R. 344 at http://scc.lexum.org/en/1995/1995scr4-344/1995scr4-344.html; *Guerin v. The Queen,* [1984] 2 S.C.R. 335 at http://scc.lexum.org/en/1984/1984scr2-335/1984scr2-335.html.

31 *Goodswimmer v. Canada (Minister of Indian Affairs and Northern Development),* [1997] 1 S.C.R. 309 at http://scc.lexum.org/en/1997/1997scr1-309/1997scr1-309.html.

32 *Calder et al. v. Attorney-General of British Columbia,* [1973] S.C.R. 313 at http://scc.lexum.org/en/1973/1973scr0-313/1973scr0-313.html. The impact of Calder is discussed in *Delgamuukw v. British Columbia,* [1997] 3 S.C.R. 1010 at para. 106, at http://scc.lexum.org/en/1997/1997scr3-1010/1997scr3-1010.html and in *R. v. Sparrow* at http://scc.lexum.org/en/1990/1990scr1-1075/1990scr1-1075.html.

33 *St. Catherine's Milling and Lumber Co. v. The Queen* (1888), 14 App. Cas. 46, explained by the Supreme Court in *Delgamuukw v. British Columbia,* [1997] 3 S.C.R. 1010 at para. 112, at http://scc.lexum.org/en/1997/1997scr3-1010/1997scr3-1010.html:

> The starting point of the Canadian jurisprudence on aboriginal title is the Privy Council's decision in *St. Catherine's Milling and Lumber Co. v. The Queen* (1888) 14 A.C. 46, which described aboriginal title as a "personal and usufructuary right" (at p. 54). The subsequent jurisprudence has attempted to grapple with this definition, and has in the process demonstrated that the Privy Council's choice of terminology is not particularly helpful to explain the various dimensions of aboriginal title. What the Privy Council sought to capture is that aboriginal title is a *sui generis* interest in land. Aboriginal title has been described as *sui generis* in order to distinguish it from "normal" proprietary interests, such as fee simple. However, as I will now develop, it is also *sui generis* in the sense that its characteristics cannot be completely explained by reference either to the common law rules of real property or to the rules

of property found in aboriginal legal systems. As with other aboriginal rights, it must be understood by reference to both common law and aboriginal perspectives.

34 *Quebec (Attorney General) v. Moses*, 2010 SCC 17, [2010] 1 S.C.R. 557 at http:// scc.lexum.org/en/2010/2010scc17/2010scc17.html; *Beckman v. Little Salmon/ Carmacks First Nation*, 2010 SCC 53, [2010] 3 S.C.R. 103 at http://scc.lexum.org/ en/2010/2010scc53/2010scc53.html.

35 *Constitution Act, 1982* at http://laws.justice.gc.ca/eng/Const/Const_index.html.

36 *R. v. Adams*, [1996] 3 S.C.R. 101, at para. 33, at http://scc.lexum.org/en/1996/1996scr3-101/1996scr3-101.html.

37 *R. v. Sundown*, [1999] 1 S.C.R. 393 at http://scc.lexum.org/en/1999/1999scr1-393/1999scr1-393.html.

38 *R. v. Sparrow*, [1990] 1 S.C.R. 1075 at http://scc.lexum.org/en/1990/1990scr1-1075/1990scr1-1075.html.

39 Ibid.

40 In *R. v. Badger*, [1996] 1 S.C.R. 771, at para. 80, at http://scc.lexum.org/en/1996/1996scr1-771/1996scr1-771.html, citing with approval the Ontario Court of Appeal in *R. v. Agawa*, (1988) 65 O.R. (2d) 505 (C.A.) at 524, at http://www.canlii.org/en/on/onca/do c/1988/1988canlii148/1988canlii148.html.

41 *R. v. Sparrow*, [1990] 1 S.C.R. 1075 at http://scc.lexum.org/en/1990/1990scr1-1075/1990scr1-1075.html.

42 *Mikisew Cree First Nation v. Canada (Minister of Canadian Heritage)*, 2005 SCC 69, [2005] 3 S.C.R. 388 at para. 58, at http://scc.lexum.org/en/2005/2005scc69/2005scc69. html.

43 *R. v. Sparrow*, [1990] 1 S.C.R. 1075 at http://scc.lexum.org/en/1990/1990scr1-1075/1990scr1-1075.html.

44 *R. v. Badger*, [1996] 1 S.C.R. 771, at http://scc.lexum.org/en/1996/1996scr1-771/1996scr1-771.html.

45 Ibid., at para. 82.

46 *Calder et al. v. Attorney-General of British Columbia*, [1973] S.C.R. 313, at http://scc. lexum.org/en/1973/1973scr0-313/1973scr0-313.html.

47 See Indian and Northern Affairs Canada, *General Briefing Note on Canada's Self-Government and Land Claims Policies and the Status of Negotiations January 2012* at http://www.aadnc-aandc.gc.ca/DAM/DAM-INTER-HQ/STAGING/texte-text/ al_ldc_ccl_gbnjan2012_1324327698586_eng.pdf

48 *Beckman v. Little Salmon/Carmacks First Nation*, 2010 SCC 53, [2010] 3 S.C.R. 103 at para. 12, at http://scc.lexum.org/en/2010/2010scc53/2010scc53.html.

49 Ibid., at para. 46.

50 *The James Bay and Northern Quebec Agreement* at http://www.gcc.ca/pdf/ LEG000000006.pdf.

51 *Inuvialuit Final Agreement* at http://www.eco.gov.yk.ca/pdf/wesar_e.pdf.

52 *Gwich'in Comprehensive Land Claim Agreement* at http://www.gwichin.nt.ca/docu-ments/GCLCA.pdf.

53 *Nunavut Land Claims Agreement* at http://nlca.tunngavik.com/.

54 *Tlicho Land Claims and Self Government Agreement* at http://www.tlicho.ca/sites/ tlicho/files/TlichoAgreement.pdf.

55 *Labrador Inuit Land Claims Agreement* at http://www.exec.gov.nl.ca/exec/igas/land_claims/agreement.html and http://www.laa.gov.nl.ca/laa/DELETE%20land_claims/.

56 *Nunavik Inuit Land Claims Agreement* at http://www.aadnc-aandc.gc.ca/DAM/DAM-INTER-HQ/STAGING/texte-text/ldc_ccl_fagr_nk_lca_1309284365020_eng.pdf.

57 *Beckman v. Little Salmon/Carmacks First Nation*, 2010 SCC 53, [2010] 3 S.C.R. 103 at para. 54, at http://scc.lexum.org/en/2010/2010scc53/2010scc53.html.

58 *The James Bay and Quebec Northern Agreement*, at http://www.gcc.ca/pdf/LEG000000006.pdf.

59 *James Bay and Northern Quebec Native Claims Settlement Act*, S.C. 1976-77 c. 32 at http://laws.justice.gc.ca/eng/acts/J-0.3/FullText.html.

60 *Act Approving the Agreement Concerning James Bay and Northern Quebec*, R.S.Q. c. C67 at http://www.canlii.org/en/qc/laws/stat/rsq-c-c-67/latest/rsq-c-c-67.html.

61 *Umbrella Final Agreement between the Government of Canada, the Council for Yukon Indians and the Government of the Yukon* at http://www.eco.gov.yk.ca/pdf/umbrellafinalagreement.pdf.

62 *Yukon First Nations Self-Government Act*, S.C. 1994 c. 35 at http://laws-lois.justice.gc.ca/eng/acts/Y-2.6/FullText.html.

63 Yukon Executive Council Office, *The Umbrella Final Agreement, First Nation Final Agreements and Treaty Rights* at http://www.eco.gov.yk.ca/landclaims/about.html.

64 *Little Salmon/Carmacks First Nation Final Agreement* at http://www.eco.gov.yk.ca/pdf/little_salmon_carmacks_fa.pdf.

65 *Western Arctic Claim—The Inuvialuit Final Agreement* at http://www.daair.gov.nt.ca/_live/documents/documentManagerUpload/InuvialuitFinalAgreement1984.pdf.

66 *Western Arctic (Inuvialuit) Claims Settlement Act*, S.C. 1984 c. 24 at http://laws.justice.gc.ca/en/W-6.7.

67 *Gwich'in Comprehensive Land Claim Settlement Agreement* at http://www.gwichin.nt.ca/documents/GCLCA.pdf.

68 *Gwich'in Land Claim Settlement Act*, S.C. 1992 c. 53 at http://laws.justice.gc.ca/eng/acts/G-11.8/.

69 *Sahtu and Dene Land Claim Settlement Agreement* at http://www.aadnc-aandc.gc.ca/DAM/DAM-INTER-HQ/STAGING/texte-text/sahmet_1100100031148_eng.pdf.

70 *Sahtu Dene and Metis Land Claim Settlement Act*, S.C. 1994 c. 27 at http://laws.justice.gc.ca/en/S-1.5/index.html.

71 *Tlicho Land Claims and Self Government Agreement* at http://www.tlicho.ca/sites/tlicho/files/TlichoAgreement.pdf.

72 *Tlicho Land Claims and Self-Government Act*, S.C. 2005 c. 1 at http://laws-lois.justice.gc.ca/eng/acts/T-11.3/FullText.html.

73 *Mackenzie Valley Resource Management Act*, S.C. 1998 c. 25 at http://laws.justice.gc.ca/en/M-0.2/index.html.

74 *Nunavut Land Claims Agreement Act*, S.C. 1993 c. 29 at http://laws-lois.justice.gc.ca/eng/acts/N-28.7/FullText.html.

75 *Nunavut Act*, S.C. 1993 c. 28 at http://laws-lois.justice.gc.ca/eng/acts/N-28.6/FullText.html.

76 *Nunavut Waters and Nunavut Surface Rights Tribunal Act*, S.C. 2002 c. 10 at http://laws-lois.justice.gc.ca/eng/acts/N-28.8/FullText.html.

77 The Nunavut Water Board maintains a website at http://www.nunavutwaterboard.org/.

78 These are briefly described at http://www.nunavutwaterboard.org/en/links.

79 *Land Claims Agreement between the Inuit of Labrador and Her Majesty the Queen in Right of Newfoundland and Labrador and Her Majesty the Queen in Right of Canada* at http://www.aadnc-aandc.gc.ca/DAM/DAM-INTER-HQ/STAGING/texte-text/al_ldc_ccl_fagr_labi_labi_1307037470583_eng.pdf.

80 *Labrador Inuit Land Claims Agreement Act*, S.C. 2005, c. 27 at http://laws.justice.gc.ca/eng/acts/L-4.3/FullText.html.

81 *Labrador Inuit Land Claims Agreement Act*, SNL 2004 c. L-3.1 at http://www.canlii.org/en/nl/laws/stat/snl-2004-c-l-3.1/latest/snl-2004-c-l-3.1.html.

82 The *Labrador Inuit Lands Claims Agreement* and the *Overlap Agreement* are available at http://www.laa.gov.nl.ca/laa/DELETE%20land_claims/.

83 *Quebec (Attorney General) v. Moses*, 2010 SCC 17, [2010] 1 S.C.R. 557 at http://scc.lexum.org/en/2010/2010scc17/2010scc17.html; and *Beckman v. Little Salmon/Carmacks First Nation*, 2010 SCC 53, [2010] 3 S.C.R. 103 at http://scc.lexum.org/en/2010/2010scc53/2010scc53.html.

84 The majority in *Quebec (Attorney General) v. Moses* was Binnie J. with McLachlin C.J. and Fish, Rothstein, and Cromwell JJ. concurring. The majority in *Beckman v. Little Salmon/Carmacks First Nation* was Binnie J. with McLachlin C.J. and Fish, Abella, Charron, Rothstein, and Cromwell JJ. concurring.

85 The minority in *Quebec (Attorney General) v. Moses* was LeBel and Deschamps JJ. with Abella and Charron JJ. concurring. The minority in *Beckman v. Little Salmon/Carmacks First Nation* was Deschamps J. with LeBel J. concurring.

86 *Beckman v. Little Salmon/Carmacks First Nation*, 2010 SCC 53, [2010] 3 S.C.R. 103 at para. 54, at http://scc.lexum.org/en/2010/2010scc53/2010scc53.html.

87 *Treaty Negotiations in British Columbia: An Assessment of the Effectiveness of British Columbia's Management and Administrative Processes*, Report No. 3, (November 2006) at http://www.bcauditor.com/pubs/2006 and http://www.bcauditor.com/pubs/2006/report3/treaty-negotiations-british-columbia-first-nations.

88 *R. v. Morris*, 2006 SCC 59, [2006] 2 S.C.R. 915 at para. 16, at http://scc.lexum.org/decisia-scc-csc/scc-csc/scc-csc/en/item/2334/index.do?r=AAAAAQAOZG91Z2xhcyBocmVhdHHkAAAAAAAAB.

89 *Nisga'a Final Agreement* at http://www.nnkn.ca/files/u28/nis-eng.pdf, with supporting documents at http://www.aadnc-aandc.gc.ca/eng/1100100031292/1100100031293.

90 *Nisga'a Final Agreement Act*, S.C. 2000 c. 7 at http://laws-lois.justice.gc.ca/eng/acts/N-23.3/.

91 *Nisga'a Final Agreement Act*, SBC 1999 c. 2 at http://www.bclaws.ca/EPLibraries/bclaws_new/document/ID/freeside/99002_01.

92 *2006 November Report of the Auditor General of Canada to the House of Commons*, "Chapter 7: Federal Participation in the British Columbia Treaty Process—Indian and Northern Affairs Canada" at 1 at http://www.oag-bvg.gc.ca/internet/docs/20061107ce.pdf and http://www.fns.bc.ca/pdf/AGofCanada20061107ce.pdf.

93 *British Columbia Treaty Commission Act*, S.C. 1995 c. 45 at http://laws-lois.justice. gc.ca/eng/B-8.5/index.html; *Treaty Commission Act*, R.S.B.C. 1996 c. 461 at http:// www.bclaws.ca/EPLibraries/bclaws_new/document/ID/freeside/00_96461_01.

94 The BC Treaty Commission maintains its own website at http://www.bctreaty.net/.

95 BC Treaty Commission, Annual Reports at http://www.bctreaty.net/files/annuals.php.

96 Described in the website of the BC Treaty Commission at http://www.bctreaty.net/ index.php. The progress of First Nations participating in that process is described at http://www.bctreaty.net/files/updates.php.

97 The *Tsawwassen Final Agreement*, federal and provincial implementing legislation, and background materials are available at http://www.gov.bc.ca/arr/firstnation/tsaw-wassen/default.html#final. The Tsawwassen First Nation maintains a website at http:// www.tsawwassenfirstnation.com/, where it refers to the Final Agreement at http:// www.tsawwassenfirstnation.com/finalagreement.php. A speech delivered by Chief Kim Baird to the BC legislature in 2007, as it began debate on the treaty, is available at http://www.tsawwassenfirstnation.com/071015_Chief_Baird_Speech.pdf.

98 See Maa-nulth First Nations at http://www.treaties.gov.bc.ca/treaties_maa-nulth. html. The *Maa-Nulth First Nations Final Agreement* is at http://www.gov.bc.ca/ arr/firstnation/maa_nulth/default.html#final, with supporting documents at http:// www.gov.bc.ca/arr/firstnation/maa_nulth/default.html#final. Federal legislation is the *Maanulth First Nations Final Agreement Act,* S.C. 2009 c. 18 at http://laws-lois. justice.gc.ca/eng/acts/M-0.55/page-1.html. Provincial legislation is the *Maa-Nulth First Nations Final Agreement Act*, SBC 2007 c. 43 at http://www.bclaws.ca/EPLibraries/ bclaws_new/document/ID/freeside/07043_01.

99 *2006 November Report of the Auditor General of Canada to the House of Commons*, "Chapter 7: Federal Participation in the British Columbia Treaty Process—Indian and Northern Affairs Canada" at http://www.oag-bvg.gc.ca/internet/docs/20061107ce.pdf and http://www.fns.bc.ca/pdf/AGofCanada20061107ce.pdf.

100 *Treaty Negotiations in British Columbia: An Assessment of the Effectiveness of British Columbia's Management and Administrative Processes*, Report No. 3 (November 2006) at http://www.bcauditor.com/pubs/2006 and http://www.bcauditor.com/pubs/2006/ report3/treaty-negotiations-british-columbia-first-nations.

101 *2006 November Report of the Auditor General of Canada to the House of Commons*, "Chapter 7: Federal Participation in the British Columbia Treaty Process—Indian and Northern Affairs Canada" at 1–2 at http://www.oag-bvg.gc.ca/internet/ docs/20061107ce.pdf and http://www.fns.bc.ca/pdf/AGofCanada20061107ce.pdf.

102 *2006 November Report of the Auditor General of Canada to the House of Commons*, "Chapter 7: Federal Participation in the British Columbia Treaty Process—Indian and Northern Affairs Canada" at 2 at http://www.oag-bvg.gc.ca/internet/docs/20061107ce. pdf and http://www.fns.bc.ca/pdf/AGofCanada20061107ce.pdf.

103 *R. v. Van der Peet*, [1996] 2 S.C.R. 507 at http://scc.lexum.org/en/1996/1996scr2-507/1996scr2-507.html.

104 Ibid., at para. 44.

105 *R. v. Adams*, [1996] 3 S.C.R. 101 at http://csc.lexum.org/en/1996/1996scr3-101/1996scr3-101.html.

106 *R. v. Côté*, [1996] 3 S.C.R. 139 at http://scc.lexum.org/decisia-scc-csc/scc-csc/scc-csc/ en/item/1421/index.do.

107 *R. v. Adams*, [1996] 3 S.C.R. 101 at para. 3, at http://csc.lexum.org/en/1996/1996scr3-101/1996scr3-101.html.

108 Ibid., at para. 26.

109 *Delgamuukw. v. The Queen* (BCSC), BCSC 79 D.L.R. (4th) 185, [1991] 3 W.W.R. 97, [1991] 5 C.N.L.R. 5, at http://www.canlii.org/en/bc/bcsc/doc/1991/1991canlii2372/1991canlii2372.pdf and 1991 CanLII 2372 (BCSC), (1991), 79 D.L.R. (4th) 185. *Delgamuukw. v. The Queen* (BCCA) decision is reported as (1993), 30 B.C.A.C. 1, 49 W.A.C. 1, 104 D.L.R. (4th) 470, [1993] 5 W.W.R. 97, [1993] 5 C.N.L.R. 1, and is viewable at http://www.canlii.org/en/bc/bcca/doc/1993/1993canlii4516/1993canlii4516.pdf.

110 *Delgamuukw v. British Columbia,* [1997] 3 S.C.R. 1010 at para. 1, at http://scc.lexum.org/en/1997/1997scr3-1010/1997scr3-1010.html.

111 Ibid., at paras. 108-09.

112 *R. v. Marshall; R. v. Bernard,* 2005 SCC 43, [2005] 2 S.C.R. 220 at http://scc.lexum.org/en/2005/2005scc43/2005scc43.html.

113 Ibid., at para. 65.

114 Ibid., at para. 67.

115 Ibid., at para. 70.

116 *Delgamuukw v. British Columbia,* [1997] 3 S.C.R. 1010 at para. 128, at http://scc.lexum.org/en/1997/1997scr3-1010/1997scr3-1010.html.

117 *R. v. Powley,* 2003 SCC 43, [2003] 2 S.C.R. 207 at http://scc.lexum.org/en/2003/2003scc43/2003scc43.html.

118 *R. v. Blais,* 2003 SCC 44, [2003] 2 S.C.R. 236 at http://scc.lexum.org/en/2003/2003scc44/2003scc44.html.

119 *R. v. Powley,* 2003 SCC 43, [2003] 2 S.C.R. 207 at para. 14, at http://scc.lexum.org/en/2003/2003scc43/2003scc43.html.

120 Ibid., at para. 23.

121 Ibid., at para. 37.

122 Ibid., at para. 24.

123 Ibid., at para. 23.

124 Ibid.

125 Ibid., at para. 29.

126 Ibid., at para. 30.

127 Ibid., at paras. 31-33.

128 See Kirk N. Lambrecht, *The Administration of Dominion Lands, 1870-1930* (Regina: Canadian Plains Research Center, 1991) at 8-11.

129 See *Manitoba Metis Federation v. Canada (Attorney General),* 2013 SCC 14 at http://scc.lexum.org/decisia-scc-csc/scc-csc/scc-csc/en/item/12888/index.do?r=AAAAAQAObWFuaXRvYmEgbWV0aXMAAAAAAAAB.

130 *Royal Proclamation of 1763,* viewable at http://www.solon.org/Constitutions/Canada/English/PreConfederation/rp_1763.html

131 The treaties were concluded over a period of decades beginning in 1871 and ending in 1911. Adhesions from time to time brought additional Indians into the existing treaties.

132 *R. v. Badger,* [1996] 1 S.C.R. 771 at para. 39, at http://scc.lexum.org/en/1996/1996scr1-771/1996scr1-771.html.

133 *R. v. Horse*, [1988] 1 S.C.R. 187 at para. 26, at http://scc.lexum.org/en/1988/1988scr1-187/1988scr1-187.html.

134 *R. v. Côté*, [1996] 3 S.C.R. 139 at http://scc.lexum.org/en/1996/1996scr3-139/1996scr3-139.html.

135 *R. v. Marshall; R. v. Bernard*, 2005 SCC 43, [2005] 2 S.C.R. 220 at http://scc.lexum.org/en/2005/2005scc43/2005scc43.html.

136 *R. v. Sundown*, [1999] 1 S.C.R. 393 at para. 28, at http://scc.lexum.org/en/1999/1999scr1-393/1999scr1-393.html.

137 *R. v. Badger*, [1996] 1 S.C.R. 771 at para. 40, at: http://scc.lexum.org/en/1996/1996scr1-771/1996scr1-771.html.

138 See Kirk N. Lambrecht, *The Administration of Dominion Lands, 1870–1930* (Regina: Canadian Plains Research Center, 1991).

139 *Constitution Act, 1930*, 20-21 George V, c. 26 (U.K.) at http://www.solon.org/Constitutions/Canada/English/ca_1930.html. Schedule 1 (Manitoba), clause 13; Schedule 2 (Alberta), clause 12; Schedule 3 (Saskatchewan), clause 12.

140 *Moosehunter v. The Queen*, [1981] 1 S.C.R. 282 at http://scc.lexum.org/en/1981/1981scr1-282/1981scr1-282.html.

141 *R. v. Horseman*, [1990] 1 S.C.R. 901 at http://scc.lexum.org/en/1990/1990scr1-901/1990scr1-901.html, citing with approval *Frank v. The Queen*, [1978] 1 S.C.R. 95 at 100, at http://scc.lexum.org/en/1977/1978scr1-95/1978scr1-95.html.

142 *R. v. Blais*, 2003 SCC 44, [2003] 2 S.C.R. 236 at para. 32, at http://scc.lexum.org/en/2003/2003scc44/2003scc44.html.

143 *R. v. Badger*, [1996] 1 S.C.R. 771, at para. 72, at http://scc.lexum.org/en/1996/1996scr1-771/1996scr1-771.html.

144 *R. v. Horseman*, [1990] 1 S.C.R. 901 at http://scc.lexum.org/en/1990/1990scr1-901/1990scr1-901.html.

145 *Frank v. The Queen*, [1978] 1 S.C.R. 95 at http://scc.lexum.org/en/1977/1978scr1-95/1978scr1-95.html.

146 *The Queen v. Sutherland et al.*, [1980] 2 S.C.R. 451 at http://scc.lexum.org/en/1980/1980scr2-451/1980scr2-451.html.

147 *Moosehunter v. The Queen*, [1981] 1 S.C.R. 282 at http://scc.lexum.org/en/1981/1981scr1-282/1981scr1-282.html.

148 *R. v. Horse*, [1988] 1 S.C.R. 187 at http://scc.lexum.org/en/1988/1988scr1-187/1988scr1-187.html

149 *R. v. Horseman*, [1990] 1 S.C.R. 901 at http://scc.lexum.org/en/1990/1990scr1-901/1990scr1-901.html.

150 *R. v. Badger*, [1996] 1 S.C.R. 771 at http://scc.lexum.org/en/1996/1996scr1-771/1996scr1-771.html.

151 *R. v. Blais*, 2003 SCC 44, [2003] 2 S.C.R. 236 at http://scc.lexum.org/en/2003/2003scc44/2003scc44.html.

152 *R. v. Horseman*, [1990] 1 S.C.R. 901 at http://scc.lexum.org/en/1990/1990scr1-901/1990scr1-901.html.

153 *Mikisew Cree First Nation v. Canada (Minister of Canadian Heritage)*, 2005 SCC 69, [2005] 3 S.C.R. 388 at para. 24, at http://scc.lexum.org/en/2005/2005scc69/2005scc69.html.

154 GPS mapping technology, if linked to land titles records and adopted by Indian hunters, might ultimately alter this test, but that is for a future day.

155 *R. v. Badger*, [1996] 1 S.C.R. 771 at para. 65, at http://scc.lexum.org/en/1996/1996scr1-771/1996scr1-771.html.

156 *Treaty Land Entitlement Framework Agreement* (Saskatchewan) at http://www.publications.gov.sk.ca/details.cfm?p=10238 and http://web.archive.org/web/20120404131515/http://www.fnmr.gov.sk.ca/documents/lands/tle-agreements/.

157 *Treaty Land Entitlement Implementation Act*, S.S. 1993 c. T-20.1, as amended by S.S. 2002, c. S-35.02 and 2005 c. S-35.03, at http://www.qp.gov.sk.ca/documents/English/Statutes/Statutes/T20-1.pdf.

158 *An Act to Confirm an Agreement between the Government of Canada and the Government of Saskatchewan Varying the Saskatchewan Natural Resources Transfer Agreements*, S.S. 1993 c. S-31.1 at http://www.qp.gov.sk.ca/documents/English/Statutes/Statutes/S31-1.pdf.

159 *Saskatchewan Treaty Land Entitlement Act*, S.C. 1993 c. 11 at http://laws.justice.gc.ca/PDF/Statute/S/S-4.3.pdf.

160 *Treaty Land Entitlement Master Agreement* (Manitoba) at http://www.gov.mb.ca/ana/interest/tle_framework_agreement_1997.pdf.

161 Specific Claims Process (Canada) at http://www.aadnc-aandc.gc.ca/eng/1100100030291. A discussion of delays in the process, described as "institutional gridlock," can be found at Canadian Bar Association, National Aboriginal Law Section, *Examination of Canada's Specific Claims Policy* (November 2006) at http://www.cba.org/CBA/submissions/pdf/06-52-eng.pdf. Since this report, Canada has created the Specific Claims Tribunal Canada, which maintains a website at http://www.sct-trp.ca/hom/index_e.htm. This tribunal was created by the *Specific Claims Tribunal Act*, S.C. 2008 c. 22 at http://laws-lois.justice.gc.ca/eng/acts/S-15.36/FullText.html.

162 Alberta's cooperation in the process is described at http://web.archive.org/web/20120424081111/http://www.energy.alberta.ca/OurBusiness/499.asp.

CHAPTER THREE: FUNDAMENTAL PRINCIPLES OF ENVIRONMENTAL ASSESSMENT AND REGULATORY REVIEW

1 Michael Watkins, blog in *Harvard Business Review* at http://blogs.hbr.org/watkins/2010/06/global_strategy_local_policies.html.

2 Final Report to the President of the Commission Established to Inquire into the Deepwater Horizon Oil Spill and Offshore Drilling (January 2011) at http://www.oilspillcommission.gov/sites/default/files/documents/DEEPWATER_ReporttothePresident_FINAL.pdf.

3 According to the Department of Foreign Affairs and International Trade at http://www.international.gc.ca/trade-agreements-accords-commerciaux/ds/csr.aspx,

> Corporate Social Responsibility (CSR) is defined as the way companies integrate social, environmental, and economic concerns into their values and operations in a transparent and accountable manner. It is integral to long-term business growth and success, and it also plays an important role in promoting Canadian values internationally and contributing to the sustainable development of communities. The Government of Canada works with the Canadian business community, civil society groups, with foreign governments and communities as well as other stakeholders to foster and promote CSR.

4   Neil McCrank , *Road to Improvement: The Review of the Regulatory Systems across the North* (May 2008) at http://www.reviewboard.ca/upload/ref_library/1217612729_rio8-eng.pdf.

5   Ibid., at 5–6.

6   See Council of Canadian Administrative Tribunals at http://www.ccat-ctac.org/en/index.php.

7   See Society of Ontario Adjudicators and Regulators at https://soar.on.ca/index.php

8   World Commission on Environment and Development, "Brundtland Report," in *Report of the National Task Force on Environment and Economy* (1987) at http://www.un-documents.net/wced-ocf.htm.

9   For example, *Quebec (Attorney General) v. Canada (National Energy Board)*, [1994] 1 S.C.R. 159 at http://scc.lexum.org/en/1994/1994scr1-159/1994scr1-159.html: "The Board retains the power, through s. 119.093(1) of the *National Energy Board Act,* to revoke the licences if the conditions are not fulfilled."

10 See, for example, *National Energy Board Act,* R.S. 1985 c. N-7, s. 52 at http://laws-lois.justice.gc.ca/eng/acts/N-7/20100712/P1TT3xt3.html: "The Board may, subject to the approval of the Governor in Council, issue a certificate in respect of a pipeline ..."; and *Oil Sands Conservation Act,* R.S.A. 2000 c. O-7, s. 10 (3) at http://www.canlii.org/en/ab/laws/stat/rsa-2000-c-o-7/latest/rsa-2000-c-o-7.html: "The Board may, with respect to an application referred to in subsection (1), if in its opinion it is in the public interest to do so, and with the prior authorization of the Lieutenant Governor in Council, grant an approval on any terms and conditions that the Board considers appropriate."

11 See, for example, Madame Justice Constance C. Hunt, "Toward the Twenty-First Century: A Canadian Legal Perspective on Resource and Environmental Law," *Osgoode Hall Law Journal* 31 (1993): 297.

12 *Friends of the Oldman River Society v. Canada (Minister of Transport)*, [1992] 1 S.C.R. 3 at http://scc.lexum.org/en/1992/1992scr1-3/1992scr1-3.html.

13 *MiningWatch Canada v. Canada (Fisheries and Oceans)*, 2010 SCC 2, [2010] 1 S.C.R. 6 at http://scc.lexum.org/en/2010/2010scc2/2010scc2.html.

14 *Quebec (Attorney General) v. Moses*, 2010 SCC 17, [2010] 1 S.C.R. 557 at http://scc.lexum.org/en/2010/2010scc17/2010scc17.html.

15 *Friends of the Oldman River Society v. Canada (Minister of Transport)*, [1992] 1 S.C.R. 3 at 71, at http://scc.lexum.org/en/1992/1992scr1-3/1992scr1-3.html.

16 Both passages are from the *2009 Fall Report of the Commissioner of the Environment and Sustainable Development*, "Chapter 1: Applying the *Canadian Environmental Assessment Act,* Why It's Important," at http://www.oag-bvg.gc.ca/internet/English/parl_cesd_200911_01_e_33196.html.

17 World Commission on Environment and Development, "Brundtland Report," in *Report of the National Task Force on Environment and Economy* (1987) at http://www.un-documents.net/wced-ocf.htm.

18 *Friends of the Oldman River Society v. Canada (Minister of Transport)*, [1992] 1 S.C.R. 3 at 37, at http://scc.lexum.org/en/1992/1992scr1-3/1992scr1-3.html.

19 Ibid., at 64.

20 Ibid., at 66.

21 Ibid., at 69.

22 Ibid., at 66.

23 *Canadian Environmental Assessment Act, 2012*, S.C. 2012 c. 19, s. 52, at http://laws-lois.justice.gc.ca/eng/acts/C-15.21/index.html.

24 See *Alberta Wilderness Association v. Express Pipeline*, [1996] 201 N.R. 336 at 342 para. 13; *Quebec (Attorney General) v. Canada (National Energy Board)*, [1994] 1 S.C.R. 159 at 198–99, at http://scc.lexum.org/en/1994/1994scr1-159/1994scr1-159.html.

25 *NIL/TU,O Child and Family Services Society v. B.C. Government and Service Employees' Union*, 2010 SCC 45 at para. 45, at http://scc.lexum.org/en/2010/2010scc45/2010scc45.html.

26 *Inter-Church Uranium Committee Educational Co-operative v. Canada (Atomic Energy Control Board)*, 2004 FCA 218 at para. 46, at http://decisions.fca-caf.gc.ca/en/2004/2004fca218/2004fca218.html.

27 *MiningWatch Canada v. Canada (Fisheries and Oceans)*, 2010 SCC 2, [2010] 1 S.C.R. 6 at paras. 24 and 25, at http://scc.lexum.org/en/2010/2010scc2/2010scc2.html.

28 For example, the Canadian Environmental Assessment Agency and the British Columbia Environmental Assessment Office have concluded a Memorandum of Understanding on substitution pursuant to the *Canadian Environmental Assessment Act, 2012*, at http://www.eao.gov.bc.ca/pdf/EAO_CEAA_Substitution_MOU.pdf.

29 *Lavoie v. Canada (Minister of the Environment)*, FC T-1596-98 at para. 93, at http://decisions.fct-cf.gc.ca/en/2000/t-1586-98_19632/t-1586-98.html.

30 The Canadian Council of the Ministers of the Environment maintain a website at http://www.ccme.ca/.

31 Canadian Council of the Ministers of the Environment, *Canada-Wide Accord on Environmental Harmonization* at http://www.ccme.ca/assets/pdf/accord_harmonization_e.pdf.

32 Canadian Council of the Ministers of the Environment, *Sub-Agreement on Environmental Assessment* at http://www.ccme.ca/assets/pdf/envtlassesssubagr_e.pdf.

33 *Federal-Provincial/Territorial Environmental Assessment Cooperation Agreements* at http://www.ceaa.gc.ca/default.asp?lang=En&n=CA03020B-1.

34 Joint Federal-Provincial Panel on Uranium Mining Developments in Northern Saskatchewan at http://www.ceaa.gc.ca/default.asp?lang=En&n=A0159CFA-1.

35 Terra Nova Offshore Oil Development Project Assessment Report at http://www.ceaa.gc.ca/default.asp?lang=En&n=804525A3-1&xml=804525A3-BECD-47C6-84B1-A5E159125986&offset=18&toc=show.

36 Voisey's Bay Mine and Mill Environmental Assessment Panel Report at http://www.ceaa-acee.gc.ca/default.asp?lang=En&n=0A571A1A-1&xml=0A571A1A-84CD-496B-969E-7CF9CBEA16AE&offset=22&toc=show. The Voisey's Bay project and its relationship to Aboriginal peoples is discussed in Robert B. Gibson, *Sustainability Assessment: Criteria and Processes* (London: Earthscan, 2005).

37 Sydney Tar Ponds and Coke Ovens Sites Remediation Project Joint Panel Assessment Report at http://www.ceaa.gc.ca/050/documents/19345/19345E.pdf.

38 Lake Kénogami Watershed Flood Control Project JRP Report at http://www.ceaa.gc.ca/3BDE42A6-docs/report-eng.pdf.

39 Lachine Canal Decontamination Project JRP Report at http://www.ceaa.gc.ca/Content/A/4/2/A421C8F2-FEA0-40A0-A584-2C8DDFCDB497/report_e.pdf.

40 Romaine Hydroelectric Complex Project JRP Report at http://www.ceaa.gc.ca/050/documents/34664/34664E.pdf. On completion of its analysis, the joint federal-provincial review panel concluded with respect to the provincial aspect of its mandate

"that the project fulfills three of the objectives of the Quebec energy strategy, namely to enhance security of energy supply, to make greater use of energy as an engine of economic development, and to give a greater role to local and regional communities and Aboriginal groups."

41 Rabaska Project, Implementation of an LNG Terminal and Related Infrastructure JRP Main Report at http://www.ceaa.gc.ca/050/documents_staticpost/pdfs/24599E.pdf.

42 Eastmain-1-A and Rupert Diversion Project Panel Report at http://www.ceaa.gc.ca/E5260A91-docs/report-eng.pdf.

43 Cacouna Energy LNG Terminal Project JRP Inquiry and Public Hearing Report at http://www.ceaa.gc.ca/050/documents/18338/18338E.pdf.

44 Agreement to Establish a Joint Review Panel for the Marathon Platinum Group Metals and Copper Mine Project at http://www.ceaa.gc.ca/050/documents/51450/51450E.pdf.

45 EnCana's Shallow Gas Infill Development Project, Canadian Forces Base Suffield, National Wildlife Area, JRP Report at http://www.ceaa.gc.ca/050/documents/31401/31401E.pdf.

46 Glacier Power Ltd. Dunvegan Hydroelectric Project at Fairview, Alberta, JRP Report at http://www.ceaa.gc.ca/050/documents/30552/30552E.pdf.

47 Imperial Oil Kearl Oil Sands Mine Project JRP Report at http://www.ceaa.gc.ca/050/documents/21349/21349E.pdf; JRP Addendum at http://www.ceaa.gc.ca/052/document-html-eng.cfm?did=26766.

48 Muskeg River Mine Expansion (Albian Oil Sands Project) JRP Report at http://www.ceaa.gc.ca/050/documents/19760/19760E.pdf.

49 Cheviot Coal Mine Project JRP Report at http://www.ceaa.gc.ca/D9BC55EE-docs/report-eng.pdf.

50 Highwood Storage and Diversion Project JRP Report at http://www.nrcb.gov.ab.ca/nrp/LittleBow%209601%20Decision%20Report.pdf; Progress Reports at http://www.nrcb.gov.ab.ca/nrp/Decisions.aspx?id=166.

51 Horizon Oil Sands Project JRP Report at http://www.ceaa.gc.ca/Content/7/3/E/73E831C7-1781-42F6-AEBB-7F79581E012E/report_e.pdf.

52 Shell Jackpine I Oil Sands Project JRP Report at http://www.ceaa.gc.ca/Content/2/0/4/2042EA47-3261-4136-A526-9B775D961BD1/report_e.pdf.

53 Little Bow Project/Highwood Diversion Plan JRP Report at http://www.nrcb.gov.ab.ca/nrp/LittleBow%209601%20Decision%20Report.pdf.

54 Kemess North Gold–Copper Mine JRP Report at http://www.ceaa.gc.ca/050/documents_staticpost/cearref_3394/24441E.pdf.

55 David Breen, *Alberta's Petroleum Industry and the Conservation Board* (Edmonton: University of Alberta Press, 1993) at xvii: "Although it is a provincial agency, Alberta's Energy Resources Conservation Board is one of the most important regulatory bodies in Canada. Decisions of this agency have had profound consequences, often beyond Alberta."

56 See, for example, Interim Directive ID 2000-3 whereby the Alberta Energy and Utilities Board and Alberta Environment developed a Memorandum of Understanding on the harmonization of waste management in Alberta: http://www.ercb.ca/ids/pdf/id2000-03.pdf.

57 Memorandum of Understanding between the BC Utilities Commission and the BC Environmental Assessment Office: http://www.bcuc.com/Documents/Reports/MOU-EAO-BCUC-2009.pdf.

58 http://www.bcuc.com/MOU.aspx.

59 Agreement to Establish a Joint Review Panel for the New Nuclear Power Plant Project by Ontario Power Generation (Darlington) within the Municipality of Clarington, Ontario, between the Minister of the Environment and the Canadian Nuclear Safety Commission at http://www.opg.com/power/nuclear/darlington/Final%20Joint%20 Review%20Panel%20Agreement.pdf.

60 Agreement to Establish a Joint Review Panel for the Deep Geologic Repository Project by Ontario Power Generation Inc. within the Municipality of Kincardine Ontario, between the Minister of the Environment and the Canadian Nuclear Safety Commission at http://www.ceaa.gc.ca/050/documents/37943/37943E.pdf.

61 The Syncrude website at http://www.syncrude.ca/users/folder.asp?FolderID=5641 notes that Syncrude "is one of 11 companies in Canada, and the only oil sands company, to be accredited at the Gold Level in the Progressive Aboriginal Relations (PAR) Program of the Canadian Council for Aboriginal Business." The Canadian Council for Aboriginal Business maintains a website at http://www.ccab.com/.

62 Created by the *National Round Table on the Environment and the Economy Act*, S.C. 1993 c. 31 at http://laws.justice.gc.ca/PDF/Statute/N/N-16.4.pdf. That legislation is now repealed.

The National Round Table on the Environment and the Economy website is archived at http://collectionscanada.gc.ca/webarchives2/20130322140948/http://nrtee-trnee.ca/.

63 National Round Table on the Environment and the Economy, *State of the Debate: Aboriginal Communities and Non-Renewable Resource Development* (2001) at 67, at http://collectionscanada.gc.ca/webarchives2/20130322183506/http://nrtee-trnee. ca/wp-content/uploads/2013/02/aboriginal-communities.pdf.

64 World Bank, *Environmental Assessment Sourcebook 1999*, "Chapter 1: The Environmental Review Process" at http://siteresources.worldbank.org/INTSAFE-POL/1142947-1116495579739/20507372/Chapter1TheEnvironmentalReviewProcess. pdf.

65 Ibid.

66 World Bank, *Environmental Assessment in Operational Policy 4.01* at http://web. worldbank.org/WBSITE/EXTERNAL/TOPICS/ENVIRONMENT/EXTENVASS/0,,menuPK:40 7994~pagePK:149018~piPK:149093~theSitePK:407988,00.html.

67 International Council of Mining and Minerals, *Good Practice Guidance on Health Impact Assessment*, at 26, at https://www.icmm.com/document/792.

68 Ibid., at 11 and 17.

69 Ibid., at 6 and 7.

70 D. Pearce, G. Atkinson, and S. Mourato, *Cost–Benefit Analysis and the Environment: Recent Developments* (Paris: OECD, 2006) at http://books.google.com/books?id=nTP bxgsvBDoC&printsec=frontcover&source=gbs_ge_summary_r&cad=0#v=onepage& q&f=false.

71 International Association of Oil and Gas Producers, *Principles for Impact Assessment: The Environmental and Social Dimension*, Report 2.74/265 (August 1997) at http:// commdev.org/content/document/detail/709/.

72 International Petroleum Industry Environment Conservation Association (IPIECA), *Guide to Social Impact Assessment in the Oil and Gas Industry* (London: IPIECA, 2004) at http://commdev.org/content/document/detail/671/ and *Key Questions in Managing Social Issues in Oil and Gas Projects* (London: IPIECA and International Association of Oil and Gas Producers, 2002) at http://www.ogp.org.uk/pubs/332.pdf.

73 The Canadian Business Ethics Research Network maintains a website at http://www. cbern.ca/home/.

74 IBA Research Network at http://www.cbern.ca/impactandbenefit/. A bibliography on impact and benefits agreements, many with hypertext links, can be found at: http:// www.cbern.ca/impactandbenefit/Research/.

75 Irene Sosa and Karyn Keenan, *Impact Benefit Agreements between Aboriginal Communities and Mining Companies: Their Use in Canada* (October, 2001) at http://s. cela.ca/files/uploads/IBAeng.pdf. See also Woodward and Company, *Benefit Sharing Agreements in British Columbia: A Guide for First Nations, Businesses, and Governments* at http://www.woodwardandcompany.com/media/pdfs/4487_benefit_sharing_final_report_-_updated.pdf.

76 National Aboriginal Health Organization, *Impact Benefit Agreements: A Tool for Healthy Inuit Communities?* (March 2009) at http://www.naho.ca/documents/ it/2009_IBA_Summary.pdf.

77 Michael Hitch and Courtney Riley Fidler, "Impact and Benefit Agreements: A Contentious Issue for Environmental and Aboriginal Justice," *Environments Journal* 35, 2 (2007): 45–69. (Abstract viewable at http://ssrn.com/abstract=1340057.)

CHAPTER FOUR: DEVELOPMENT OF THE LAW OF ABORIGINAL CONSULTATION BY THE SUPREME COURT OF CANADA

1 The Court itself acknowledges this in it subsequent judgment in *Rio Tinto Alcan Inc. v. Carrier Sekani Tribal Council*, 2010 SCC 43, [2010] 2 S.C.R. 650 at paras. 2 and 32 at http://scc.lexum.org/en/2010/2010scc43/2010scc43.html, where the Court emphasizes the relationship between the duty to consult and the treaty claim process in British Columbia:

> [2] ... [G]overnments have a duty to consult with Aboriginal groups when making decisions which may adversely impact lands and resources to which Aboriginal peoples lay claim. In the intervening years, government–Aboriginal consultation has become an important part of the resource development process in British Columbia especially; much of the land and resources there are subject to land claims negotiations.

> [32] The duty to consult is grounded in the honour of the Crown. It is a corollary of the Crown's obligation to achieve the just settlement of Aboriginal claims through the treaty process. While the treaty claims process is ongoing, there is an implied duty to consult with the Aboriginal claimants on matters that may adversely affect their treaty and Aboriginal rights, and to accommodate those interests in the spirit of reconciliation.

2 *Rio Tinto Alcan Inc. v. Carrier Sekani Tribal Council*, 2010 SCC 43, [2010] 2 S.C.R. 650 at para. 38, at http://scc.lexum.org/en/2010/2010scc43/2010scc43.html.

3 Ibid., at para. 47.

4 Ibid., at para. 38.

5 *Haida Nation v. British Columbia (Minister of Forests)*, [2004] 3 S.C.R. 511, 2004 SCC 73 at http://scc.lexum.org/en/2004/2004scc73/2004scc73.html.

6 Ibid., at para. 32: "...the duty to consult and accommodate is part of a process of fair dealing and reconciliation that begins with the assertion of sovereignty. ..."

7 Ibid., at para. 25.

8 Ibid., at para. 20.

9   Ibid., at para. 38.

10   Ibid., at para. 20: "It is a corollary of s. 35 that the Crown act honourably in defining the rights it guarantees and in reconciling them with other rights and interests. This, in turn, implies a duty to consult and, if appropriate, accommodate";   ·

and at para. 38: "I conclude that consultation and accommodation before final claims resolution, while challenging, is not impossible, and indeed is an essential corollary to the honourable process of reconciliation that s. 35 demands."

11   See *Manitoba Metis Federation v. Canada (Attorney General)*, 2013 SCC 14 at http://scc.lexum.org/decisia-scc-csc/scc-csc/scc-csc/en/item/12888/index.do?r=AAAAAQAObwFuaxRVYmEgbwV0axMAAAAAAAAB.

12   *Haida Nation v. British Columbia (Minister of Forests)*, [2004] 3 S.C.R. 511, 2004 SCC 73 at para. 35, at http://scc.lexum.org/en/2004/2004scc73/2004scc73.html.

13   Ibid., at para. 44.

14   Ibid., at para. 47.

15   Ibid., at para. 53.

16   *Haida Nation v. B.C. and Weyerhaeuser*, [2002] B.C.J. NO. 1882 (BCCA) at para. 104, at http://www.canlii.org/en/bc/bcca/doc/2002/2002bcca462/2002bcca462.pdf.

17   Ibid., at para. 40: "Instead, this Court made what amounts to the least disruptive order that could still take account of the fact that the Haida people had not been consulted as they should have been consulted."

18   *Haida Nation v. B.C. and Weyerhaeuser*, [2002] B.C.J. NO. 378 (BCCA) at para. 54, at http://www.canlii.org/en/bc/bcca/doc/2002/2002bcca147/2002bcca147.pdf.

19   *Taku River Tlingit First Nation v. British Columbia (Project Assessment Director)*, 2004 SCC 74, [2004] 3 S.C.R. 550 at http://scc.lexum.org/en/2004/2004scc74/2004scc74.html.

20   Ibid., at para. 28.

21   Ibid., at para. 33.

22   Ibid., at para. 34.

23   Ibid., at para.40.

24   Ibid., at para. 8.

25   *Beckman v. Little Salmon/Carmacks First Nation*, 2010 SCC 53, [2010] 3 S.C.R. 103 at para. 39, at http://scc.lexum.org/en/2010/2010scc53/2010scc53.html.

26   *Taku River Tlingit First Nation v. British Columbia (Project Assessment Director)*, 2004 SCC 74, [2004] 3 S.C.R. 550 at para. 8, at http://scc.lexum.org/en/2004/2004scc74/2004scc74.html.

27   Ibid., at para. 46.

28   Ibid., at para. 2.

29   *Mikisew Cree First Nation v. Canada (Minister of Canadian Heritage)*, 2005 SCC 69, [2005] 3 S.C.R. 388 at http://scc.lexum.org/en/2005/2005scc69/2005scc69.html.

30   Ibid., at para. 1.

31   *Canada National Parks Act*, S.C. 2000 c. 32, Schedule 1(5) Wood Buffalo National Park of Canada at http://laws-lois.justice.gc.ca/eng/acts/N-14.01/FullText.html:

Saving and excepting thereout and therefrom,

Firstly: all those lands lying within Peace Point Indian Reserve No. 222 as shown on Plan 71277 recorded in the Canada Lands Surveys Records at Ottawa, a copy of which is filed in the Land Titles Office at Edmonton under number 882-0308, said reserve containing 5.18 square kilometres (518 hectares), more or less, together with all mines and minerals. ...

32 *Mikisew Cree First Nation v. Canada (Minister of Canadian Heritage)*, 2005 SCC 69, [2005] 3 S.C.R. 388 at para. 11, at http://scc.lexum.org/en/2005/2005scc69/2005scc69. html:

Parks Canada wrote Chief Poitras on April 30, 2001, stating in part: "I apologize to you and your people for the way in which the consultation process unfolded concerning the proposed winter road and any resulting negative public perception of the [Mikisew Cree First Nation]." At that point, in fact, the decision to approve the road with a modified alignment had already been taken.

33 Ibid., at para. 64.

34 Ibid., at para. 66.

35 *Beckman v. Little Salmon/Carmacks First Nation*, 2010 SCC 53, [2010] 3 S.C.R. 103 at paras. 15 and 35 respectively, at http://scc.lexum.org/en/2010/2010scc53/2010scc53. html.

36 See *Canadian Parks and Wilderness Society v. Canada (Minister of Canadian Heritage)*, (F.C.A.) [2003] 4 F.C. 672 at paras. 10–14, 22–28, 104–105, and 107, per Rothstein J.A. (as he then was) for the Court, at http://decisions.fca-caf.gc.ca/ en/2003/2003fca197/2003fca197.html.

37 The material provisions of the clause in Treaty 8 is reproduced here for convenience:

And Her Majesty the Queen HEREBY AGREES with the said Indians that they shall have right to pursue their usual vocations of hunting, trapping and fishing throughout the tract surrendered as heretofore described, subject to such regulations as may from time to time be made by the Government of the country, acting under the authority of Her Majesty, and saving and excepting such tracts as may be required or taken up from time to time for settlement, mining, lumbering, trading or other purposes.

38 *Mikisew Cree First Nation v. Canada (Minister of Canadian Heritage)*, 2005 SCC 69, [2005] 3 S.C.R. 388 at para. 31, at http://scc.lexum.org/en/2005/2005scc69/2005scc69. html.

39 Ibid., at para. 54.

40 Ibid., at para. 48.

41 Ibid., at para. 64.

42 Ibid., at para. 65.

43 *Beckman v. Little Salmon/Carmacks First Nation*, 2010 SCC 53, [2010] 3 S.C.R. 103 at http://scc.lexum.org/en/2010/2010scc53/2010scc53.html.

44 *Little Salmon/Carmacks First Nation Final Agreement* at http://www.eco.gov.yk.ca/ pdf/little_salmon_carmacks_fa.pdf.

45 *Umbrella Final Agreement between the Government of Canada, the Council for Yukon Indians, and the Government of the Yukon* at http://www.eco.gov.yk.ca/pdf/ umbrellafinalagreement.pdf.

46 *Beckman v. Little Salmon/Carmacks First Nation*, 2010 SCC 53, [2010] 3 S.C.R. 103 at para. 38, at http://scc.lexum.org/en/2010/2010scc53/2010scc53.html.

47 *Little Salmon/Carmacks First Nation Final Agreement, S. 12.2.0, Definitions, Development Assessment Legislation* at http://www.eco.gov.yk.ca/pdf/little_salmon_carmacks_fa.pdf.

48 *Beckman v. Little Salmon/Carmacks First Nation*, 2010 SCC 53, [2010] 3 S.C.R. 103 at para. 87, at http://scc.lexum.org/en/2010/2010scc53/2010scc53.html.

49 A map of the Kemano facilities is located on page 7 of the British Columbia Utilities Commissions decision at http://www.bcuc.com/Documents/Decisions/2008/DOC_17815_BCH-Alcan_2007EPA-Web.pdf.

50 The smelter is described at http://www.riotintoalcaninbc.com/pages/our-products/smelter-operations.php.

51 *Utilities Commission Act*, R.S.B.C. 1996 c. 473 at http://www.bclaws.ca/EPLibraries/bclaws_new/document/ID/freeside/00_96473_01 or http://www.canlii.org/en/bc/laws/stat/rsbc-1996-c-473/latest/rsbc-1996-c-473.html.

52 The Supreme Court described the factors that the Commission is required to consider under section 71 of the *Utilities Commission Act* as "focused mainly on economic issues." See *Rio Tinto Alcan Inc. v. Carrier Sekani Tribal Council*, 2010 SCC 43, [2010] 2 S.C.R. 650 at para. 70, at http://scc.lexum.org/en/2010/2010scc43/2010scc43.html.

53 See *Public Hearing Process* at http://www.bcuc.com/Hearing.aspx and *Understanding Utility Regulation: A Participants' Guide to the British Columbia Utilities Commission* at http://www.bcuc.com/Documents/Guidelines/Participant_Guide.pdf.

54 The Scoping Order is Appendix C of British Columbia Utilities Commission, Decision in the Matter of a Filing of Electricity Purchase Agreement with Alcan Inc. as an Energy Supply Contract Pursuant to Section 71 (January 29, 2008) at http://www.bcuc.com/Documents/Decisions/2008/DOC_17815_BCH-Alcan_2007EPA-Web.pdf.

55 Reconsideration is provided for in section 99 of the *Utilities Commission Act*, R.S.B.C. 1996 c. 473.

56 British Columbia Utilities Commission, Decision in the Matter of a Filing of Electricity Purchase Agreement with Alcan Inc. as an Energy Supply Contract Pursuant to Section 71 (January 29, 2008) at http://www.bcuc.com/Documents/Decisions/2008/DOC_17815_BCH-Alcan_2007EPA-Web.pdf.

57 Ibid., at 118.

58 Ibid., sec. 8 at 117–125.

59 Ibid., at 122–23.

60 National Energy Board, In the Matter of Terasen Pipelines (Trans Mountain Inc.), OH-1-2006 at 17, at http://dsp-psd.pwgsc.gc.ca/Collection/NE22-1-2006-4E.pdf.

61 British Columbia Utilities Commission, Decision in the Matter of a Filing of Electricity Purchase Agreement with Alcan Inc. as an Energy Supply Contract Pursuant to Section 71 (January 29, 2008) at Appendix D, at http://www.bcuc.com/Documents/Decisions/2008/DOC_17815_BCH-Alcan_2007EPA-Web.pdf.

62 Ibid., at Appendix D at 3.

63 Rio Tinto had acquired the shares of Alcan, though Alcan maintained ownership of the Kemano facilities. Rio Tinto shareholders approved the acquisition of Alcan on September 28, 2007, and the acquisition was announced as complete on November 14, 2007. See the media releases at http://www.riotinto.com/media/18435_media_releases_6764.asp and http://www.riotinto.com/media/18435_media_releases_6881.asp. According to *The Economist*, the Rio Tinto acquisition of Alcan was "a disastrous purchase. ... Rio overpaid greatly for the Canadian aluminium producer and the debts it ran up to

finance the deal, just as the credit crisis hit, were nearly fatal for the company." See http://mobile.economist.com/newsbook-21014202.php.

64 *The Carrier Sekani Tribal Council v. The B.C. Utilities Commission,* 2008 BCCA 385 at http://www.canlii.org/en/bc/bcca/doc/2008/2008bcca385/2008bcca385.html; *Carrier Sekani Tribal Council v. British Columbia (Utilities Commission),* 2009 BCCA 67 (CanLII) at http://www.canlii.org/en/bc/bcca/doc/2009/2009bcca67/2009bcca67.html.

65 *Rio Tinto Alcan Inc. v. Carrier Sekani Tribal Council,* 2010 SCC 43, [2010] 2 S.C.R. 650 at para. 81, at http://scc.lexum.org/en/2010/2010scc43/2010scc43.html: "BC Hydro's proposal to enter into an agreement to purchase electricity from Alcan is clearly proposed Crown conduct. BC Hydro is a Crown corporation. It acts in place of the Crown. No one seriously argues that the 2007 EPA does not represent a proposed action of the Province of British Columbia."

66 Ibid., at para. 60.

67 Brian Slattery, "Aboriginal Rights and the Honour of the Crown," *Supreme Court Law Review* 20 (2005): 433–45 at http://papers.ssrn.com/sol3/papers.cfm?abstract_id=1572569. Professor Slattery was expressing his opinion on the Court's view of section 35 as reflected in the *Haida Nation* and *Taku River* decisions.

68 Dwight G. Newman, *The Duty to Consult: New Relationships with Aboriginal Peoples* (Saskatoon: Purich Publishing, 2009) at 30. Professor Newman goes on to state in the same paragraph that

> Although the Supreme Court seemingly offered an easily triggered duty … the triggering of a duty to consult by every government action that could, through some remote process, have some minimal adverse effect on an Aboriginal right would set up an impractical scenario for government decision-making. To say this much is not to undermine the purposes of the duty to consult, but to make it workable and efficacious in furthering reconciliation process.

69 *Rio Tinto Alcan Inc. v. Carrier Sekani Tribal Council,* 2010 SCC 43, [2010] 2 S.C.R. 650 at para. 50, at http://scc.lexum.org/en/2010/2010scc43/2010scc43.html.

70 Ibid., at para. 83.

71 Ibid.

72 Ibid., at para. 90.

73 Ibid.

74 Ibid., at paras. 90 and 63 respectively.

75 Ibid., at para. 63.

76 Ibid., at para. 45.

77 Ibid., at para. 46.

78 Ibid., at para. 48.

79 Ibid., at para. 35.

80 Ibid., at para. 87.

81 Ibid., at paras. 85–93.

82 Ibid., at para. 58. In arriving at this conclusion, the Court emphasized the narrow definition of the term "constitutional question" in provincial legislation that purported to withdraw from the tribunal any capacity to determine constitutional questions. See para. 72.

83   Ibid., at para. 60.

CHAPTER FIVE: CASE STUDIES INVOLVING ABORIGINAL CONSULTATION AND THE NATIONAL ENERGY BOARD OF CANADA

1   *National Energy Board Act*, R.S. 1985 c. N-7 at http://laws-lois.justice.gc.ca/eng/N-7/index.html.

2   The acts and regulations that apply to the National Energy Board are listed at http://www.neb-one.gc.ca/clf-nsi/rpblctn/ctsndrgltn/ctsndrgltn-eng.html.

3   The mandate of the Northern Pipeline Agency is described at http://www.appointments.gc.ca/prflOrg.asp?OrgID=NPA&lang=eng.

4   The National Energy Board's process is described in plain language in *Pipeline Regulation in Canada: A Guide for Landowners and the Public* (revised September 30, 2010) at http://www.neb.gc.ca/clf-nsi/rthnb/pblcprtcptn/pplnrgltncnd/pplnrgltncnd_ndx-eng.html.

5   National Energy Board, *Canadian Pipeline Transportation System: Transportation Assessment* (June 2008) at 44, at http://www.neb.gc.ca/clf-nsi/rnrgynfmtn/nrgyrprt/trnsprttn/trnsprttnssssmnt2008/trnsprttnssssmnt2008-eng.pdf.

6   Earle Gray, *Forty Years in the Public Interest: A History of the National Energy Board* (Vancouver: Douglas & McIntyre Ltd. in cooperation with the National Energy Board, 2000) at 2.

7   National Energy Board, *Canadian Pipeline Transportation System: Transportation Assessment* (July 2009) at viii, at http://www.neb.gc.ca/clf-nsi/rnrgynfmtn/nrgyrprt/trnsprttn/trnsprttnssssmnt2009/trnsprttnssssmnt2009-eng.html.

8   Ibid., at sec. 2.1.1.

9   Memorandum of Guidance (March 4, 2002) at https://www.neb-one.gc.ca/ll-eng/livelink.exe/fetch/2000/90463/522930/523056/Memorandum_Of_Guidance_(A0C8Q3).pdf?nodeid=522841&vernum=0.

10   Consultation with Aboriginal Peoples (April 3, 2002) at https://www.neb-one.gc.ca/ll-eng/livelink.exe/fetch/2000/90463/522930/522833/Information_Request_(A0D6S0).pdf?nodeid=524604&vernum=0.

11   *Implications of Supreme Court of Canada Decisions on the NEB's Memorandum of Guidance on Consultation with Aboriginal People* (August 3, 2005) at https://www.neb-one.gc.ca/ll-eng/livelink.exe/fetch/2000/90463/522930/523055/Letter_(A0R5U7).pdf?nodeid=524481&vernum=0.

12   The National Energy Board's Aboriginal Engagement program was described by Board member Strater Crowfoot at the First Nations Energy Summit in April 2007. According to the PowerPoint presentation, "its goal is to increase the understanding of Aboriginal people so that, in the future, they may participate more effectively in the NEB's processes to present their views on a proposed project directly to the Board. The AE program involves NEB staff visiting Aboriginal communities on their request to answer questions about NEB processes and upcoming applications." See *Regulatory Processes: Issues and Opportunities* at http://www.neb.gc.ca/clf-nsi/archives/rpblctn/spchsndprsnttn/2007/rgltryprcss/rgltryprcss-eng.html.

13   National Energy Board Filing Manual at http://www.neb-one.gc.ca/clf-nsi/rpblctn/ctsndrgltn/flngmnl/flngmnl-eng.html.

14   *Consideration of Aboriginal Concerns in National Energy Board Decisions* (July 2008) at https://www.neb-one.gc.ca/ll-eng/livelink.exe/fetch/2000/90463/522930/522832/

Consideration_of_Aboriginal_Concerns_in_National_Energy_Board_Decisions_ (AoT5X3).pdf?nodeid=524268&vernum=0. It states that the NEB did not have funds for participant funding. This changed with the coming into force of the 2010 federal budget. See *NEB Participant Funding Program Guide: Guide to the National Energy Board Participant Funding Program under the National Energy Board Act* (2010) at http://www.neb-one.gc.ca/clf-nsi/rthnb/pblcprtcptn/prtcpntfndngprgrm/prgrmgd-eng. pdf.

15   At the same time, a parallel but less well-known inquiry was conducted by Kenneth Lysyk into the possible routing of a pipeline from Alaska through the Yukon. The Alaska Highway Pipeline Inquiry of Kenneth M. Lysyk, dated July 29, 1977, and the report of the Mackenzie Valley Pipeline Inquiry, entitled *Northern Frontier, Northern Homeland*, dated April 15, 1977, are viewable at https://www.neb-one.gc.ca/ll-eng/ livelink.exe?func=ll&objId=238336&objAction=browse. The commercial history of the proposals to ship northern gas to southern markets, and the relationship between the Lysyk and Berger Inquiries and the National Energy Board, are discussed at National Energy Board, Northern Pipelines, Reasons for Decision, GH-1-76, at https://www. neb-one.gc.ca/ll-eng/livelink.exe?func=ll&objId=239633&objAction=browse&sort= name&redirect=3.

16   The final report included a note on terminology. The phrase "the North" was used to refer to the Northwest Territories and the Yukon unless otherwise stated. The phrase "Mackenzie Valley" was used to refer to "the whole of the Region from the Alberta border to the Mackenzie Delta, including the Great Slave Lake and Great Bear Lake areas." See *Northern Frontier, Northern Homeland: Mackenzie Valley Pipeline Inquiry Report*, vol. 1, Chapter 12, Epilogue, Bibliographic Note and Terminology at https://www.neb-one.gc.ca/ll-eng/livelink.exe/fetch/2000/90463/238336/234916/ AoF3K7_-_BergerV1ch12_-_English_Version.pdf?nodeid=234950&vernum=0.

17   Standing Committee on Aboriginal Affairs and Northern Development, Evidence (November 18, 1997) at http://www2.parl.gc.ca/HousePublications/Publication.asp x?DocId=1038170&Language=E&Mode=1.

18   36th Parliament, 1st Session, Bill C-6, House of Commons Standing Committee on Aboriginal Affairs and Northern Development, Witnesses and Evidence to Standing Committee on Aboriginal Affairs and Northern Development at http://www.parl. gc.ca/committee/CommitteePublication.aspx?SourceId=49453.

19   The Deh Cho process, and the settlement agreement with the Deh Cho, as seen from the Government of Canada perspective, is described at http://www.aadnc-aandc.gc.ca/ DAM/DAM-INTER-NWT/STAGING/texte-text/ntr_pubs_pfdpn_1331052268915_eng.pdf, http://www.aadnc-aandc.gc.ca/aiarch/mr/nr/m-a2005/2-02689-eng.asp, and http:// www.aadnc-aandc.gc.ca/aiarch/mr/nr/m-a2005/02689bk-eng.asp. The Government of the Northwest Territories contains a description at http://www.daair.gov.nt.ca/_live/ pages/wpPages/Dehcho.aspx. A description of the process from the Deh Cho perspective can be found at http://www.dehcho.org/negotiations.htm.

20   The 2001 *Framework Agreement* with the Deh Cho is at http://www.aadnc-aandc. gc.ca/DAM/DAM-INTER-HQ/STAGING/texte-text/dcf_1100100032119_eng.pdf. The Deh Cho *Interim Measures Agreement*, sec. 57, is at http://www.aadnc-aandc.gc.ca/DAM/ DAM-INTER-HQ/STAGING/texte-text/dci_1100100032115_eng.pdf. The website for the Mackenzie Valley Environmental Impact Review Board at http://reviewboard.ca/about/ members.php does identify a Deh Cho nominee in the 2003–04 period.

21   The Aboriginal Pipeline Group is described at http://www.mackenziegasproject.com/ moreInformation/publications/documents/Who_We_Are.pdf and at its website at http://www.mvapg.com/index.php.

22 Information on the Mackenzie Gas Project is available at http://www.mackenziegaspro-ject.com/.

23 The Regulatory Roadmap Project was supported by the Government of Canada and the Canadian Association of Petroleum Producers. It generated a number of individual publications prepared by Erlandson and Associates from 2000 to 2002:

(1) *Oil and gas approvals in the Northwest Territories—southern Mackenzie Valley: a guide to regulatory approval processes for oil and natural gas exploration and production on public lands in the southern Mackenzie Valley*;

(2) *Oil and gas approvals in the Northwest Territories—Sahtu Settlement Area: a guide to regulatory approval processes for oil and natural gas exploration and production on Sahtu lands and Crown lands in the Sahtu Settlement Area of the Northwest Territories*;

(3) *Oil and gas approvals in the Northwest Territories—Inuvialuit Settlement Region: a guide to regulatory approval processes for oil and natural gas exploration and production in the Inuvialuit Settlement Region*; and

(4) *Guide to Oil and Gas Approvals in the Gwich'in Settlement Area*.

24 Accessible today through the Internet archive at http://web.archive.org/web/20050415080111/www.neb-one.gc.ca/newsroom/Speeches/KWVEnergyEnvNaturalResourcesCC2001_04_24_e.htm at accompanying text for slide 19 of the PowerPoint presentation.

25 The Mackenzie Valley Environmental Impact Review Board maintains a website at http://www.reviewboard.ca/.

26 The Mackenzie Valley Land and Water Board maintains a website at http://www.mvlwb.com/.

27 The Northwest Territories Water Board maintained a website, viewable today at http://web.archive.org/web/20110207033240/http://www.nwtwb.com/.

28 The Environmental Impact Screening Committee maintains a website at http://www.screeningcommittee.ca/.

29 The Environmental Impact Review Board maintains a website at http://www.eirb.ca/.

30 The Inuvialuit Land Administration maintains a website at http://www.inuvialuitland.com/.

31 The Inuvialuit Game Council maintains a website at http://www.jointsecretariat.ca/igc.html.

32 The Sahtu Land and Water Board maintains a website at http://slwb.com/.

33 The Gwich'in Land and Water Board maintains a website at http://glwb.com/.

34 The text is available today through the Internet archive at http://web.archive.org/web/20040824080506/www.neb.gc.ca/newsroom/Speeches/KWVNorthernEA_RegulatoryCooperationCERI2002_03_04_e.htm.

35 The text of the address by Kenneth Vollman, entitled "Northern Environmental Assessment and Regulatory Cooperation" (March 4, 2002) is available today through the Internet archive at http://web.archive.org/web/20040824080506/www.neb.gc.ca/newsroom/Speeches/KWVNorthernEA_RegulatoryCooperationCERI2002_03_04_e.htm.

36 Ibid.

37 *National Energy Board Act*, R.S. 1985 c. N-7 at http://laws.justice.gc.ca/eng/N-7/index.html.

38 *Canada Oil and Gas Operations Act,* R.S. 1985 c. O-7 at http://laws.justice.gc.ca/
    eng/O-7/FullText.html. Known by its acronym COGOA, and administered by the National
    Energy Board, this statute provides in section 3 that it applies, *inter alia,* "in respect
    of the exploration and drilling for and the production, conservation, processing and
    transportation of oil and gas in the Northwest Territories."

39 The Inuvialuit Settlement Region, though straddling the delta of the Mackenzie River,
    is outside the "Mackenzie Valley" as defined in the *Mackenzie Valley Resource Man-
    agement Act.*

40 Written Submissions of the Attorney General of Canada in A-561-06.

41 *Cooperation Plan for the Environmental Impact Assessment and Regulatory Review
    of a Northern Gas Pipeline Project through the Northwest Territories* at http://www.
    neb-one.gc.ca/clf-nsi/rthnb/pplctnsbfrthnb/mcknzgsprjct/cprtnpln-eng.pdf and also
    at http://www.ceaa.gc.ca/Content/1/5/5/155701CE-6B5C-4F54-84E3-5D9B8297CD15/
    coop-plan_e.pdf.

42 Available at http://www.mackenziegasproject.com/theProject/regulatoryProcess/
    pipSubmission/Documents/Volume%201%20PIP.pdf.

43 See maps showing Nova Gas Transmission Limited interconnect facility at http://www.
    mackenziegasproject.com/theProject/regulatoryProcess/applicationSubmission/Images/
    MGP_EIS_Vol4_Figure_6.13.jpg and http://www.mackenziegasproject.com/theProject/
    regulatoryProcess/applicationSubmission/Images/0829-08-ML-03-010.jpg.

44 Application 1467403.

45 In 2008, TransCanada PipeLines Limited, the parent company of Nova Gas Transmis-
    sion Limited, applied to the NEB requesting that the TransCanada's Alberta pipeline
    system (also known as the Nova system) be declared under federal jurisdiction and that
    the NEB issue a Certificate of Public Convenience and Necessity for it under section 52
    of the *National Energy Board Act,* R.S. 1985 c. N-7. The NEB issued Hearing Order
    GH-5-2008 for this application and announced its intention to hold a public hearing
    process. On February 26, 2009, the NEB issued its Reasons for Decision confirming
    that it would assume jurisdiction over the Nova system. See National Energy Board
    Reasons for Decision in GH-5-2008 at https://www.neb-one.gc.ca/ll-eng/livelink.exe/fetch/2
    000/90464/90550/90715/518313/518500/549090/549124/A1I9K3_-_GH-5-2008_Rea-
    sons_for_Decision.pdf?nodeid=549125&vernum=0.

46 *Agreement for the Coordination of the Regulatory Review of the Mackenzie Gas
    Project* at http://www.neb-one.gc.ca/clf-nsi/rpblctn/ctsndrgltn/mmrndmndrstndng/
    mcknzgsprjct2004_04_22-eng.pdf ; also available in the Internet archive at http://
    web.archive.org/web/20061209215416/http://www.ngps.nt.ca/documents/Agreement-
    fortheCoordinationoftheRegulatoryReview_signed.pdf.

47 *Agreement for the Environmental Impact Review of the Mackenzie Gas Project* at
    http://www.reviewboard.ca/upload/project_document/EIR0405-001_Agreement_for_
    the_Environmental_Impact_Review_of_the_Mackenzie_Gas_Project_1254158065.
    pdf.

48 In the summer of 2003, a commercial decision was made by the project proponents
    to establish a southern terminus for the interprovincial pipeline of the Mackenzie
    Gas Project at a point just south of the Alberta/Northwest Territories border but
    still some 103 kilometres from the nearest connection point with the existing Nova
    pipeline system. A separate company, Nova, was to construct in Alberta a section
    of intraprovincial pipeline that would connect the existing Nova Gas Transmission
    Limited system with the southern terminus of the Mackenzie Gas Project pipeline and
    fall under the provincial regulatory authority of the Alberta Energy and Utilities Board
    (now the Alberta Energy Resources Conservation Board).

49 The *Rules of Procedure for the Conduct of the Environmental Impact Assessment of the Mackenzie Gas Project by a Joint Review Panel* are today referred to, though not available, at http://web.archive.org/web/20070623231621/http://www.ngps.nt.ca/registryDetail_e.asp?CategoryID=69.

50 National Energy Board Hearing Order GH-1-2004 at https://www.neb-one.gc.ca/ll-eng/livelink.exe/fetch/2000/90464/90550/338535/338661/343021/340839/NEB-1a_-_Hearing_Order_GH-1-2004_(NEB-1)_-_AoL3X9.pdf?nodeid=340840&vernum=0. The Supreme Court judgment in *Haida Nation* was rendered the week before, on November 28, 2004.

51 *National Energy Board Rules of Practice and Procedure, 1995*, SOR/95-208 at http://laws.justice.gc.ca/en/N-7/SOR-95-208/index.html.

52 The Agency distributed funding in several phases. Reports describing each phase and the funding recipients, including the Deh Cho and the Dene Tha', are public. Phase I Funding Report is at http://www.ceaa.gc.ca/default.asp?lang=en&xml=B2E2DFA2-59C7-46CA-90E1-E2F0A754F2F2. The Phase II Funding Report is at http://www.ceaa.gc.ca/default.asp?lang=en&xml=8E995396-D732-4DC4-AB3E-A00C6A182B7F. The Phase III Funding Report is at http://www.ceaa.gc.ca/default.asp?lang=en&xml=41843454-B358-476B-A308-07529FAF44E7. The Additional Phase III Funding Report is at http://www.ceaa.gc.ca/default.asp?lang=en&xml=1914FE7F-66ED-437A-B118-826FE571419A.

53 "Federal Funding Assists Dene Tha' First Nation to Participate in the Mackenzie Gas Project," Indian and Northern Affairs Canada press release (January 14, 2005) at http://www.aadnc-aandc.gc.ca/aiarch/mr/nr/j-a2005/2-02562-eng.asp. See also the funding programs described in the Indian and Northern Affairs Canada Backgrounder, Mackenzie Gas Project, at http://www.aadnc-aandc.gc.ca/eng/1100100016358.

54 Federal Court Application T-1686-04.

55 Action No. S-0001-CV-2004000291.

56 The settlement is accessible today at http://web.archive.org/web/20101123034933/http://www.dehcho.org/documents/negotiations/Settlement_Agmt[1].Signed_July_8.05%20(1).pdf. A Government of Canada perspective is described at http://www.aadnc-aandc.gc.ca/aiarch/mr/nr/m-a2005/02689bk-eng.asp.

57 The Environmental Impact Statement is located electronically at http://www.mackenziegasproject.com/theProject/regulatoryProcess/applicationSubmission/Applicationscope/EIS.html. A project update was filed in November 2005 at http://www.mackenziegasproject.com/theProject/regulatoryProcess/applicationSubmission/Applicationscope/projectupdate.html, and then a further project update in May 2007 at http://www.mackenziegasproject.com/theProject/regulatoryProcess/applicationSubmission/Applicationscope/projectupdate2007.html.

58 A massive amount of information was filed with the NEB and is available through the NEB website at Facilities, Gas, Imperial Oil Resources Ventures Limited (Mackenzie Gas Project), 2004-10-07—Application for the Construction and Operation of the Mackenzie Gas Pipeline—GH-1-2004 (Folder 338661). Information filed with the Joint Review Panel was available through the public registry maintained by the Northern Gas Project Secretariat, no longer in existence. The basic structure of the registry can be accessed today via the Internet archives at http://web.archive.org/web/20070608034406/http://www.ngps.nt.ca/registryDetail_e.asp. Some documents are located at http://www.ceaa.gc.ca/default.asp?lang=En&n=155701CE-1.

59 Notice of Application in Federal Court, Judicial Review Application T-867-05.

60 Ibid.

61 *Dene Tha' First Nation v. Canada (Minister of Environment)*, 2006 FC 307 (March 9, 2006) at http://decisions.fct-cf.gc.ca/en/2006/2006fc307/2006fc307.html.

62 NEB-028 - 05-01-13 - GH-1-2004 - Ruling No. 2 - Dene Tha' Motion 1 December 04 - Reasons for Decision (A0L8R4) at https://www.neb-one.gc.ca/ll-eng/livelink.exe/fe tch/2000/90464/90550/338535/338661/343021/347499/NEB-028_-_05-01-13_-_GH-1-2004_-_Ruling_No._2_-_Dene_Tha_Motion_1_Dec_04_-_Reasons_for_Decision_(A0 L8R4)?nodeid=347500&vernum=0.

63 The Joint Review Panel ruling on the motion was filed by the Dene Tha' First Nation on June 22, 2006.

64 At this time, under its Memorandum of Guidance as it was prior to the *Haida Nation* judgment of the Supreme Court, the NEB had included the adequacy of Aboriginal consultation by the Crown as an issue in its Hearing Order for the Mackenzie Gas Project. See NEB-001 - Hearing Order GH-1-2004, Mackenzie Gas Project (A08561) NEB-1 at https://www.neb-one.gc.ca/ll-eng/livelink.exe/fetch/ 2000/90464/90550/3385 35/338661/343021/340839/NEB-1a_-_Hearing_Order_GH-1-2004_(NEB-1)_-_A0L3X9. pdf?nodeid=340840&vernum=0.

65 *Dene Tha' First Nation v. Canada (Minister of Environment)*, 2006 FC 1354 (November 10, 2006) at http://decisions.fct-cf.gc.ca/en/2006/2006fc1354/2006fc1354.pdf.

66 Ibid., at para. 49.

67 Ibid., at para. 69.

68 Ibid., at para. 121.

69 The relief granted was described as "extraordinary" by Justine Duncan, Anastasia Lintner, and Hugh Wilkins in "Fracas Borealis: Consultation, Planning, and Managing Use of Canada's Northern Forests," in S. Berger and D. Saxe, eds., *Environmental Law: The Year in Review 2006* (Aurora: Canada Law Book, 2006), at 50.

70 A CBC article in regard to the settlement is located at http://www.cbc.ca/news/canada/ calgary/story/2007/07/23/mackenzie-pipeline.html. Contemporaneous private sector comment on the settlement is at http://www.millerthomson.com/assets/files/newsletter_attachments/issues/Aboriginal_Law_Update_March_2007.pdf.

71 *Canada (Environment) v. Imperial Oil Resources Ventures Ltd.*, 2008 FCA 20 (January 17, 2008) at para. 11, at http://decisions.fca-caf.gc.ca/en/2008/2008fca20/2008fca20. pdf.

72 *Rio Tinto Alcan Inc. v. Carrier Sekani Tribal Council*, 2010 SCC 43, [2010] 2 S.C.R. 650 at para. 44, at http://scc.lexum.org/en/2010/2010scc43/2010scc43.html.

73 *Foundation for a Sustainable Northern Future* at http://www.ceaa.gc.ca/155701CE-docs/Mackenzie_Gas_Panel_Report_Vol1-eng.pdf.

74 See *Foundation for a Sustainable Northern Future* at Chapter 15.4, Procurement and Business Opportunities, at http://www.ceaa.gc.ca/155701CE-docs/Mackenzie_Gas_Panel_Report_Vol2-eng.pdf, at 449: "These Access and Benefits Agreements that the Proponents are negotiating with NWT Aboriginal groups are confidential documents that the Panel has not seen or reviewed. ..."; and at 452-3:

> The Panel considers that ... the Benefits Agreements ... have the potential to provide important procurement and business opportunities within the NWT. However as their contents were not disclosed to the Panel, the Panel is unable to determine the magnitude and likelihood of these benefits. The Panel assumes that if negotiated agreements are acceptable to both parties, then the implied benefits in those agreements must also be acceptable to those parties.

75 *Foundation for a Sustainable Northern Future* at Chapter 16.9.6, Panel Views and Recommendations, at http://www.ceaa.gc.ca/155701CE-docs/Mackenzie_Gas_Panel_Report_Vol2-eng.pdf.

76 *Foundation for a Sustainable Northern Future* at Chapter 16.9, Mackenzie Gas Project Impacts Fund, at http://www.ceaa.gc.ca/155701CE-docs/Mackenzie_Gas_Panel_Report_Vol2-eng.pdf.

77 *Mackenzie Gas Project Socio-Economic Agreement* at http://www.iti.gov.nt.ca/publications/2007/miningoilgas/070119_GNWT-MGP_SEA_Final_Signed.pdf.

A legal analysis of the *Agreement* was prepared by Nigel Bankes of the University of Calgary for Alternatives North; see Nigel Bankes, *A Policy Review of the Mackenzie Gas Project Socio-Economic Agreement* (August 2007) at http://aged.alternativesnorth.ca/pdf/BankesMGPSEAReviewforAlternativesNorthAug15.pdf.

78 *Foundation for a Sustainable Northern Future* at Chapter 16.8, Socio-Economic Agreement, at http://www.ceaa.gc.ca/155701CE-docs/Mackenzie_Gas_Panel_Report_Vol2-eng.pdf.

79 *Mackenzie Gas Project Impacts Act*, S.C. 2006 c. 4, s. 208 at http://www.canlii.org/en/ca/laws/stat/sc-2006-c-4-s-208/latest/sc-2006-c-4-s-208.html. The Parliamentary Secretary to the Minister of Indian and Northern Affairs said that the legislation was intended "to support regional projects that help to alleviate the socio-economic impacts on communities affected by this project." See http://www2.parl.gc.ca/HousePublications/Publication.aspx?DocId=2449784&Language=E&Mode=1&Parl=39&Ses=1.

80 *Mackenzie Valley Resource Management Act*, S.C. 1998 c. 25 at http://laws.justice.gc.ca/en/M-0.2/index.html.

Consideration of report by agencies

137. (1) A designated regulatory agency shall, after considering the report of a review panel,

(a) adopt the recommendation of the review panel or refer it back to the panel for further consideration; or

(b) after consulting the review panel, adopt the recommendation with modifications or reject it.

81 Available at http://www.ec.gc.ca/bpgm-mgpo/default.asp?lang=En&n=EFF97846-1.

82 National Energy Board, Reasons for Decision, sec. 2.4.5 at http://www.neb-one.gc.ca/clf-nsi/rthnb/pplctnsbfrthnb/mcknzgsprjct/rfd/rfdv2ch2-eng.html.

83 Covering letter at https://www.neb-one.gc.ca/ll-eng/livelink.exe/fetch/2000/90464/90550/338535/338661/343021/603209/NEB-210A__-_Letter_to_GH1-2004_Parties_re_Proposed_Conditions_(A1S0T9).pdf?nodeid=603210&vernum=0. Mackenzie Gas Project—GH-1-2004 Hearing—Proposed Conditions for the Mackenzie Valley Pipeline and Mackenzie Gathering System Conditions at https://www.neb-one.gc.ca/ll-eng/livelink.exe/fetch/2000/90464/90550/338535/338661/343021/603209/NEB-210C_-_Proposed_Conditions_to_GH-1-2004_(A1S0U1_).pdf?nodeid=603329&vernum=0.

84 See the letter from the Assistant Deputy Minister, Mackenzie Gas Project, to the Joint Review Panel, dated September 1, 2010, at https://www.ec.gc.ca/bpgm-mgpo/default.asp?lang=En&n=244F3A14-1&wsdoc=7883685B-CE63-448B-9E5F-32E6117EB3CA; and the letter from the Joint Review Panel to the Assistant Deputy Minister for the Mackenzie Gas Project, September 3, 2010, at http://www.naturecanada.ca/pdf/Letter%20from%20JRP-%20Response%20to%20Government%20-%20September%203.pdf.

85   Consult to Modify Process: Next Steps at http://www.ec.gc.ca/bpgm-mgpo/default. asp?lang=En&n=BABFA30A-1.

86   The response of the Joint Review Panel is at http://www.ec.gc.ca/bpgm-mgpo/9F636D2E-16F4-4194-A908-85A9B891F4E7/Letter---Response-to-Government---October-4.pdf and http://www.ec.gc.ca/bpgm-mgpo/default. asp?lang=En&n=9F636D2E-1.

87   The final response is at http://www.ceaa.gc.ca/Content/1/5/5/155701CE-6B5C-4F54-84E3-5D9B8297CD15/MGP_Final_Response.pdf:

It was initially anticipated that the Joint Review Panel would issue its final report within ten months of the commencement of the public hearings [on February 14, 2006]. The hearings, which ended November 29, 2007, took place over 115 days across 26 northern communities and in Edmonton, Alberta. The Joint Review Panel released its report on December 30, 2009, twenty-five months after the hearings concluded.

88   The *Joint Review Panel Agreement* was amended to fix a definite date (the end of December of 2009) for the JRP report. See *Amendment to the Agreement for an Environmental Impact Review of the Mackenzie Gas Project* at http://www.ceaa.gc.ca/Content/1/5/5/155701CE-6B5C-4F54-84E3-5D9B8297CD15/amendment-eng.pdf; and Office of the Auditor General of Canada, Environmental Petition No. 278, Concerns about the Mackenzie Gas Project Joint Review Panel's Funding and Contractual Arrangements at http://www.oag-bvg.gc.ca/internet/English/pet_278_e_32998.html. The JRP report issued in December 2009 described the project schedule, according to the most recent information filed with the JRP, as anticipating receipt of a Certificate of Public Convenience and Necessity and development plan approvals for the anchor fields in 2008 and receipt of all remaining regulatory approvals in 2008 and 2009.

89   Neil McCrank, *Road to Improvement: The Review of the Regulatory Systems Across the North* (May 2008) at http://www.reviewboard.ca/upload/ref_library/1217612729_ri08-eng.pdf.

90   Government of the Northwest Territories, *Approach to Regulatory Improvement* at http://www.executive.gov.nt.ca/documents/GNWTRegulatoryPositionsIntermediateMar20-09.pdf.

91   *Up Here Business* at http://www.upherebusiness.ca/node/261. See also the commentary at http://www.canada.com/calgaryherald/news/calgarybusiness/story.html?id=d5355f99-9916-40f5-b6ac-141147824db5&k=67541.

92   Canadian Northern Economic Development Agency at http://www.cannor.gc.ca/pr/faq-eng.asp.

93   National Energy Board, Mackenzie Gas Project, Reasons for Decision, GH-1-2004, at http://www.one-neb.gc.ca/clf-nsi/rthnb/pplctnsbfrthnb/mcknzgsprjct/rfd/rfd-eng. html; vol. 1: *Respecting All Voices: Our Journey to a Decision* at http://www.one-neb. gc.ca/clf-nsi/rthnb/pplctnsbfrthnb/mcknzgsprjct/rfd/rfdv1-eng.pdf; vol. 2: *Technical Considerations: Implementing the Decision* at http://www.one-neb.gc.ca/clf-nsi/rthnb/pplctnsbfrthnb/mcknzgsprjct/rfd/rfdv2-eng.pdf.

94   Letter and Order DP-01-2010 to Shell Canada Limited as managing partner of Shell Canada Energy—Development Plan for the Niglintgak gas field (A27756) at https://www.neb-one.gc.ca/ll-eng/livelink.exe/fetch/2000/90464/90550/338535/338661/343021/659035/A1W9G5_-_Letter_and_Order_DP-01-2010.pdf?nodeid=659036&vernum=0; letter and Order DP-02-2010 to Imperial Oil Resources Limited—Development Plan for the Taglu gas field (A27757) at https://www.neb-one.gc.ca/ll-eng/livelink.exe/fetch/2000/90464/90550/338535/338661/343021/659223/A1W9G8_-_Letter_and_Order_DP-02-2010.pdf?nodeid=659224&vernum=0; letter and Order DP-03-2010 to

ConocoPhillips Canada and ExxonMobil Canada Properties—Development Plan for the Parsons Lake gas field (A27758) at https://www.neb-one.gc.ca/ll-eng/livelink.exe/ fetch/2000/90464/90550/338535/338661/343021/659227/A1W9H1_-_Letter_and_Order_DP-03-2010.pdf?nodeid=659228&vernum=0.

95 National Energy Board, Mackenzie Gas Project, Reasons for Decision, GH-1-2004, vol. 1, Chapter 1.3 at http://www.neb-one.gc.ca/clf-nsi/rthnb/pplctnsbfrthnb/mcknzgsprjct/rfd/rfd-eng.html.

96 Ibid., vol. 1, Chapter 1.3, at 13.

97 Ibid., vol. 2, Chapter 9.5, at 206.

98 Ibid., vol. 1, Chapter 1, at 13.

99 Ibid., vol. 2, Chapter 9.

100 Ibid., vol. 2, Chapter 9, at 207.

101 Ibid., vol. 2, Chapter 10.1.2.

102 Ibid., vol. 2, Chapter 9.5.2.

103 PC 2011-0260 at http://www.pco-bcp.gc.ca/oic-ddc.asp?lang=eng&Page=&txtOICID =&txtFromDate=&txtToDate=&txtPrecis=mackenzie+gas&txtDepartment=&txtA ct=&txtChapterNo=&txtChapterYear=&txtBillNo=&rdoComingIntoForce=&DoS earch=Search+%2F+List&viewattach=24023&blnDisplayFlg=1\.

104 PC 2011-0259 at http://www.pco-bcp.gc.ca/oic-ddc.asp?lang=eng&Page=&txtOICID =&txtFromDate=&txtToDate=&txtPrecis=mackenzie+gas&txtDepartment=&txtA ct=&txtChapterNo=&txtChapterYear=&txtBillNo=&rdoComingIntoForce=&DoS earch=Search+%2F+List&viewattach=24022&blnDisplayFlg=1.

105 PC 2011-0258 at http://www.pco-bcp.gc.ca/oic-ddc.asp?lang=eng&Page=&txtOICID =&txtFromDate=&txtToDate=&txtPrecis=mackenzie+gas&txtDepartment=&txtA ct=&txtChapterNo=&txtChapterYear=&txtBillNo=&rdoComingIntoForce=&DoS earch=Search+%2F+List&viewattach=24021&blnDisplayFlg=1.

106 National Energy Board, Mackenzie Gas Project, Reasons for Decision, GH-1-2004, vol. 1, Chapter 4.1 at http://www.neb-one.gc.ca/clf-nsi/rthnb/pplctnsbfrthnb/mcknzgsprjct/rfd/rfd-eng.html.

107 See Governor in Council Appointments, Corporation for the Mitigation of Mackenzie Gas Project Impacts at http://www.appointments-nominations.gc.ca/prflOrg.asp?OrgID=MKZ&type-typ=&lang=eng.

108 The Alberta Clipper Pipeline Project is described at http://www.enbridge.com/Alberta-Clipper-and-Southern-Lights.aspx and at http://www.neb-one.gc.ca/clf-nsi/archives/rthnb/pplctnsbfrthnb/pplctnsbfrthnbrchv/nbrdglbrtclppr_oh_4_2007/nbrdglbrtclppr_oh_4_2007-eng.html.

109 The Southern Lights Pipeline Project is described at http://www.enbridge-expansion.com/expansion/main.aspx?id=1216 and at http://www.neb-one.gc.ca/clf-nsi/archives/rthnb/pplctnsbfrthnb/pplctnsbfrthnbrchv/nbrdgsthrnlghts_oh_3_2007/nbrdgsthrnlghts_oh_3_2007-eng.html#s2.

110 The Keystone Pipeline Project is described at http://www.transcanada.com/keystone.html and at http://www.neb-one.gc.ca/clf-nsi/archives/rthnb/pplctnsbfrthnb/pplctnsbfrthnbrchv/trnscndkystnxlppln_oh_1_2009-eng.html/trnscndkystnxlppln_oh_1_2009-eng.html.

111 The National Energy Board process for the Mackenzie Gas Project, in comparison, was initiated under the pre-*Haida Nation* Memorandum of Guidance.

112 *Brokenhead Ojibway First Nation v. Canada (Attorney General)*, 2009 FC 484 at http://decisions.fct-cf.gc.ca/en/2009/2009fc484/2009fc484.html.

113 Four appeals were filed with the Federal Court of Appeal from the National Energy Board decisions to issue certificates in regard to the three pipeline projects. These four appeals were all heard together, and a single judgment was rendered on October 23, 2009, in *Standing Buffalo Dakota First Nation v. Enbridge Pipelines Inc.*, 2009 FCA 308 at http://decisions.fca-caf.gc.ca/en/2009/2009fca308/2009fca308.html. Four applications for leave to appeal were filed with the Supreme Court from this single Federal Court of Appeal decision, and all were dismissed. See (1) *Standing Buffalo Dakota First Nation, et al. v. TransCanada Keystone Pipeline GP Ltd., et al.*, SCC Case 33482 at http://www.scc-csc.gc.ca/case-dossier/cms-sgd/dock-regi-eng.aspx?cas=33482; (2) *Standing Buffalo Dakota First Nation, et al. v. Enbridge Southern Lights GP Inc. on behalf of Enbridge Southern Lights LP, et al.*, SCC Case 33481 at http://www.scc-csc.gc.ca/case-dossier/cms-sgd/dock-regi-eng.aspx?cas=33481; (3) *Standing Buffalo Dakota First Nation, et al. v. Enbridge Pipelines Inc., et al,.* SCC Case 33480 at http://www.scc-csc.gc.ca/case-dossier/cms-sgd/dock-regi-eng.aspx?cas=33480; and (4) *Sweetgrass First Nation, et al. v. National Energy Board, et al.*, SCC Case 33462 at http://www.scc-csc.gc.ca/case-dossier/cms-sgd/dock-regi-eng.aspx?cas=33462.

114 Hearing Order OH-3-2007, Application for the Southern Lights Pipeline Project at https://www.neb-one.gc.ca/ll-eng/livelink.exe/fe ch/2000/90464/90552/441806/456607/459848/459189/A-1a__Hearing_OH-3-2007_re_Enbridge_Southern_Lights_Project__A0Y5R6__.pdf?nodeid=459190&vernum=0;

Hearing Order OH-1-2007, TransCanada Keystone Pipeline GP Ltd. Application at https://www.neb-one.gc.ca/ll-eng/livelink.exe/fetch/2000/90464/90552/418396/446070/446078/451448/A-1a_-__Letter_and_Hearing_Order_OH-1-2007__(A0X6Y1_).pdf?nodeid=451449&vernum=0;

and Hearing Order OH-4-2007, Enbridge Pipelines Inc. Alberta Clipper Expansion Project Application of May 30, 2007, at https://www.neb-one.gc.ca/ll-eng/livelink.exe/fetch/2000/90464/90552/92263/452395/465178/465117/468138/A-1A_Hearing_Order_OH-4-2007_-_Enbridge_Pipelines_Inc._-_Alberta_Clipper_Expansion_Project_(A0Z4I6)?nodeid=468139&vernum=0.

115 The Southern Lights regulatory documents are at https://www.neb-one.gc.ca/ll-eng/livelink.exe?func=ll&objId=456607&objAction=browse&sort=name; the Keystone regulatory documents are at https://www.neb-one.gc.ca/ll-eng/livelink.exe?func=ll&objId=446070&objAction=browse&sort=-name; the Alberta Clipper regulatory documents are at https://www.neb-one.gc.ca/ll-eng/livelink.exe?func=ll&objId=465178&objAction=browse.

116 Southern Lights Pipeline Project, Applications by Enbridge Southern Lights GP Inc. on Behalf of Enbridge Southern Lights LP and Enbridge Pipelines Inc., Vol. 1, Chapter 6.3 at https://www.neb-one.gc.ca/ll-eng/livelink.exe/fet ch/2000/90464/90552/441806/456607/459768/456266/B-1b_Southern_Lights_Application_-_Vol_I_A0Y1Q0.pdf?nodeid=456267&vernum=0;

Keystone Application, Sec. 11.3.4 and Table 4.0 at https://www.neb-one.gc.ca/ll-eng/livelink.exe/fetch/2000/90464/90552/418396/446070/446079/444693/B-1n_-_Consultation_(Tab_11)__A0X2H4_.pdf?nodeid=444733&vernum=0;

Alberta Clipper Expansion Project, Application by Enbridge Pipelines Inc., Vol. 1, Chapter 6.3 and Tables 6-12 and 6-13 at https://www.neb-one.gc.ca/ll-eng/livelink.exe/fetch/2000/90464/90552/92263/452395/465178/465179/464927/B-1B_Volume_1__-_Alberta_Clipper_Expansion_Project_Application_(A0Z0V6).pdf?nodeid=464931&vernum=0.

117 National Energy Board, TransCanada Keystone Pipeline GP Ltd., Reasons for Decision, OH-1-2007, at 41, at https://www.neb-one.gc.ca/ll-eng/livelink.exe/fet ch/2000/90464/90552/418396/446070/478070/477791/A1A4H2_-_Reasons_for_Deci-sion_OH-1-2007.pdf?nodeid=477856&vernum=0.

118 Pursuant to section 35 of the National Energy Board *Rules of Practice and Procedure, 1995,* SOR 95/2008.

119 Notice of Motion by Standing Buffalo Dakota First Nation at https://www.neb-one.gc.ca/ll-eng/livelink.exe/fetch/2000/90464/90552/441806/456607/459849/461439/481619/C-13-11b_SBDFN_s._35_Notice_of_Motion-October_10-07_-_A1A6T3__?nodeid=4816 23&vernum=0.

120 The National Energy Board decision on the Motion filed by the Standing Buffalo is located within National Energy Board, Reasons for Decision in the Matter of Enbridge Southern Lights GP on Behalf of Enbridge Southern Lights LP and Enbridge Pipelines Inc., H-3-2007, Chapter 2.2 at 10, at https://www.neb-one.gc.ca/ll-eng/livelink.exe/fet ch/2000/90464/90552/441806/456607/499885/499563/A1D4Q5_-_Reasons_For_Deci-sion.pdf?nodeid=499564&vernum=0.

121 Ibid., at 11.

122 Ibid., at 11.

123 See National Energy Board, Alberta Clipper Pipeline Project, Reasons for Decision, OH-4-2007 at https://www.neb-one.gc.ca/ll-eng/livelink.exe/fech/2000/90464/90552/ 92263/452395/465178/500099/500012/A1D5A3_-_Reasons_for_Decision_OH-4-2007. pdf?nodeid=500013&vernum=0;

the Southern Lights Pipeline Project, Reasons for Decision, OH-3-2007 at https://www.neb-one.gc.ca/ll-eng/livelink.exe/fetch/2000/90464/90552/441806/456607/499885/499563/ A1D4Q5_-_Reasons_For_Decision.pdf?nodeid=499564&vernum=0;

and the Keystone Pipeline Project, Reasons for Decision, OH-1-2007 at https://www.neb-one.gc.ca/ll-eng/livelink.exe/fetch/2000/90464/90552/418396/446070/478070/477791/ A1A4H2_-_Reasons_for_Decision_OH-1-2007.pdf?nodeid=477856&vernum=0.

124 The Governor in Council approval of the Keystone Pipeline Project was evidenced in P.C. 2007-1786 dated November 22, 2007, at http://www.pco-bcp.gc.ca/OIC-DDC.as p?lang=eng&Page=secretariats&txtOICID=2007-1786&txtFromDate=&txtToDate= &txtPrecis=&txtDepartment=&txtAct=&txtChapterNo=&txtChapterYear=&txtBi llNo=&rdoComingIntoForce=&DoSearch=Search+%2F+List&viewattach=17553.

Approval of the Southern Lights Pipeline Project was evidenced in P.C. 2008-856 dated May 8, 2008, at http://www.pco-bcp.gc.ca/OIC-DDC.asp?lang=eng&Page=secretariat s&txtOICID=2008-856+&txtFromDate=&txtToDate=&txtPrecis=&txtDepartment= &txtAct=&txtChapterNo=&txtChapterYear=&txtBillNo=&rdoComingIntoForce= &DoSearch=Search+%2F+List&viewattach=18694.

Approval of the Alberta Clipper Pipeline Project was evidenced in P.C. 2008-857, also dated May 8, 2008, at http://www.pco-bcp.gc.ca/OIC-DDC.asp?lang=eng&Page=secr etariats&txtOICID=2008-857+&txtFromDate=&txtToDate=&txtPrecis=&txtDepa rtment=&txtAct=&txtChapterNo=&txtChapterYear=&txtBillNo=&rdoComingIn toForce=&DoSearch=Search+%2F+List&viewattach=18695.

125 *Brokenhead Ojibway First Nation v. Canada (Attorney General),* 2009 FC 484 at http://decisions.fct-cf.gc.ca/en/2009/2009fc484/2009fc484.html.

126 Ibid., at paras. 42 and 43.

127 Ibid., at para. 45.

128 *Standing Buffalo Dakota First Nation v. Enbridge Pipelines Inc.*, 2009 FCA 308 at http://decisions.fca-caf.gc.ca/en/2009/2009fca308/2009fca308.html.

129 Ibid., at para. 46.

130 *Quebec (Attorney General) v. Canada (National Energy Board)*, [1994] 1 S.C.R. 159 at 184.

131 *Rio Tinto Alcan Inc. v. Carrier Sekani Tribal Council*, 2010 SCC 43, [2010] 2 S.C.R. 650 at http://scc.lexum.org/en/2010/2010scc43/2010scc43.html.

132 Supreme Court of Canada Notice, Judgment in Leave Applications, December 2, 2010, at http://scc.lexum.org/en/news_release/2010/10-12-02.3a/10-12-02.3a.html.

CHAPTER SIX: CONCLUDING OBSERVATIONS

1   The archived webcast can be viewed at the Supreme Court of Canada website at http://www.scc-csc.gc.ca/case-dossier/cms-sgd/webcast-webdiffusion-eng.aspx?cas=33132. The quoted question appears at 03:02:22 of the webcast as the conclusion of a longer series of questions beginning at 02:59:50.

2   *2747-3174 Québec Inc. v. Québec (Régie des permis d'alcool)*, [1996] 3 S.C.R. 919 at http://scc.lexum.org/en/1996/1996scr3-919/1996scr3-919.html: "Both the rules of natural justice and the duty of fairness are variable standards. Their content will depend on the circumstances of the case, the statutory provisions and the nature of the matter to be decided."

3   *Taku River Tlingit First Nation v. British Columbia (Project Assessment Director)*, 2004 SCC 74, [2004] 3 S.C.R. 550 at para. 12, at http://scc.lexum.org/en/2004/2004scc74/2004scc74.html:

> Through the environmental assessment process, the TRTFN's concerns with the road proposal became apparent. Its concerns crystallized around the potential effect on wildlife and traditional land use, as well as the lack of adequate baseline information by which to measure subsequent effects. It was the TRTFN's position that the road ought not to be approved in the absence of a land use planning strategy and away from the treaty negotiation table. The environmental assessment process was unable to address these broader concerns directly, but the project assessment director facilitated the TRTFN's access to other provincial agencies and decision makers. For example, the Province approved funding for wildlife monitoring programs as desired by the TRTFN (the Grizzly Bear Long-term Cumulative Effects Assessment and Ungulate Monitoring Program). The TRTFN also expressed interest in TRTFN jurisdiction to approve permits for the project, revenue sharing, and TRTFN control of the use of the access road by third parties. It was informed that these issues were outside the ambit of the certification process and could only be the subject of later negotiation with the government.

4   *Mikisew Cree First Nation v. Canada (Minister of Canadian Heritage)*, 2005 SCC 69, [2005] 3 S.C.R. 388, at para. 54, at http://scc.lexum.org/en/2005/2005scc69/2005scc69.html.

5   *Quebec (Attorney General) v. Canada (National Energy Board)*, [1994] 1 S.C.R. 159 at http://scc.lexum.org/en/1994/1994scr1-159/1994scr1-159.html.

6   *In re Canadian Radio-Television Commission and in re London Cable TV Ltd.*, [1976] 2 F.C. 621 (FCA) at 624–25.

7   *Halfway River First Nation v. British Columbia (Minister of Forests)*, 1999 BCJ No. 1880 at para. 160, per Finch J.A. (as he then was), at http://www.canlii.org/en/bc/bcca/doc/1999/1999bcca470/1999bcca470.html.

8   *Beckman v. Little Salmon/Carmacks First Nation*, 2010 SCC 53, [2010] 3 S.C.R. 103 at http://scc.lexum.org/en/2010/2010scc53/2010scc53.html.

9   Ibid., at para. 33.

10 *Haida Nation v. British Columbia (Minister of Forests)*, 2004 SCC 73, [2004] 3 S.C.R. 511 at para. 53, at http://scc.lexum.org/en/2004/2004scc73/2004scc73.html.

11 *Taku River Tlingit First Nation v. British Columbia (Project Assessment Director)*, 2004 SCC 74, [2004] 3 S.C.R. 550 at para. 22, at http://scc.lexum.org/en/2004/2004scc74/2004scc74.html.

12 *Mikisew Cree First Nation v. Canada (Minister of Canadian Heritage)*, 2005 SCC 69, [2005] 3 S.C.R. 388 at para. 64, at http://scc.lexum.org/en/2005/2005scc69/2005scc69.html.

13 Ibid., at para. 66.

14 Objectives of the development process described in Chapter 12 include that in 12.1.1.7, which is to provide for a development assessment process that "avoids duplication in the review process for Projects and, to the greatest extent practicable, provides certainty to all affected parties and Project proponents with respect to procedures, information requirements, time requirements and costs." See *Little Salmon/Carmacks First Nation Final Agreement* at http://www.eco.gov.yk.ca/pdf/little_salmon_carmacks_fa.pdf.

15 The citations that follow in this paragraph are taken from Beverley McLachlin, "The Evolution of the Law of Private Obligation: The Influence of Justice LaForest," in *Gerard v. La Forest at the Supreme Court of Canada 1985–1997*, edited by Rebecca Johnson and John P. McCoy, with Thomas Kuttner and H. Wade MacLauchlan (Winnipeg: University of Manitoba, 2000) at 22 ff.

16 *R. v. Sparrow*, [1990] 1 S.C.R. 1075 at http://scc.lexum.org/en/1990/1990scr1-1075/1990scr1-1075.html.

17 *Taku River Tlingit First Nation v. British Columbia (Project Assessment Director)*, 2004 SCC 74, [2004] 3 S.C.R. 550, at http://scc.lexum.org/en/2004/2004scc74/2004scc74.html.

18 *Mikisew Cree First Nation v. Canada (Minister of Canadian Heritage)*, 2005 SCC 69, [2005] 3 S.C.R. 388 at http://scc.lexum.org/en/2005/2005scc69/2005scc69.html.

19 *R. v. Sparrow*, [1990] 1 S.C.R. 1075 at 1119, at http://scc.lexum.org/en/1990/1990scr1-1075/1990scr1-1075.html.

20 *Douglas/Kwantlen Faculty Assn. v. Douglas College*, [1990] 3 S.C.R. 570 at http://csc.lexum.org/en/1990/1990scr3-570/1990scr3-570.html.

21 *Cuddy Chicks Ltd. v. Ontario (Labour Relations Board)*, [1991] 2 S.C.R. 5 at http://scc.lexum.org/en/1991/1991scr2-5/1991scr2-5.html; *Douglas/Kwantlen Faculty Assn. v. Douglas College*, [1990] 3 S.C.R. 570 at http://scc.lexum.org/en/1990/1990scr3-570/1990scr3-570.html; and *Tétreault-Gadoury v. Canada (Employment and Immigration Commission)*, [1991] 2 S.C.R. 22 at http://scc.lexum.org/en/1991/1991scr2-22/1991scr2-22.html.

22 *Tétreault-Gadoury v. Canada (Employment and Immigration Commission)*, [1991] 2 S.C.R. 22 at http://scc.lexum.org/en/1991/1991scr2-22/1991scr2-22.html.

23 *Douglas/Kwantlen Faculty Assn. v. Douglas College*, [1990] 3 S.C.R. 570 at http://csc.lexum.org/en/1990/1990scr3-570/1990scr3-570.html.

24 *R. v. Conway*, 2010 SCC 22, [2010] 1 S.C.R. 765 at http://scc.lexum.org/en/2010/2010scc22/2010scc22.html.

25 *Rio Tinto Alcan Inc. v. Carrier Sekani Tribal Council,* 2010 SCC 43 [2010] 2 S.C.R. 650 at http://scc.lexum.org/en/2010/2010scc43/2010scc43.html.

26 Ibid., at para. 55:

> [55] The duty on a tribunal to consider consultation and the scope of that inquiry depends on the mandate conferred by the legislation that creates the tribunal. Tribunals are confined to the powers conferred on them by their constituent legislation: *R. v. Conway,* 2010 SCC 22, [2010] 1 S.C.R 765. It follows that the role of particular tribunals in relation to consultation depends on the duties and powers the legislature has conferred on it.

27 *National Energy Board Act,* R.S. 1985 c. N-7, s. 11(3).

28 Ibid., s. 12(2).

29 *Quebec (Attorney General) v. Canada (National Energy Board),* [1994] 1 S.C.R. 159 at http://scc.lexum.org/en/1994/1994scr1-159/1994scr1-159.html.

30 *Consideration of Aboriginal Concerns in National Energy Board Decisions* (July 2008) at https://www.neb-one.gc.ca/ll-eng/livelink.exe/fetch/2000/90463/522930/522832/Consideration_of_Aboriginal_Concerns_in_National_Energy_Board_Decisions_(A0T5X3).pdf?nodeid=524268&vernum=0.

31 *Public Inquiries Act,* R.S.A. 2000, c. P-39, s. 5 at http://www.canlii.org/en/ab/laws/stat/rsa-2000-c-p-39/latest/rsa-2000-c-p-39.html: "The commissioner or commissioners have the same power to enforce the attendance of persons as witnesses and to compel them to give evidence and to produce documents and things as is vested in a court of record in civil cases, and the same privileges and immunities as a judge of the Court of Queen's Bench."

32 *Energy Resources Conservation Act,* R.S.A. 2000 c. E-10 s. 36 at http://www.canlii.org/en/ab/laws/stat/rsa-2000-c-e-10/latest/rsa-2000-c-e-10.html: "For the purpose of any hearing, inquiry or investigation pursuant to this Act, the Board and any member of it and any other person authorized by the Board to conduct a hearing, or to make an inquiry or investigation, has all the powers of a commissioner appointed under the *Public Inquiries Act.*"

33 Letter to the Chair of the Energy Resources Conservation Board from the Office of the Minister of Alberta Energy (mailed December 20, 2007) at http://www.energy.alberta.ca/Electricity/pdfs/ERCB_Mand.pdf.

34 *Quebec (Attorney General) v. Canada (National Energy Board),* [1994] 1 S.C.R. 159 at http://scc.lexum.org/en/1994/1994scr1-159/1994scr1-159.html.

35 *Rio Tinto Alcan Inc. v. Carrier Sekani Tribal Council,* 2010 SCC 43, [2010] 2 S.C.R. 650 at para. 74, at http://scc.lexum.org/en/2010/2010scc43/2010scc43.html.

36 Ibid.

37 *Quebec (Attorney General) v. Canada (National Energy Board),* [1994] 1 S.C.R. 159 at http://scc.lexum.org/en/1994/1994scr1-159/1994scr1-159.html, approving Reed J. of the Trial Division of the Federal Court in *Friends of the Island Inc. v. Canada (Minister of Public Works),* [1993] 2 F.C. 229 at 264.

38 *Rio Tinto Alcan Inc. v. Carrier Sekani Tribal Council,* 2010 SCC 43, [2010] 2 S.C.R. 650 at para. 58, at http://scc.lexum.org/en/2010/2010scc43/2010scc43.html.

39 *Mikisew Cree First Nation v. Canada (Minister of Canadian Heritage),* 2005 SCC 69, [2005] 3 S.C.R. 388 at para. 34, at http://scc.lexum.org/en/2005/2005scc69/2005scc69.html.

40 *Weber v. Ontario Hydro,* [1995] 2 S.C.R. 929, at para. 15, at http://scc.lexum.org/en/1995/1995scr2-929/1995scr2-929.html.

Bibliography

Alvarez Sloan and Associates. "Guide to Oil and Gas Approvals in the Inuvialuit Settlement Region." 2001.

Auditor General of British Columbia. Treaty Negotiations in British Columbia: An Assessment of the Effectiveness of British Columbia's Management and Administrative Processes. Report No. 3, November 2006.

Auditor General of Canada. "Chapter 7: Federal Participation in the British Columbia Treaty Process." In 2006 November Report of the Auditor General of Canada to the House of Commons. November 2006.

Bankes, Nigel. "A Policy Review of the Mackenzie Gas Project Socio-Economic Agreement." August 2007.

Breen, David. Alberta's Petroleum Industry and the Conservation Board. Edmonton: University of Alberta Press, 1993.

British Columbia Utilities Commission. "A Participants' Guide to the British Columbia Utilities Commission." N.d.

——. "Public Hearing Process." N.d.

Brown, Howard L. "Expanding the Effectiveness of the European Union's Environmental Impact Assessment Law." Boston College International and Comparative Law Review 20, 2 (1997): 313–34.

Canadian Bar Association. National Aboriginal Law Section. Examination of Canada's Specific Claims Policy. 2006.

Canadian Council of Ministers of the Environment. Canada Wide Accord on Environmental Harmonization. N.d.

——. *Sub-Agreement on Environmental Assessment.* N.d.

Commissioner of the Environment and Sustainable Development. "Chapter 1: Applying the *Canadian Environmental Assessment Act, Why It's Important.*" In 2009 *Fall Report of the Commissioner of the Environment and Sustainable Development,* by the Auditor General of Canada, 2009.

Duncan, Justine, Anastasia Lintner, and Hugh Wilkins. "Fracas Borealis: Consultation, Planning, and Managing Use of Canada's Northern Forests." In *Environmental Law: The Year in Review 2006,* edited by Stanley D. Saxe and Dianne Berger, 43–58. Toronto: Canada Law Book, 2006.

Erlandson and Associates. "Guide to Oil and Gas Approvals in the Gwich'in Settlement Area." 2002.

——. "Guide to Oil and Gas Approvals in the Sahtu Settlement Area." 2002.

——. "Guide to Oil and Gas Approvals in the Southern Mackenzie Valley NWT." 2000.

Gray, Earle. *Forty Years in the Public Interest: A History of the National Energy Board.* Vancouver: Douglas and McIntyre in cooperation with the National Energy Board, 2000.

Hitch, Michael, and Courtney Riley Fidler. "Impact Benefit Agreements: A Contentious Issue for Environmental and Aboriginal Justice." *Environmental Journal* 25, 2 (2007): 45–69.

Hogg, Peter. "The Constitutional Basis of Aboriginal Rights." In *Aboriginal Law since Delgamuukw,* edited by Maria Morellato, 3–16. Toronto: Canada Law Book, 2009.

Hunt, Madame Justice Constance C. "Toward the Twenty-First Century: A Canadian Legal Perspective on Resource and Environmental Law." *Osgoode Hall Law Journal* 31 (1993): 297–325.

International Association of Oil and Gas Producers. *Principles for Impact Assessment: The Environmental and Social Dimension.* August 1997.

International Council on Mining and Metals. "Good Practice Guide on Health Impact Assessment." N.d.

International Petroleum Industry Environment Conservation Association. *Guide to Social Impact Assessment in the Oil and Gas Industry.* 2004.

——. *Key Questions in Managing Social Issues in Oil and Gas Projects.* 2002.

Keenan, Irene, and Karyn Sosa. "Impact Benefit Agreements between Aboriginal Communities and Mining Companies: Their Use in Canada." October 2001.

Lambrecht, Kirk N. *The Administration of Dominion Lands, 1870–1930.* Regina: Canadian Plains Research Center, 1991.

Low, Cecilia A. *Energy and Utility Regulation in Alberta: Like Oil and Water?* Occasional Paper 25, Canadian Institute of Resources Law. N.d.

McCrank, Neil. *Road to Improvement: The Review of the Regulatory Systems across the North.* Report of the Minister's Special Representative, Public Works and Government Services. 2008.

McLachlin, Beverley. "The Evolution of the Law of Private Obligation: The Influence of Justice LaForest." In *Gerard v. LaForest at the Supreme Court of Canada 1985–1997,* edited by Rebecca Johnson and John P. McCoy, with Thomas Kuttner and H. Wade MacLauchlan, 21–46. Winnipeg: University of Manitoba Press, 2000.

National Aboriginal Health Organization. "Impact Benefit Agreements: A Tool for Healthy Inuit Communities?" March 2009.

National Energy Board. "Canadian Pipeline Transportation System: Transportation Assessment." June 2008.

——. "Consideration of Aboriginal Concerns in National Energy Board Decisions." July 2008.

——. "Consultation with Aboriginal Peoples." April 2002.

——. "Implications of the Supreme Court of Canada Decisions on the NEB's Memorandum of Guidance on Consultation with Aboriginal Peoples." August 2005.

——. "Memorandum of Guidance." March 2002.

National Round Table on the Environment and the Economy. "State of the Debate: Aboriginal Communities and Non-Renewable Resource Development." N.d.

Newman, Dwight G. *The Duty to Consult: New Relationships with Aboriginal Peoples.* Saskatoon: Purich Publishing, 2009.

Pape, Arthur. "The Duty to Consult and Accommodate: A Judicial Innovation Intended to Promote Reconciliation." In *Aboriginal Law since Delgamuukw,* edited by Maria Morellato, 313–332. Toronto: Canada Law Book, 2009.

Pearce, D., G. Atkinson, and S. Mourato. *Cost Benefit Analysis and the Environment: Recent Developments.* Paris: OECD, 2006.

Ray, Arthur J., and Donald J. Freeman. *An Economic Analysis of Relations between the Indians and the Hudson's Bay Company before 1763.* Toronto: University of Toronto Press, 1978.

Slattery, Brian. "Aboriginal Rights and the Honour of the Crown." *Supreme Court Law Review* 20 (2005): 433–45.

——. "Making Sense of Aboriginal and Treaty Rights." *Canadian Bar Review* 79 (2000): 196–224.

——. "Understanding Aboriginal Rights." *Canadian Bar Review* 66 (1987): 727–783.

Vollman, Kenneth. "Northern Environmental Assessment and Regulatory Cooperation." National Energy Board, March 2002.

Woodward and Company. "Benefit Sharing Agreements in British Columbia: A Guide for First Nations, Businesses, and Governments." N.d.

World Bank. "Environmental Assessment Sourcebook." 1999.

World Commission on Environment and Development. "Brundtland Report." In *Report of the National Task Force on Environment and Economy.* 1987.

MAP RESOURCES

Aboriginal Mapping Network

http://www.nativemaps.org/

Land Claims Agreement Coalition

http://www.landclaimscoalition.ca/

Government of Canada

    Timelines and Maps for Historical Treaties

    http://www.aadnc-aandc.gc.ca/eng/1100100032297

    Historical Indian Treaties in Canada

    http://www.aadnc-aandc.gc.ca/DAM/DAM-INTER-HQ/STAGING/
    texte-text/htoc_1100100032308_eng.pdf

Treaty Negotiations in British Columbia

http://www.aadnc-aandc.gc.ca/DAM/DAM-INTER-BC/STAGING/texte-text/
trynegc_1100100021020_eng.pdf

Treaty Commission of British Columbia (Annual Reports)

http://www.bctreaty.net/files/annuals.php

Natural Resources Canada, Historical Indian Treaties

http://atlas.nrcan.gc.ca/site/english/maps/reference/national/hist_trea-
ties/

Index

For Cases, Statutes, Constitutional Provisions and
Tribunal Decisions, see Tables on pages xv–xxii.

A

Aboriginal avocations, 32–33, 109; hunting, fishing, trapping, 78, 99, 108, 141n37; and NRTAS, 34–35

Aboriginal claims: impact of projects on, 71–72, 88

Aboriginal communities: and mineral, oil and gas exploration, 47; relationship-building with, 15; and the role of industry, 47

Aboriginal Communities and Non-renewable Resource Development Program, 47

Aboriginal concerns, 108, 118; as addressed in assessment and review, 101, 110; as addressed through NEB processes, 102; as balanced through accommodation, 59–60; as integrated into regulatory process, 94

Aboriginal consultation, 5, 23, 48, 92, 107, 112; adequacy of, 84, 87, 98, 105, 111; as defined, xxv, 3; on energy agreements, 70; and environmental assessment, 39; evidence of, 10; as honour of the Crown, 77; and industry, xxvi; as integrated, 9–10; law of, 1–2, 6, 11, 13, 18–20, 47, 53–55, 77, 108, 110;

and Mackenzie Gas Project, 90; and modern treaties, 25; as obligation, 65, 76; opportunities for, 103; as part of planning, 12; and pipeline projects, 95; on project impacts, 120; and reconciliation, 13; and regulatory review, 39; scope of, 72; and tribunals, 54, 110, 113, 118–19

Aboriginal Consultation and Accommodation: Updated Guidelines for Federal Officials to Fulfill the Duty to Consult 2011, 126n29

Aboriginal Consultation Policy (Ontario Energy Board), 125n24

Aboriginal engagement, 13, 91, 96–97; with pipeline projects, 96

Aboriginal interests, 6; and duty to consult and accommodate, 63; and impact benefit agreements, 117; project impacts on, 98

Aboriginal land claims, 15, 27, 56, 78, 86, 98, 100; agreements for, 22, 90, 113; negotiation of, 25, 27; policies for, 22, 78; processes for, 20; and tribunals, 46. *See also* comprehensive land claims

comprehensive land claims, 15, 79, 86, 90; policy, historical origin of, 22, 78. *See also* Aboriginal land claims

compromise, 115; as related to reconciliation process, 60, 116

Concerns about the Mackenzie Gas Project Joint Review Panel's Funding and Contractual Arrangements, 152n88

ConocoPhillips Canada, 152n94

Consideration of Aboriginal Concerns in National Energy Board Decisions, 77, 145n14, 158n30

constitutional law, 14, 114; protections of, 19; and rights, 20

constitutional obligations: of consultation, 13; of NRTAS, 35

constitutional protection: for Aboriginal and Treaty rights, 21, 30, 33; for Aboriginal avocations, 34

Consult to Modify Process, 89–90, 152n85

consultation: benefits of, 50; as constitutional obligation, 71; as defined, 65, 71; as enabling reconciliation, 141n10; as meaningful, 111; as part of project lifecycle, 59; public, 47, 109; and social and environmental assessment, 50; through NEB processes, 102

consultation process: as preserving Aboriginal interests, 56; as reciprocal, 102

contextual analysis, xxv, 4, 35, 113, 117–19; as related to duty to consult, 21, 112

Cooperative Plan for the Environmental Impact Assessment and Regulatory Review of a Northern Gas Pipeline Project through the Northwest Territories, 82, 148n41

corporate business model, 5–8

corporate social responsibility, 52, 135n3

Corporation for the Mitigation of Mackenzie Gas Project Impacts, 89, 94, 153n107

Council of Canadian Administrative Tribunals, 38, 136n6

courts: role in oversight of tribunal process, 14, 66, 113, 120

Crown: accommodation by for pipeline projects, 95; decision-making related to projects, 108, 110; decisions as adversely affecting Aboriginals, 108; duties toward reserve land, 19; and duty to consult, 96, 98, 101, 103–4, 115, 119; governance functions of, 4; as having fiduciary obligation to Aboriginal peoples, 76; as indifferent to Mikisew people, 61–62; and infringement of Haida's rights, 58; and negotiated treaties, 21; and obligation to consult, 57, 66, 108, 115, 119; responsiveness of, 13, 120

Crown consultation, 70, 76, 92, 119; adequacy of, 69, 72, 77, 87, 105, 116–17, 120; and approval of energy agreement, 68; as assessed by tribunals, 118; and assessments, 112; power to conduct, 74; process of, 118

Crown lands: administration and control of, 33

Crown sovereignty: as reconciled with Aboriginal sovereignty, 55

D

Dakota Nations of Manitoba, 97–98

Dakota Plains First Nation, 97

Dakota Tipi First Nation, 97

Deh Cho First Nations, 79–80, 85–86, 91

Deh Cho Process, 79, 85, 146n19

Dene Tha' First Nation, 80, 86, 150n63; and aboriginal consultation, 87; judicial review of case, 87

Development Plan for Niglintgak gas field, 152n94

Development Plan for Parsons Lake gas field, 94, 152n94

Development Plan for Taglu gas field, 94, 152n94

doctrine of *stare decisis*, 2

Dominion Lands Act, 31–32

Draft Aboriginal Consultation Guide for Preparing a Renewable Energy Approval (REA) Application (Ontario), 10, 125n26 duplicative process: reduction of, 38, 43–45, 80–83, 119, 157n14

duty to accommodate, xxv, 58; and Aboriginal interests, 63; constitutional nature of, 71; as part of consultation, 57

duty to consult, xxv, 6, 12, 14, 21, 58, 72, 110, 112; and Aboriginal interests, 63; constitutionality of, 54, 71; described, 63; as fostering reconciliation, 54; fulfilled by NEB process, 95; as honour of the Crown, 56, 141n10; in numbered treaties, 60; as obligation, 54, 64–65; on possible effects on Aboriginal rights, 144n68; regarding energy agreement, 69; regarding rights, 19; regarding Scoping Order, 68; scope of, 88

E

Eastmain-1-A and Rupert Diversion Project, 46

economic planning: as related to environmental planning, 40–42

Electricity Purchase Agreement (EPA), 67–73, 117, 119

Enbridge Pipelines Inc., 76, 95, 101, 154nn114,116

EnCana Shallow Gas Infill Development Project, 46, 126n33

environmental assessment, xxv–xxvi, 57, 79, 125n24; and Aboriginal concerns, 95, 101, 103; Aboriginal engagement in, 13, 91, 97; as addressing project impacts, 100; and administrative law principles, 66; as advisory, 42; as assessing impacts, 73; avoiding duplication of, 81; conducting of, 41; and constitutional responsibility, 40; and consultation, 47, 49, 119; as contributing to sustainable development, 39; costs of, 38; as decision-making process, 40; as defined, 48; and duty to consult, 111; functions of, 7, 11, 39; and gas development projects, 78; and impact and benefit agreements, 52; and impacts on Aboriginal peoples, 110; and industry, 111; as informing regulatory decision-making, 43; as integrated, 96; and joint review panels, 83; as law, 2; and Mackenzie Gas Project, 90; and natural resource development, 20; by

Parks Canada, 60; as part of project development, 1, 4, 9, 120; processes of, 45, 58–59, 62, 80, 82; and public consultation, 41; and reconciliation with Aboriginal peoples, 11; and reducing duplicative process, 44–45, 81, 83; responsibilities for, 8; as separate from regulatory review, 81; as spanning jurisdictions, 43–44; and sustainable development, 3, 5, 37; and tribunals, 10, 14, 46, 107–8, 114

Environmental Assessment and Review Process Guidelines Order, 124n15

Environmental Assessment Certificate, 46

environmental assessment law, 39

environmental impact assessment (EIA), 51, 80; panel for, 81; protection of, 37, 44

environmental impact review, 84

Environmental Impact Review Board, 80; website, 147n29

Environmental Impact Screening Committee, 80, 147n28

Environmental Impact Statement (EIS), 85–86, 149n57

environmental protection, xxvi, 3–5, 45–46

Environmental Screening Report, 96

Examination of Canada's Specific Claims Policy, 135n161

F

Facilities, Gas, Imperial Oil Resources Ventures Limited, 149n58

federalism, cooperative, 40, 43–44

First Nation of Nacho Nyak Dun, 24

First Nations Energy Summit, 145n12

First Nations Summit (BC), 26

formalism, 112–13

formalistic interpretation: and danger of logical fallacy in *Rio Tinto,* 118

Foundation for a Sustainable Northern Future, 150nn73,74, 151nn75,76,78

fur trade, 2, 32

O

oil and gas development, 46–47, 75

Ontario: joint review panels in, 46

Ontario Energy Board, 46, 125n25; *Aboriginal Consultation Policy*, 125n25

Ontario Power Generation Inc., 47

Organization for Economic Co-operation and Development, 49

P

Participant Funding Program Guide: Guide to the National Energy Board Participant Funding Program under the National Energy Board Act, 145n14

Peace Point reserve, 61, 141n31

pipeline projects: and litigation cases, 95, 117; potential infringement on rights by, 98, 102

Pipeline Regulation in Canada: A Guide for Landowners and the Public, 145n4

pipeline transportation system, 76

Policy Review of the Mackenzie Gas Project Socio-Economic Agreement, A, 151n77

pre-control: as test for asserting Métis rights, 31

Principles for Impact Assessment: The Environmental and Social Dimension, 139n71

procedural fairness, 67, 69, 108–9; and Aboriginal intervenors, 68, 84, 97; as administrative law principle, 66; in NEB processes, 99

Progressive Aboriginal Relations (PAR) Program, 139n61

project approval, xxv, 5, 38, 154n114; authority for, 13, 75, 95; conditions for, 8, 39, 58–59, 62; and Crown, 120; as informed by assessments, 7, 48–49, 51–52; as part of project development, 4, 13, 59; and regard for Aboriginal rights, 104; regulatory conditions of, 11, 43, 109, 111; responsibilities for, 8, 39; and tribunals, 9, 12, 118

project development, 7–8, 10–12, 108, 111; and Aboriginal concerns, 84; and Aboriginal engagement, 96; and Aboriginal title to lands, 30; as affecting Aboriginal

rights, 15; and assessed impacts, 116; and benefit and impact agreements, 52; environmental effects of, 42, 83; functions of, 113; governance of, 5, 23–24; as impacted by treaties, 23; impacts on Aboriginal peoples, 77, 96, 110, 120–21; as process, 4–6, 9, 114, 117, 119, 157n14; and reconciliation, 52; regulatory model of, 6–9; regulatory review of, xxvi; and relationship building, 110; stages of, 10; and Treaty rights, 32, 96; and tribunal process, 115, 118

project lifecycle, 5–6, 13, 50, 59, 93, 108, 117; and Aboriginal engagement, 91; planning process in, 9, 13

Proposed Conditions for the Mackenzie Valley Pipeline and Mackenzie Gathering System Conditions, 151n83

public consultation: as part of environmental assessment, 41. *See also* Aboriginal consultation; consultation; Crown consultation

public hearings: by independent regulatory body, 109; and joint review panels, 88

Q

Quebec: and Aboriginal rights and title, 28; joint review panels in, 45; modern treaties in, 20; projects in, 45

Quebec Régie de l'énergie, 46

R

Rabaska Project—Implementation of an LNG Terminal and Related Infrastructure, 46

railway, transcontinental, 32

reciprocal onus: as related to duty to consult, 64

reconciliation, xxvi, 3, 12, 32, 54, 141n10; of Aboriginal concerns and project development, 52; and Aboriginal consultation, 13; and Aboriginal peoples, 11, 53; achieved by impact and benefit agreements, 52; causes of, 47; as compromise, 60–61, 144n68; as fostered by integration, 110; supported by duty to consult, 140n6; through accommodation, 140nn1,6; through assessment and review processes, 108

INDEX

treaties: as creating and protecting reserves, 36; as impacting project development, 23; infringement of, 63; negotiation of, 13, 22, 27, 59, 64, 140n1; rights defined in, 23

treaties, historical, 15–16, 19–20, 26, 64, 107

treaties, modern, 15, 17, 19–20, 107, 111; and asserted Aboriginal rights and title, 27; in British Columbia, 26; and consultation, 53; and governance, 79; as having constitutional status, 23; making of, 25

treaties, numbered, 22, 60; and ceding of land, 32; and constitutional protection, 33–34; as extinguishing Aboriginal rights and title, 32; and right to land access, 35

Treaty 1 First Nations, 100–102

Treaty 8 Alberta Chief's Position Paper on Consultation, 126n30

Treaty Land Entitlement Agreements, 36

Treaty Land Entitlement (Saskatchewan) Fund, 36

Treaty Negotiations in British Columbia: An Assessment of the Effectiveness of British Columbia's Management and Administrative Processes, 131n87, 132n100

Treaty rights, 32, 107, 113, 120; to Aboriginal avocations, 35, 62; and accommodation, 53; adverse impacts on, 118; as asserted, 116–18; boundaries of, 63; breach of, 63; and constitutional law, 1, 20; defined, 16, 19; impacts on, xxvi, 13, 95, 113; infringement of, 21–22, 76–77; and judgments, 18; project impacts on, 14, 96, 99, 114, 116, 119; protection for, 21, 23, 35, 72, 105, 121

tribunal process, 110, 113, 120–21; as assessing project impacts, 113; and public record, 14; as robust, 118–20

tribunals, 8, 12, 25, 54, 111; and Aboriginal consultation, 108, 118–19, 158n26; and accommodation, 108; authority of, 14; as balancing competing interests, 66; as consultation, 71, 74; creation of, 24; and duty to consult, 56; and environmental assessment, 46, 114; function of, xxvi, 9, 11, 108, 112, 115, 117–18; funding of, 38; and governance

responsibilities, 23; and land claims agreements, 46; of the National Energy Board, 77; obligations of, 66, 80; participation in, 86; for project governance, 24, 39; and project impacts, 116, 121; as public hearing process, 25, 80; regarding energy agreement, 69; regulatory processes of, xxv, 2; for regulatory review, 44, 46, 114

Tr'ondëk Hwëch'in First Nation, 24

Tsawwassen First Nation, 26, 132n97; website, 132n97

2001 Framework Agreement with the Deh Cho, 146n20

2006 November Report of the Auditor General of Canada to the House of Commons, 26, 131n92, 132nn99,101,102

2009 Fall Report of the Commissioner of the Environment and Sustainable Development, 136n16

U

Umbrella Final Agreement, First Nation Final Agreements and Treaty Rights, The, 130n63

Understanding Utility Regulation: A Participants' Guide to the British Columbia Utilities Commission, 143n53

United Nations Environment Programme, 124n11

United Nations University, 4, 124n11

universalism, 112

uranium-mining projects, 45

usufructuary rights: as defined by Supreme Court of Canada, 20, 128n33

V

visible, incompatible land use: as defined, 35

Voisey's Bay Mine and Mill Project, 45, 137n36

Vuntut Gwitchin First Nation, 24